Germany from Defeat to Partition, 1945–1963

Pearson Education

We work with leading authors to develop the strongest educational materials in history, bringing cutting-edge thinking and best learning practice to a global market.

Under a range of well-known imprints, including Longman, we craft high-quality print and electronic publications which help readers to understand and apply their content, whether studying or at work.

To find out more about the complete range of our publishing please visit us on the World Wide Web at: www.pearsoneduc.com

SEMINAR STUDIES | IN HISTORY

Germany from Defeat to Partition 1945–1963

D. G. WILLIAMSON

An imprint of **Pearson Education**

Harlow, England · London · New York · Reading, Massachusetts · San Francisco · Toronto · Don Mills, Ontario · Sydney
Tokyo · Singapore · Hong Kong · Seoul · Taipei · Cape Town · Madrid · Mexico City · Amsterdam · Munich · Paris · Milan

Pearson Education Limited
Edinburgh Gate
Harlow
Essex CM20 2JE
England
and Associated Companies throughout the world.

Visit us on the World Wide Web at:
www.pearsoneduc.com

First published 2001

© Pearson Education Limited 2001

ISBN 0-582-29218-2 PPR

British Library Cataloguing-in-Publication Data
A catalogue record for this book is
available from the British Library

Library of Congress Cataloging-in-Publication Data
A catalog record for this book is available from the Library of Congress

Set by 7 in 10/12 Sabon Roman
Printed in Malaysia

CONTENTS

Introduction to the Series   x
Note on Referencing System   xi
Acknowledgements   xii
List of Abbreviations   xiii
Maps   xv–xvii

PART ONE: THE BACKGROUND   1

1 Plans and Reality: The Allies and Germany, 1943–45   3
   Zonal Division   3
   The Future of Germany   3
   The Revolutionary Impact of War on German Society   4
   The 'Interregnum', May–July 1945   5
   The Potsdam Conference   7

PART TWO: THE OCCUPATION, 1945–49   9

2 Allied Occupation Policy, August 1945–December 1947   11
   Denazification and Re-education   11
   The Decentralization and Democratization of Local Government   15
   The Economy   17
   The Revival of Political Parties and the Trade Unions   21
   The Legacy of the Occupation   24

3 The Division of Germany   25
   The Bizone and the German Economic Commission   25
   The Impact of the Marshall Plan and the Soviet Response   26
   The Momentum to Partition Accelerates, November 1947–June 1948   27
   Currency Reform and the Berlin Blockade   29
   The Emergence of the two Germanies   30

PART THREE: THE COLD WAR AND THE TWO GERMANIES,
1949–63   37

4 Two Rival States   39
   Western Integration: The ECSC and EDC   39
   The FRG Achieves Sovereignty and Enters NATO   41
   The Reaction of the GDR and the USSR to Western Integration   43
   The FRG as a Sovereign State, 1955–58   45
   The Berlin Crisis, 1958–61   48
   The Consequences   50

**PART FOUR: RECONSTRUCTION AND CONSOLIDATION:
THE FRG, 1949–63**   51

5 Politics: Developing a Democracy   53
   The Formation of the Adenauer Government and its Initial Prospects 55
   The Adenauer–Schumacher Duel   55
   Adenauer's Re-election, September 1953   58
   Coalition Politics, September 1953–February 1956   59
   The Creation of the *Bundeswehr*: A Citizens' Army   61
   Adenauer Re-asserts his Authority   62
   The Last Years of the Adenauer Era, 1958–63   63

6 The West German 'Economic Miracle', 1948–63   67
   The Social Market Economy   67
   Currency and Economic Reform, June–December 1948   68
   The Role of Marshall Aid   70
   Structural Problems, 1949–51   71
   Economic Reconstruction and Modernization, 1951–63   72

7 Social and Cultural Developments, 1949–63   76
   The Condition of the People   76
   Changing Social Structures   77
   The Partial Americanization of West German Culture   79

**PART FIVE: THE GDR FROM ITS FOUNDATION TO THE
BERLIN WALL, 1949–61**   81

8 Political Developments in the GDR, 1949–61   83
   The Creation of the SED Dictatorship   83
   17 June 1953 and its Consequences   86
   The Crisis of De-Stalinization, 1956   91
   The Construction of the Berlin Wall   93

9 The Economy in the GDR, 1948–61   95
   The Planned Economy, 1948–61   95
   Agriculture and Collectivization   98

10 Socialism and the East German People   101
   Education, Culture and the Creation of a new Elite   101
   The Workers' and Peasants' State   104
   The Opposition   105

PART SIX: ASSESSMENT   109

11 Germany from Defeat to Partition: A Retrospective View   111
   The Federal Republic   112
   The German Democratic Republic   113
   A Comparison between the Two States   115

PART SEVEN: DOCUMENTS   **117**

Chronology   149
Glossary   152
Who's Who   154
Bibliography   160
Index   167

INTRODUCTION TO THE SERIES

Such is the pace of historical enquiry in the modern world that there is an ever-widening gap between the specialist article or monograph, incorporating the results of current research, and general surveys, which inevitably become out of date. *Seminar Studies in History* is designed to bridge this gap. The series was founded by Patrick Richardson in 1966 and his aim was to cover major themes in British, European and world history. Between 1980 and 1996 Roger Lockyer continued his work, before handing the editorship over to Clive Emsley and Gordon Martel. Clive Emsley is Professor of History at the Open University, while Gordon Martel is Professor of International History at the University of Northern British Columbia, Canada, and Senior Research Fellow at De Montfort University.

All the books are written by experts in their field who are not only familiar with the latest research but have often contributed to it. They are frequently revised, in order to take account of new information and interpretations. They provide a selection of documents to illustrate major themes and provoke discussion, and also a guide to further reading. The aim of *Seminar Studies in History* is to clarify complex issues without over-simplifying them, and to stimulate readers into deepening their knowledge and understanding of major themes and topics.

NOTE ON REFERENCING SYSTEM

Readers should note that numbers in square brackets [5] refer them to the corresponding entry in the Bibliography at the end of the book (specific page numbers are given in italics). A number in square brackets preceded by *Doc*. [*Doc*. 5] refers readers to the corresponding item in the Documents section which follows the main text.

ACKNOWLEDGEMENTS

We are grateful to the following for permission to reproduce copyright material:

Berg Publishers for extracts from *Politics, Society and Government in the GDR* by J.K.A. Thomanek and J. Mellis (1988) and *The West German Economy* (1st edition) by A. Kramer (1991); Berghahn Books for extracts from *Uniting Germany: Documents and Debates* edited by K. Jarausch and V. von Gransow; The Controller of Her Majesty's Stationery Office for extracts from PRO (Public Records Office) FO 371 76652 by the British High Commissioner. Crown Copyright, *Diary of a Tour through the British Zone, 1–6 July 1945* by W. Strang FO 371 46933. Crown Copyright and *Letter to Deputy Military Governor* by Air Vice Marshall H.V. Champion de Crespigni 30.5.47. Crown Copyright.

We have been unable to trace the copyright holder of the poem 'Welcome Liberators' and would appreciate any information which would enable us to do so.

We are also grateful for permission to reproduce:

Plate 1: Airplane lands over a crowd of children, 1948; Plate 2: Portrait of Otto Grotewohl and Walter Ulbricht, 4 December 1954; Plate 3: Big four leaders at Western Summit Meeting, 19 December 1959; and Plate 4: Youth lies dying 17 August 1962; all plates reproduced courtesy of Corbis, all © Bettmann/CORBIS.

LIST OF ABBREVIATIONS

BHE	*Bund der Heimatvertriebenen und Entrechteten* (League of Expellees and Disenfranchised)
BP	*Bayernpartei* (Bavarian Party)
CC	Central Committee
CDU	*Christlich Demokratische Union* (Christian Democratic Union)
CDUD	*Christlich Demokratische Union Deutschlands* (German Christian Democratic Union in the GDR)
CSU	*Christlich-Soziale Union* (Christian Social Union)
DBD	*Demokratischer Bauernpartei Deutschlands* (German Democratic Farmers' Party)
DGB	*Deutscher Gewerkschaftsbund* (German Trades Union Federation)
DM	*Deutschmark* (West German mark)
DP	*Deutsche Partei* (German Party)
DRP	*Deutsche Reichspartei* (German Reich Party)
DWK	*Deutsche Wirtschaftskommission* (German Economic Commission)
ECSC	European Coal and Steel Community
EDC	European Defence Community
EEC	European Economic Community
ERP	European Recovery Programme (Marshall Plan)
FDGB	*Freier Deutscher Gewerkschaftsbund* (Federation of Free German Trades Unions)
FDJ	*Freie Deutsche Jugend* (Free German Youth)
FDP	*Freie Demokratische Partei* (Free Democratic Party)
FRG	Federal Republic of Germany
GDP	Gross Domestic Product
GDR	German Democratic Republic
KPD	*Kommunistische Partei Deutschlands* (Communist Party of Germany)
LDPD	*Liberaldemokratische Partei Deutschlands* (Liberal Democratic Party of Germany in the GDR)

LPG	*Landwirtschaftliche Produktionsgenossenschaft* (agricultural production cooperative)
Mfs	*Ministerium für Staatssicherheit* (Ministry for State Security)
NATO	North Atlantic Treaty Organization
NDPD	*National-Demokratische Partei Deutschlands* (National Democratic Party of Germany)
NKVD	People's Commissariat of Internal Affairs in the USSR
NVA	*Nationale Volksarmee* (National People's Army)
OEEC	Organization for European Economic Cooperation
RM	*Reichsmark*
SA	*Sturm-Abteilung* (Nazi storm-troops)
SAG	*Sowjetische Aktiengesellschaft* (Soviet limited company)
SED	*Sozialistische Einheitspartei Deutschlands* (Socialist Unity Party of Germany)
SMAD	Soviet Military Administration in Germany
SPD	*Sozialistische Partei Deutschlands* (Social Democratic Party of Germany)
SRP	*Sozialistische Reichspartei Deutschlands* (Socialist Reich Party)
UN	United Nations
USSR	Union of Soviet Socialist Republics
VdgB	*Vereinigung der gegenseitigen Bauernhilfe* (Association for Farmers' Mutual Help)
VEB	*Volkseigener Betrieb* (nationalized enterprise)

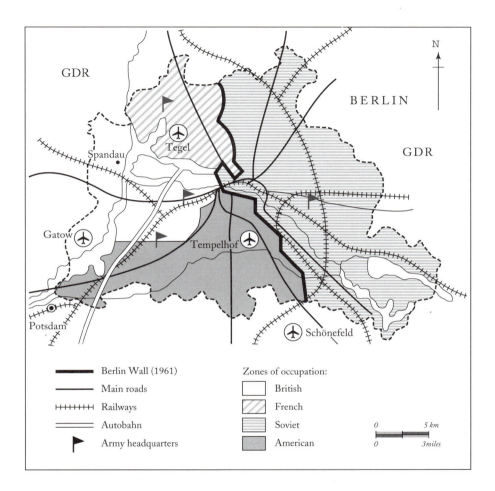

Map 1   Berlin, 1945–61

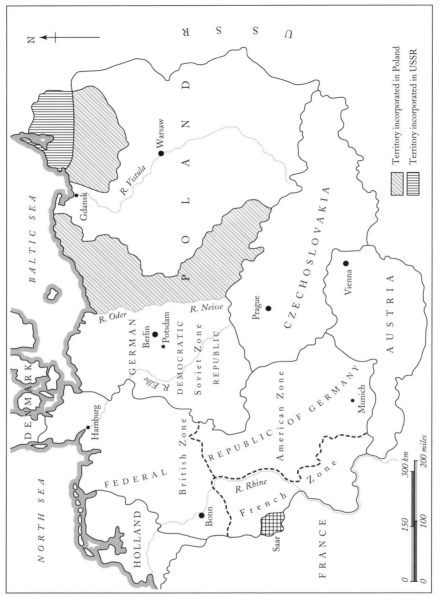

Map 2   Germany, 1945–63

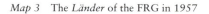

Map 3 The *Länder* of the FRG in 1957

PART ONE | THE BACKGROUND

PLANS AND REALITY: THE ALLIES AND GERMANY, 1943–45

ZONAL DIVISION

By the summer of 1943 after the defeat of the German armies in North Africa and Stalingrad, it was clear that the future of Continental Europe and its strongest state, Germany, would be decided by the USSR, Great Britain and the USA. In January 1944 these three powers set up the European Advisory Commission to begin work on detailed planning for post-war Europe. By the autumn plans both for an Allied Control Council to supervise a post-Nazi German central administration and the division of Germany into zones of occupation were drawn up. Most of the eastern half of the pre-war Reich was envisaged as the Soviet Zone of occupation. In further negotiations the Soviet Union was ceded the northern half of East Prussia. The rest of Germany to the east of the Oder was to be annexed by Poland in exchange for the territory which had been allotted to the USSR under the Nazi–Soviet pact of August 1939. The British Zone was to comprise the Ruhr and most of north-west Germany, while the Americans were to occupy the predominantly rural areas of Bavaria, Hesse and Württemberg-Baden in addition to the northern port of Bremen through which their occupying army would be supplied. Each of the three occupying powers was also to have a zone in Berlin. These plans were confirmed at Yalta where it was also belatedly agreed to allocate small zones to France in both Berlin and Western Germany [62].

THE FUTURE OF GERMANY

Right up to the Potsdam Conference the great powers oscillated between enforcing a Carthaginian peace on Germany that would, as Stalin succinctly expressed it, eliminate 'forever its ability to function as a single state in the centre of Europe' [53 *p. 9*] and pursuing a more conciliatory policy which, through re-education and disarmament, would ultimately allow a chastened but independent Germany to survive. In America this debate was particularly vigorous. Initially, President Roosevelt's intention was to destroy the economic nationalism of the Nazis and force Germany to take its place in a new liberal world order of free trade and democracy dominated by the United States. However, pressure from the Treasury Secretary, Henry Morgenthau, led to Roosevelt and Churchill accepting a plan which envisaged the eventual partition of Germany into several states in which higher education would be initially banned and heavy industry destroyed. The Morgenthau Plan remained official Anglo-American policy up to the early spring of 1945, when it was replaced with the more practical aim of creating a decentralized federal Germany. In Britain, too, by 1945, a consensus had emerged that once Germany was disarmed and denazified, British interests would best be served by a controlled revival of the German economy – 'security from attack and then business as usual', as one historian has expressed it [103 *p. 48*]. Similarly, in Russia, plans for the partition of Germany were dropped, and at Yalta Stalin accepted the prospect of a united but neutral and probably non-Communist Germany. Stalin was ready to exploit any favourable situation in Germany as it arose to bring Germany into the Soviet sphere of influence, but he was primarily concerned to turn Russian gains in Eastern Europe into a protective shield against any future attack from the West. Above all he wanted to extract reparations from Germany to help rebuild the war-shattered Soviet Union. By the spring of 1945 it was the French who were the fiercest opponents of a united Germany. Essentially, their intention was to turn the Rhineland and the Saar into satellite states dependent on Paris, while the rest of Germany would only be a loose confederation of states [41; 48; 68]. The Ruhr would also be detached and put under international control.

Each of the Allied powers drew up radical plans for fundamentally restructuring German society. The British, Americans and later the French set up teams composed of civil and military experts who would, on the defeat of Germany, move into the relevant zones and assume the complex tasks of administration, denazification and re-education. Although the advice of *émigrés* had been sought in London and Washington, and the American security services had compiled a 'white book' of reliable Germans who could be given administrative posts, it was only the Russians who had trained groups of German *émigré* Communists to follow the Red Army into Germany to assist the Soviet Military Government in its initial task of setting up reliable local administrations. Their leader was Walther Ulbricht, a 52-year-old cabinet-maker who had gone to Moscow in 1938. Later, in building up the GDR, he was to show political skills rivalled only by Adenauer in the West [13; 53] [*Doc. 6*].

THE REVOLUTIONARY IMPACT OF WAR ON GERMAN SOCIETY

Since 1943 Germany had been undergoing a social revolution which continued unabated until the early 1950s. What remained of the influence of the Prussian Junkers was destroyed. The decimation of the traditional officer class on the eastern front finally broke their grip on the army, while their houses, estates and often their families were liquidated in Eastern Germany by the advancing Russians and Poles. The urban evacuees from the bombed-out cities and then the twelve million Germans expelled from East Prussia, Pomerania, Lower Silesia and the Sudetenland irrevocably destroyed the traditional structure and isolation of rural and small-town Germany [*Docs 3–5*]. 'The uprooted person ... became the typical figure of the immediate post-war period' [*41 p. 62*], while another symbolic figure of this period was the *Trümmerfrau*, the female rubble clearer. By 1945 the position of women in German society had undergone a dramatic change. With so many of the men dead or prisoners of war there was a numerical surplus of 70 per cent women over men. Females were therefore 'catapulted' [*102 p. 12*] into a life for which the Third Reich had hardly prepared them. They had to work at back-breaking tasks and find food and shelter for their families [*Doc. 2*].

Yet amid this destruction and misery it is possible to see in hindsight that preconditions for the future (West) German economic and political renaissance were already in place. Despite heavy bombing, much industrial machinery was intact. For instance, in May 1945 German machine tool holdings were double the sum of those in Britain [103]. Even before the end of the war some businessmen were beginning to move away from the concept of autarky and centralized planning to make clandestine contact with free market economists such as Ludwig Erhard. It can also be argued that paradoxically a 'democratic transformation had already begun in the institutions created by Nazi Germany' [*45 p. 109*]. The Nazi Labour Front, for instance, had created a language of harmony which later helped defuse class warfare, while many former members of the Hitler Youth were to find a home in the Social Democratic Party of Germany (SPD) through which some of the more egalitarian and democratic elements of Nazi ideology were later absorbed and transferred into the Federal Republic [39; 45; 103].

THE INTERREGNUM, MAY–JULY 1945

As the Allies advanced into Germany they were confronted by what could only be called 'indescribable, impenetrable chaos' [*10 p. 19*]. Virtually every town as far east as Berlin with a population over 50,000 had been destroyed by British and American bombers. In Cologne, for instance, 72 per cent of the buildings were destroyed and in Berlin 75 per cent, while just under one per cent of the buildings of the city of Hanover were undamaged [*Doc. 1*]. Throughout the former Reich the whole transport system had been paralysed by Allied bombing. The main roads were blocked with never-ending columns of refugees and the concourses and platforms of the stations became at night enormous communal dormitories.

By the time Hitler had committed suicide in his Berlin bunker on 30 April 1945 British troops had already crossed the Elbe and further south American and Russian troops had met up at Torgau. Grand Admiral Dönitz, whom Hitler had designated as his successor, had little option but to accept Allied demands for unconditional surrender on 8 May. Two weeks later his government, which had been allowed to survive in Schleswig-Holstein, was dissolved and its members arrested. On 5 June the Allied commanders officially announced the assumption of supreme authority over Germany by the occupying powers, its division into four zones and the setting up of the Allied Control Commission, which was, or so it seemed, to be the executive body of the Military Government. It took another month to re-deploy the British and American armies from the points they had reached when hostilities ended, back into the zones agreed upon at Yalta, and to finalize the borders of the French Zone. It was only then, on 5 July, that the Russians allowed the Western Allies to take over their zones in Berlin, and it was not until 29 July that the Control Council first met in Berlin [12].

The preceding three months were something of an 'interregnum' in which the occupying troops tried to establish order within the chaos that was Germany. Contrary to expectations, the advancing troops had met with no opposition or partisan activities from Nazi *Werwolf* units. Instead, in many areas anti-Fascist action committees had been formed, which were ready to cooperate with the Allies in stamping out the last remnants of Nazism. They were predominantly Socialist or Communist and had developed their own programmes for the future of Germany.

Some wished to set up a soviet republic with the help of the Red Army, others wanted to form broadly based anti-Fascist fronts. The anti-Fascist committees were 'the first and only political initiatives with revolutionary potential' [41 *p.107*] and were therefore dissolved by the occupying authorities after a few weeks. The Western Allies were determined to prevent revolution while the Russians saw them as 'sectarian' and a threat to their own policies, which at that time were aimed at winning over the bourgeoisie and establishing a broadly based coalition or bloc of anti-Nazi groups.

In the absence, until the end of July, of a centrally established control council in Berlin, the local commanders had no option but to try to solve the daunting problems of the occupation in their own way. The immediate priorities facing the occupying forces were to restore the basic services of water, gas, electricity and sewerage, repair the railways, bridges and canals, and ensure that the population was provided with a minimum ration and housed. In the Western zones military engineers working with Germans achieved considerable success. For instance, in Hanover, water and electricity services were fully restored by 1 July [51]. Feeding and rehousing the population was a much more complex task, complicated by the new zonal divisions, the claims of the millions of displaced persons released from forced labour or the concentration camps and the constant stream of refugees coming from the East. Cellars, lofts, ruins, corrugated iron huts and camps were all used to house the millions of homeless.

Faced with emergencies on this scale the local commanders sought out experienced German administrators. In the West, the advice of the local clergy was often followed in appointing officials who had been either dismissed by the Nazis or were living in retirement [41]. In the Soviet Zone the local commandants' work was made easier by the presence of the *émigré* groups which were able to recommend suitable German civil administrators, with a proven anti-Fascist past. To stop looting and to help the Allies maintain civil order, local police forces were rapidly set up in all four zones. Efforts were made to ensure that the senior German officers were untainted by Nazism, but at the lower levels a considerable number of ex-Nazis were accepted. Inevitably, in those early chaotic days, when faced with the choice between 'efficiency and political purity' [51 *p. 37*] all the Allies chose the former [53].

THE POTSDAM CONFERENCE

Some two weeks before the first meeting of the Control Council the Allied leaders met at Potsdam. The American State Department's growing interest in 'multilateralism' or the creation of a free capitalist global economy, in which Germany would play its part, intensified Russian suspicions of American economic imperialism. There was also sharp disagreement over Poland's western frontiers where the Poles, against the expressed wishes of Britain and America but with Soviet backing, had annexed German territory right up to the Western Neisse and were already beginning to expel or indeed starve to death the German population [*Doc. 3*]. The statesmen at Potsdam, far from providing concise and practical guidelines for the Control Council, could only paper over their deep mutual disagreements with generalizations. There was a consensus on the need to enforce the 'four d's' – denazification, demilitarization, decartelization and democratization – but no agreement on how this should be carried out in practice. The Allies also committed themselves to a united, but decentralized Germany. There was 'for the time being' [*Doc. 7*] to be no central government, but only central departments headed by German civil servants were to be set up in the areas of finance, transport, communications, foreign trade and industry. In the key question of reparations the Western powers rejected the figure of $20 billion, which Stalin had first put forward at Yalta, but did agree that 50 per cent of the eventual total should go to Russia. The Russians had already begun to remove materials and industrial plant from their zone to help rebuild their own war-shattered economy, but the Americans and the British were convinced that the German economy must be left sufficiently strong to pay for imports of food and raw materials – the so-called 'first charge principle' [48 *p. 134*]. A compromise was agreed upon whereby Russia and the Western powers would take reparations from their own zones, but Britain and America would grant 10 per cent of these to the Russians and a further 15 per cent in exchange for the supply of food and raw materials from the Soviet Zone. The failure to agree on a joint reparation policy was a major step towards ultimate partition. Molotov, the Soviet Foreign Minister, was quick to ask what 'if reparations were not treated as a whole ... would happen to overall treatment of economic matters?' [48 *p. 157; 63*].

PART TWO THE OCCUPATION, 1945–49

CHAPTER TWO

ALLIED OCCUPATION POLICY, AUGUST 1945–DECEMBER 1947

The guidelines laid down at Potsdam were to be interpreted and applied in detail by the Allied Commanders on the Control Council in Berlin. The drafting of the future peace treaty with Germany would, it was assumed, eventually be dealt with by the Council of Foreign Ministers. As the four Commanders-in-Chief exercised supreme power in their own zones, and were responsible to their own governments at home, the Control Council never developed into an inter-Allied executive body and became merely an instrument of inter-zonal coordination, and that only briefly. Each power interpreted the Potsdam Agreement and the subsequent laws of the Control Council differently, and began to create a 'new order' [50 *p. 29*] in its zone based on its own conceptions of what was good for the Germans. Theoretically, they all shared the same general aims, the 'four ds', to which they had subscribed in Potsdam, but their individual approaches were radically different; inevitably, the philosophy of each occupying power was conditioned by its own history. They all saw the victorious conclusion of the war as confirming the inherent virtues of their own political systems and consequently their programmes for institutional, economic and educational reform were modelled on their own political and social structures. It rapidly became apparent, however, that for all the theoretical omnipotence of the occupiers, they enjoyed in reality only a limited power. To repair communications, restore an effective administration at the local level and to avoid the disasters of famine and disease, the few thousand military government officials in each zone were in fact dependent on German cooperation. As Klessmann has pointed out, the essence of the history of the occupation was not so much dictatorship by the Allies as 'interaction between the occupiers and the occupied, which developed out of parallel interests and struggles' [46 *p. 66*].

DENAZIFICATION AND RE-EDUCATION

Denazification aimed at removing a discredited ruling class and replacing it in due course with a new democratic elite, yet by 1948 Western observers were united in believing that it had not just failed, but become a 'full-fledged fiasco' [66 *p. 240*], which had left many Nazis in responsible positions and alienated the German population. At Potsdam it had been agreed that the Nazi Party, and organizations linked to it, were to be destroyed, that war criminals were to be arrested and put on trial and that all Nazis were to be removed from positions of responsibility in both the public and private sectors [*Doc. 7*]. Twenty-two Nazi leaders, of whom twelve were condemned to death, were tried by the International Military Tribunal at Nuremberg for conspiracy against peace and crimes against humanity. The Nuremberg trials were seen by some Western lawyers as a travesty of justice, as they applied law restrospectively, a view which many Germans also shared. The philosopher Karl Jaspers, for example, argued that the Allies, far from vindicating the rule of law, merely succeeded in making the Germans more sceptical of it [46]. Nevertheless, these trials did destroy the Nazi political leadership and, through the immense amount of documentation that was compiled, made clear to the German people the sheer scale of the Nazi atrocities. Later the West Germans were to use this material for further prosecutions of Nazi war criminals [29 Vol. 1].

Of more immediate impact on the German population were the denazification processes which were carried out in all four zones albeit in an arbitrary and inefficient way. Denazification started off as a purge rigorously enforced by at least three out of the four of the occupying powers, but then increasingly it was delegated to the Germans themselves, and finally dropped when the Cold War turned the Western and Eastern zones of Germany into allies of their respective occupiers. The Russians, convinced that Nazism was a product of German capitalism, developed the most coherent denazification programme of all the former Allies. They did not just weed out Nazi officials, judges, teachers and industrialists, but also consciously implemented what the German revolution of 1918 had failed to achieve: a series of radical, structural reforms which decisively broke the power of the traditional elites in East Germany [53]. The Americans hoped to purge Nazism from all aspects of German life while preserving, apart from the cartels, the existing capitalist structure of the German economy intact. Initially, they pursued this with an almost missionary-like zeal. By December 1945 they had arrested nearly double the number of Germans interned by the British or indeed the Russians. To assist the Military Government in its task, questionnaires or *Fragebogen* were distributed to the relevant German personnel, 1.3 million of which were returned by March 1946. However, they had set themselves a bureaucratic task which 'offered almost no possibilities of even fairly satisfactory solution' [69 *p. 160*] [*Doc. 8*]. The British and French were more pragmatic in their approach to denazification. Both believed that Nazism was a consequence of the German character and could not immediately, in Vermeil's words, be thrown off 'like a garment that has gone out of style' [68 *p. 163*]. Ultimately, they were convinced that only long-term re-education would change German attitudes. Denazification in the British Zone was therefore more a surgical operation aimed at removing former Nazis in responsible positions in industry or public administration [66]. In the French Zone, denazification was firmly subordinated to France's dual policy of building up her power at the cost of Germany and seeking security from any future German threats. Only in Württemberg-Hohenzollern, which for a time gained a reputation as 'the Eldorado of tolerance' for ex-Nazis, did the French, under American pressure, conduct a rigorous and effective denazification policy [41 *p. 118*].

Denazification quickly ran into major problems. It denuded German local and provincial administration of personnel and, by removing managers from the mines and other vital industrial plants, impeded even the low level of reconstruction permitted by the Allied Control Council. Out of sheer necessity and self-interest all four occupying powers at times turned a selective blind eye to the employment of Nazis in key positions. Thus, after a major pit disaster in the Ruhr, the British suspended denazification in the mines and the Russians continued to employ Nazis in leading positions in the Soviet limited companies (SAGs), which they set up in January 1946 (see *p. 19*) [43; 53; 66].

To ease the pressure the Control Council in October 1946, in what has been called 'the most important law passed in Germany during the occupation' [29 Vol. 1, *p. 75*], divided the Germans into five categories ranging from major offenders to non-offenders. It then handed over the responsibility for their denazification to German tribunals which worked under only very general Allied supervision. Although permitting the Germans to purge themselves of Nazism was a major step in the democratization of Germany, almost inevitably serious abuses took place. In the American Zone, for example, the Munich Denazification Tribunal had to be dismissed and replaced with new personnel because of its unwillingness to prosecute former Nazis. The demand by the courts that all Germans seeking employment in official positions should produce written statements confirmed by oath (*affidavits*) attesting to their good character was easily abused. As the Cold War intensified denazification gradually became an irrelevance and by early 1948 the four occupying powers had each declared the process to be at an end. Left-wing critics in West Germany have argued that denazification failed because, in the words of Lutz Niethammer, it was so superficial that it enabled many ex-Nazis to regain their position in society 'with a fresh white waistcoat' [55 *p. 13*]. On the other hand they returned to a society where, through defeat and occupation, the appeal of Nazism had been irreparably shattered, even if that society, at any rate in the West, remained for a time deeply conservative and apolitical [29 Vol. 1].

Denazification went hand in hand with an ambitious attempt to re-educate the German people. The Potsdam Agreement laid down that both militarism and National Socialism were to be eliminated in German education so as 'to make possible the development of democratic ideas' [66 p. 222]. There was agreement among the powers that secondary education should be free and that the way to grammar school (*Gymnasium*) education, which was the key to entry into a university, should be made as accessible as possible. The schools began to open in late summer 1945. Everywhere the conditions were appalling. In Schleswig-Holstein, for instance, there were classes of over 120 [44]. Right across Germany Nazi teachers were suspended and replaced at first by elderly staff, most of whom had not been in a classroom since 1933. Nazi textbooks were destroyed – or at least the offending pages were removed – and replaced with either specially written new books or with old pre-1933 editions, many of which had to be discarded because they were themselves so nationalistic. Teacher training colleges were hastily opened to produce more teachers – by Easter 1946, 28 had been set up in the British Zone. The Russians made great efforts to recruit workers and peasants with impeccable anti-Fascist credentials and set up crash courses to train them [44; 53].

In the Soviet Zone a central German educational administration was formed in mid-July 1945 under the German Communist, Paul Wandel, which attempted to democratize the whole school system from nursery schools to universities. In April 1946 a compromise was reached with the local CDU (Christian Democratic Union) leaders that out of a twelve-year school system only the last four years would be selective. Religion would not be part of the syllabus but could still be taught in the school buildings after the school day by outside teachers. In fact the school system for the next three years was so overwhelmed by material difficulties that these reforms failed dismally 'to create a classroom that produced the socialist values [the Russians] hoped to instil in the Germans' [53 p. 457]. The French attempted to modify the elitism of the German Gymnasium system in a more subtle way by delaying the teaching of Latin for three years, so that students could transfer from the elementary schools at a later stage. They also introduced the study of French as a compulsory foreign language, but their plans to abolish religious teaching in schools met with heavy opposition from the Germans and failed [53; 68].

Paradoxically, the educational policies of the American Military Government assumed a higher profile just at the time when increasingly more powers were being handed over to the *Länder* (see below, p. 16). Thus, in January 1947, the Americans suddenly produced 'elaborate paper plans' [69 p. 203] for a free, fully comprehensive secondary school system, which formed the basis of a belated law issued by the Allied Control Council on 25 July. General Lucius Clay, Military Governor of the American Zone, put immense pressure on the *Länder* but, with the exception of Bremen, all managed to procrastinate until 1949–50 by which time the Americans were powerless to act as the West German state had been set up [43; 69].

The British were less ambitious than the Americans. Once they handed over responsibility for education to the *Länder*, the work of their education officers was to advise and to persuade rather than to dictate policies, although they did take the precaution of laying down certain fundamental guidelines for educational reform, involving the abolition of school fees, giving teacher training colleges university status, retaining church schools and keeping the way open for extending the period spent by pupils at a primary school from four to six years [44; 66].

The Western Allies paid considerably less attention to the universities, which for the most part survived the occupation period unreformed. The French created two new universities at Saarbrücken and Mainz, but they respected the academic autonomy of both institutions. The Russians, on the other hand, aimed to turn the universities in their zone into 'instruments of the party' [53 *p. 446*] both by encouraging the children of workers and peasants, whom they hoped would become reliable Communists, to study for degrees, and by ensuring that the Socialist Unity Party (SED) dominated the student organizations.

In the 1960s it became commonplace in Western Germany to argue that the Western powers had left intact an old-fashioned, elitist and class-ridden system both at school and university level. However, while some of the teaching staff were certainly conservative, the West German universities did not become breeding grounds for the far right, as they did in the 1920s, but in fact produced generations of democratic students anxious to build a liberal and outward-looking Germany [29 Vol. 1].

THE DECENTRALIZATION AND DEMOCRATIZATION OF LOCAL GOVERNMENT

The Potsdam Agreement committed the occupying powers to decentralize the political structure of Germany and to restore democratic local government [*Doc. 7*]. The subsequent Allied decision to break up Prussia in February 1947 ensured that the *Länder* boundaries of Germany would have to be drastically redrawn. This allowed the non-Prussian states in Western Germany to break free from a Prussian hegemony that had been ruthlessly enforced in the nineteenth century, and to create a genuinely federal system that reflected their own cultures and traditions. In the British Zone three new states – Schleswig-Holstein, Lower Saxony and North Rhine-Westphalia – were carved out of the former Prussian territory [29 Vol. 1].

The demarcation lines of the French and American Zones had been drawn up with scant regard to the historic borders of the south German

Länder. Although virtually the whole of Bavaria was included in the American Zone, its western part 'was made up of such an assortment of legs, arms, fingers, ears and other stray pieces of dismembered body that one could hardly believe one's eyesight' [69 *p. 177*]. Out of this administrative chaos the Americans constructed Hesse and Württemberg-Baden, while the French, faced with a similar problem of truncation, cobbled together two territories, Baden and Württemberg-Hohenzollern (only in 1952 was the *Land* of Baden-Württemberg created). The Russians quickly moved to create five new *Länder* in July 1945: Saxony, Mecklenburg, Saxony-Anhalt, Thuringia and Brandenburg [53].

Each power approached the problem of rebuilding local government differently. The British treated their zone as a unified whole and created a Central Economic Office, which was run by German officials subject to Military Government instructions. In February 1946 they also set up a consultative Zonal Advisory Council composed of leading zonal politicians and administrators. The French, on the other hand, who actively encouraged separatism and hoped to detach the Saar, had no coordinating body above the *Land* level. The French and the British believed, however, that political power should be given only 'in small doses' [68 *p. 180*] from the bottom upwards. The British therefore appointed unelected members to the governments and provisional parliaments of the *Länder*, while the French initially restricted German participation in local government to purely nominated officials, and it was not until the autumn of 1946 that municipal elections took place in both zones [66; 68].

The Americans, true to their own political traditions, created a federal system of government in their zone. In September 1945 they set up a nominated council composed of the chief German officials of the *Länder*, which rapidly became the main channel through which their zone was administered, but they moved more quickly than either the French or the British to create local democracy. Elections were held as early as January 1946, in which communities of fewer than 20,000 inhabitants chose their councillors, and these were followed rapidly by town and county (*Bezirk*) elections three months later. They then moved on to give the *Länder* themselves democratic constitutions. Constituent assemblies were elected in June to draw up the new democratic *Land* constitutions and by the end of the year elected state legislatures met in Munich, Wiesbaden and Stuttgart. It was not until May 1947 that *Länder* elections were held in the British and French Zones [28]. The Russians were the only occupying power to create the nucleus of a central German administration. In July 1945 SMAD (Soviet Military Administration in Germany) set up eleven ministries at the same time as it authorized the setting up of local governments in the five new *Länder*. The relationship between the provincial and central administrations remained undefined until the future of Germany itself became clearer.

Initially, the central ministries were mere show-pieces which, according to an American observer, 'had only fragmentary information' about the economic situation in the provinces and had no power to influence them [*53 p. 45*].

The three Western powers also tried to de-politicize the German civil service. The civil servants' right to stand for election to any central or local assembly was banned and their unique status and privileges abolished. This, however, was rejected by the new West German Federal Government in 1949, and two years later their traditional rights and privileges were restored, thereby fuelling accusations that the Bonn Republic was really a restoration of the old regime [60; 79 Vol. 2]. In the Soviet Zone the question of 'restoration' did not arise as gradually key positions in the bureaucracy were filled with loyal SED personnel [87; 88].

THE ECONOMY

According to the Potsdam Agreement 'Common policies' covering disarmament, decartelization, and land reform were to be developed, while the Allies were also pledged to maintain a common currency and transport system as well as 'import and export programmes for Germany as a whole' [*Doc. 7*]. The reality was, however, very different. The four zones were initially, as far as the exchange of goods and services went, virtually hermetically sealed. Inter-zonal transport, if it was still running, was strictly controlled. The manufacturing industries in the Soviet Zone were thus cut off from their markets in Western Germany and goods could only be exported to Western Europe for payment of dollars, which no European country could afford. Coal production in the Ruhr, in 1946 at 178,000 tons per day, was only one-third of its 1936 daily average [66; 67].

These difficulties were compounded by the amputation of Germany's main food-producing areas in the East – Pomerania and East and West Prussia. The subsequent shortage of food became the 'greatest single source of misery' [29 Vol. 1, *p. 150*] in the period 1945–49 [46; 103]. The minimum number of calories required for a working adult according to a scale devised by the League of Nations was 2,000 calories a day. In the immediate post-war period rations fell to 800 calories per day and in July 1947 the actual daily ration distribution in the British Zone was still only 996 calories, even though it was slightly higher in Hamburg. It was not until the currency reform of 1948 that rations approaching 2,000 calories per day could be distributed. Inevitably this led to a large part of the population living on the edge of starvation and a sharp reduction in the productivity of the workers [*Docs 2 and 9*].

The *Reichsmark* currency had been destroyed by wartime inflation and was almost valueless. In 1945 it has been calculated that at least RM 300 billion were theoretically available to buy goods and services worth only

RM 50 billion. Germany would have been overwhelmed with hyper-inflation if the Allied powers had not continued the Third Reich's policy of freezing pay and prices. The solution was a drastic reduction in the amount of notes circulating and the introduction of a new currency. This, however, was not immediately possible because of Allied disagreements about the future of Germany. Germany's production also needed to be restored so that there would not be too much money chasing too few goods. Thus Germany remained in a state of what the social market economists called 'repressed inflation' [101 *p. 20*] until the currency reforms of June 1948 (see *pp. 68–9*).

There were two parallel economies in Germany: 'one was the official economy, grinding along on the basis of rations, production plans and quotas' [103 *p. 125*]; the other was the black market or the economy of barter. It was the latter that became the normal means by which individuals procured food and factories and businesses vital raw materials. Unless they were paid in kind, the workers would take time off work to scour the surrounding countryside for food. The Phoenix tyre factory at Hamburg, for instance, topped up its employees' salaries with a pair of cycle tyres which they could sell on the black market and buy food. Firms, too, sought to barter their products for raw materials. Max Grundig, for instance, swapped 3,000 radio kits for 30 million cigarettes and 5,000 boxes of cigars with the French Military Government, part of which in turn could be exchanged for the necessary materials for constructing a new factory [103] [*Doc. 12*].

In March 1946 the four occupying powers achieved a fragile consensus over the future of the German economy when they published a 'Plan for Reparations and the Level of the Post-War German Economy', which, if implemented, would have reduced post-war production to the level of that in 1932. The steel industry was to be cut to 30 per cent of its pre-war level, the chemical industry to 40 per cent, heavy engineering to 40 per cent and machine tool manufacturing to 11.4 per cent. As part of the demilitarization measures the manufacture of armaments, aircraft, ships, synthetic fuels, light metals and radioactive substances were to be banned. Surplus plant was either to be destroyed or dismantled. The 'plan represented the zenith of Allied unity' [103 *p. 60*] over the economic treatment of Germany but it was never implemented as the Allies failed to reach any agreement on the future of Germany as a political or economic entity. Instead, in the words of *The Times*, they merely 'pick[ed] from the Potsdam Agreement the phrases that suit[ed] them best', with important long-term consequences for the German economy [68 *p. 140*].

Over reparations the policies of the occupying powers diverged sharply. At the meeting of the Allied Control Council in May 1946, the Russians refused to accept an inter-zonal export–import plan proposed by General

Clay, the American Military Governor. They rejected the American argument that Germany could only pay reparations once its account was in balance, and that what they had already seized in their zone should be subtracted from the total amount eventually due to them. To put pressure on both the French, who were pursuing their own separatist policies, and the Russians, Clay announced that no further reparation deliveries would be made from the American Zone until German economic unity was restored. At the Paris Conference of Foreign Ministers in July, Byrnes, the American Secretary of State, reiterated this message, but he also went a step further and offered to amalgamate the American Zone economically with all or any one of the other zones in an effort to achieve German economic unity on terms acceptable to America. Only the British, faced with spending some $320 million per year on their zone, accepted and on 1 January 1947 a potentially viable West German economic area, the Bizone, came into existence. The new Anglo-American emphasis was now on reconstruction, and in July 1947 the Level of Industry Plan was revised to allow the Bizone economy to reach the 1936 level of production. Nevertheless, up to 1950 a modified programme of dismantling was still being carried out, which met increasing opposition from the West Germans (see *pp. 55–6*).

France and Russia continued to pursue independent reparation policies in their zones. The French set about harnessing the industries and natural resources to assist the modernization of their own economy as laid down in the Monnet Plan of 1946 [68]. It is difficult to assess the amount of material removed from the Soviet Zone. The soldiers in the first wave of the occupation looted and plundered watches, jewellery, furs, etc., as their allies in the West did on a smaller scale [*Doc. 11*]. They were then followed by trophy battalions which removed vital pieces of machinery and equipment as well as raw materials. By August 1945, 1.2 million tons of materials and some 3.6 million tons of equipment had already gone to the USSR. The removals continued until 1949 by which time the Russians had probably extracted the $10 billion reparations they had insisted upon at Yalta. The Soviet authorities also siphoned off reparations from current production by requisitioning factories and turning them into SAGs or Soviet limited companies, which were responsible by the end of 1946 for some 30 per cent of the zone's industrial production [35; 53].

The four powers also failed to devise a common policy on land reform and the restructuring of German industry. The most radical measures were taken in the Soviet Zone where by 1948 both the large estates and farms had been broken up and the key industries nationalized. In September 1945 all land belonging to those landowners who had estates of more than 100 hectares was confiscated and handed over to smallholders, expellees and industrial workers in parcels of five to ten hectares. In the short term this measure only exacerbated the food shortages because the new farmers lacked equipment and fertilizers and were harassed by requisitioning and unrealistically high production quotas. In July 1946 in Saxony, the most industrialized *Land* in the Soviet Zone, the population approved in a referendum, by a margin of 77 per cent, the proposal to hand over 'the factories of the war criminals and Nazi criminals into the hands of the people'. Some 2,341 enterprises were expropriated and the policy was extended to the other East German *Länder* without further referenda [53].

The British government was convinced that Germany could only be effectively disarmed if the great industrial trusts of the Ruhr were both nationalized and broken up into smaller units (decartelization). Consequently, the mines and steel industry were put under control of the Military Government, but nationalization was prevented by the creation of the Bizone which gave America, in effect, a veto over economic policy in the British Zone. The Americans were adamant that decartelization could only take place within the overall context of private enterprise. Ultimately, the thorny problem of decartelization was left to the new West German government to solve (see *p. 74*) [93; 94].

A similar fate befell the plans for land reform in the Western zones as a means of rooting out the big landowners. The Americans did very little, while the French handed over the initiative to the local *Landtage*. The British were more sympathetic to the demands for land reform, but they were inhibited from taking radical action by the fear that the dislocation it would cause would affect food supplies. Their main priority was to keep their zone running, whereas for the Russians, as one British Control Commission official stressed, 'political gains' were 'achieved at the expense of great economic losses' [42 *p. 55*].

By the end of 1947, in the absence of any effective central control, Germany was visibly splitting into two distinct economic entities, the American-dominated capitalist Western Germany and the Soviet-dominated socialist Eastern Germany. In the Bizone there were some signs of economic recovery. Production had reached half the 1936 level and manufacturers were repairing buildings and accumulating stocks of raw materials in the hope that eventually conditions would improve [66]. The Russians made little attempt to develop a comprehensive economic strategy for the reconstruction of their zone until June 1947 when they set up the German Economic Commission to administer the whole zonal economy (see *p. 26*). To improve production, SMAD also attempted to motivate the work force with Order 234, issued four months later, which 'amounted to a full blown transfer of Soviet style labour relations to East Germany' [117 *p. 23*]. Key factories were signalled out for special deliveries of food and improved working conditions and welfare provisions such as crèches and clinics. 'People's Control Committees' were set up to stop thefts on the factory floor, while workers were now to be paid by piece-work rates. This order began the crucial process in East Germany of 'refashioning the factory as a social and political as opposed to purely economic institution' [117 *p. 24*].

THE REVIVAL OF POLITICAL PARTIES AND THE TRADE UNIONS

The Western powers had no immediate plans for the formation of German political parties, but their hand was forced by the Russians who licensed democratic parties as early as 11 June 1945 and set up an anti-Fascist bloc comprising four parties: the Communists (KPD), the Socialists (SPD), the Christian Democrats (CDU) and the Liberals (LDPD). Their reasons for doing this were first to control political developments within their own zone and secondly, to use the parties as a means of projecting their own influence throughout Germany. The Americans agreed to the formation of democratic parties in August, the British a month later, and the French not until December 1945. In all four zones similar party grouping emerged [29 Vol. 1; 46].

Party leaders and activists, who had gained their formative political experiences during the Weimar Republic, were haunted by the divisions which had let the Nazis seize power in 1933. In the summer of 1945 the grass-root demand among the workers in both the Soviet and Western zones was for 'the organizational unity of the German working class' [46 *p. 137*]. The KPD leadership, hoping to dominate the anti-Fascist bloc of parties in the Soviet Zone, had initially declined to amalgamate with the SPD. By the autumn it was clear that this policy was failing. The KPD and its leaders were seen as 'bullies and stooges' [53 *p. 276*] who were manipulated by the Russians. The SPD remained the larger party and a potential challenge to Soviet authority. In the British Zone its branches increasingly fell under the influence of Kurt Schumacher who, as a former concentration camp inmate, became the symbolic figure of Social Democratic opposition to both Nazi and Soviet tyranny and was bitterly hostile to cooperation with the Communists [16].

In November 1945 the weakness of Communism in Central Europe was exposed by the elections in Hungary and Austria where the party did very badly. The Russians realized that the only chance of electoral success in their zone, and indeed Germany as a whole, was to force a union between the SPD and the KPD. After several months of bribery, intimidation and argument, the Central Executive of the SPD in the Soviet Zone agreed to plans for the formation of a new united party, the Socialist Unity Party (SED), by a vote of eight to three in February 1946. The Russians were then embarrassed when Pieck, the Chairman of the KPD, consented to hold a referendum on the decision in Berlin on 31 March. In East Berlin they managed to close the polling stations a mere half hour after they had opened, but in West Berlin the voting went ahead and 82 per cent of the

SPD members voted against union. Nevertheless this resounding rejection was softened by a second vote. Replying to the question of whether they supported 'an alliance ... which will guarantee continued cooperation and exclude fraternal strife' [*53 p. 282*] some 62 per cent of the membership responded positively. Thus, despite the forced amalgamation of the two parties in April 1946 [*Doc. 10*], there was still an underlying desire among the grass-root members of the SPD for close cooperation with the KPD. Pressure from SMAD ensured that the party modelled itself on the Russian Communist Party and, as the Cold War intensified, it expelled dissidents and became, as its Executive announced in June 1948, 'a fighting party of Marxism-Leninism' [*53 p. 310*] [*Doc. 13*]. At a stroke the shotgun marriage of the SPD and the KPD in the Soviet Zone demolished the claims of the SPD to be the strongest political force in Germany with the power to act as a bridge between the Soviet and Western zones. Instead, it became a rump party which drew most of its support from the industrialized areas in the British Zone [41; 46].

Apart from the SED the only party radically to break with the pre-1933 mould of party politics was the Christian Democratic Union which was set up simultaneously in Berlin and the Rhineland in June 1945. Its sister party, the CSU, was founded in Munich in October. The CDU/CSU, or Union as it was later called, attempted successfully to bridge the gap between North German Protestants and South German and Rhineland Catholics, thereby creating a powerful new Christian middle-class party, which also accepted many of the ideas of Christian Socialism. It was a coalition of forces which a French newspaper characterized as being 'socialist and radical in Berlin, clerical and conservative in Cologne, capitalist and reactionary in Hamburg and counter-revolutionary and particularist in Munich' [*46 p. 143*]. Schumacher was convinced that the movement would founder from its own contradictions, but he underestimated the political skills of Konrad Adenauer who, after being dismissed by the British from the post of *Oberbürgermeister* of Cologne, rapidly emerged as the most powerful man in the CDU. He was a pragmatist who believed that party programmes were essentially 'instruments' for winning elections [*46 p. 145*]. Although he himself was convinced that 'with the word socialism we win five people and twenty run away' [*46 p. 145*], he nevertheless agreed in 1947 to the Ahlen Programme, which was a compromise with the Christian-Socialist wing of the CDU, and conceded that the nationalization of heavy industry and even of some banks was necessary. This avoided a damaging row with Jakob Kaiser, the leader of the CDU in the Soviet Zone, who saw the party as a 'bridge between East and West' [*35 p. 32*] and enabled Adenauer to concentrate on building up the party's organization in the Western zones. With the intensification of the Cold War and Kaiser's flight to the West in December 1947, Adenauer found it increasingly easy to steer the CDU away from socialism and in the direction of the social market economy [9; 20 Vol. 1; 77].

Although the Liberal parties had only polled 3 per cent of the vote in 1932, Liberalism as a political force did revive spontaneously in 1945. It attracted those who were alienated by the CDU's close links with the Catholic Church and who wanted a capitalist rather than a socialist economy. The Russians recognized the LDPD in their zone in early July and two years later Liberals from all over Germany founded a unified German Democratic Party (DDP) at Eisenach under the joint chairmanship of Theodor Heuss and Wilhelm Külz, who were respectively the leaders of Liberalism in Western and Eastern Germany [46]. The DDP collapsed when Külz supported the German People's Congress, which was convened in Berlin in December 1947 by the Russians but boycotted by all the parties in the West except the KPD (see *p. 27*). A few months later, the Liberal rump in West Germany set up the Free Democratic Party under the chairmanship of Heuss. Like the CDU, it was a product of the Germans' desire to overcome the party divisions of the Weimar period as it appealed to both the supporters of the old right-wing National Liberal Party and the more left-wing Democratic Party. Yet, as a supporter of economic liberalism, it was to become a close ally of the CDU [29 Vol. 1; 41; 46].

At Potsdam the right to form unions was conceded, but the shape of the revived German trade union movement was in practice left to the occupying powers. The Americans and the French pursued a policy of encouraging the Germans to reconstruct the movement from the grass roots upwards. By January 1946 there were 163 different local unions in the French Zone alone. It was, however, in the Soviet and British Zones, where the greatest concentration of industry and therefore of workers were, that the future patterns of German trades unionism were to be created. From the beginning the Russians encouraged the idea of a centralized unitary trade union movement, as through it KPD members would be able to exercise a decisive influence on Germany. A preparatory trade union committee was set up in Berlin in June 1945, and in February 1946 the Free German Trade Union Association (FDGB) was formed in the Soviet Zone as a single trade union representing all German workers.

Initially, a centralized organization was also favoured by the trade unionists in the British Zone as it would avoid the divisions and weaknesses of the Weimar period. Hans Böckler, the future Chairman of the German Trades Union Federation (DGB), put forward plans for a giant general union, but the scheme ran into opposition from the Military Government and its British trade union advisors as they feared that a centralized organization would maximize Communist influence and that its very size would discourage its members from actively participating. Some German workers, particularly the miners and the office workers also wanted to revive their own unions. Böckler agreed to the principle of independent unions grouped under an umbrella federation. By April 1947 over two million workers in the British Zone were members of local zonal unions. In August, the trade unions in the American and British Zones were amalgamated, but only in December 1948 did the French allow the unions in their Zone to join. From 1946 to August 1948 regular conferences between union leaders in all four zones took place with the intention of preparing the way for a united German trade union movement, but with the onset of the Cold War contacts between the FDGB and the Western unions ceased [53; 46].

Initially the trades unionists throughout Germany shared the same general aims – full employment, the workers' right to co-determination in individual plants and nationalization of key industries – but the realization of these aims was dependent on the policies of the occupying powers. There was little that the workers themselves could do about full employment or nationalization, but in May 1945 throughout Germany they seized the opportunity to set up works councils in their factories in a bold attempt to extend democracy into the work place. The Allied Control Council recognized works councils in principle in April 1946 and the British granted co-determination rights to the unions in the iron and steel industries as part of their decartelization programme, but the Americans vetoed plans by the Hesse *Land* government for introducing co-determination into the IG Farben chemical plants in 1947. In the Russian Zone works councils survived until they were forcibly amalgamated with the plant trade union committees in late 1948 [27; 43; 66].

THE LEGACY OF THE OCCUPATION

It would be hard to exaggerate the impact of the occupation on the history of Germany up to 1990. The failure of the occupying powers to agree on German unity led to partition and the creation of two rival German states: the FRG and the GDR. Both of these states were profoundly influenced by their occupiers. By 1961 the GDR was a socialist state and part of the Russian-dominated Eastern bloc, while the FRG became a liberal democracy integrated into the global economy and increasingly adopted the values of American society [32; 35].

CHAPTER THREE

THE DIVISION OF GERMANY

THE BIZONE AND THE GERMAN ECONOMIC COMMISSION

In retrospect it can be seen that the Bizone was the 'germ cell and pre-figuration' of the later FRG [41 *p. 419*], yet initially this was by no means clear. There was no bizonal parliament and the offices responsible for food and agriculture, finance and communications were deliberately located in five different cities to allay Russian suspicions that it was a political entity. It was only with the failure of the Moscow Foreign Ministers' Conference in April 1947 that the Bizone began to acquire some of the characteristics of a provisional government.

The Moscow Conference was a 'benchmark in early post-war history' [9 *p. 26*]. The British, fearful of Communist influence in a united Germany and nearly bankrupt, played a skilful role in isolating Russia over the key issue of reparations. They persuaded the Americans to drop a proposal that would have enabled the Russians to take some reparations from the current production of coal and steel in the Ruhr and to focus instead on rebuilding the West German economy. To implement this decision the level of per-mitted industrial capacity in the Western zones was raised in July (see *p. 19*) and the administrative machinery of the Bizone improved. All five of the administrative offices were moved to Frankfurt and three new institutions were added: an Economic Council, made up of 52 members who were to be chosen by the *Land* assemblies; an Executive Committee composed of one representative from each *Land*; and a Directorate, the members of which were the executives of the Bizonal Economic Agencies. The Economic Council was empowered, subject to overall Anglo-American approval, to pass laws on economic matters and to ensure that they were carried out. It could also appoint and remove the executive directors. Reflecting the com-position of the *Land* parliaments, the SPD and CDU, together with its sister party in Bavaria, the CSU, were each given twenty seats. The remaining twelve seats were divided up among the smaller parties, most of which, with the exception of the KPD, were more sympathetic towards the Christ-ian Democrats than they were towards the Social Democrats. A preview of the political configuration of the future West German state could be glimpsed in the battle over the appointments of the key economic officials who would run the five administrative offices of the Bizone. When the SPD group failed to secure its choice of candidates in July 1947, it went into opposition, leaving the business of the Council to be carried out by the other parties led by the CDU/CSU, the so-called 'Frankfurt Coalition' [30 Vol. 1; 41; 47].

From the very beginning the Soviet government had suspected that the Bizone was a political as well as an economic entity. The formation of the Economic Council and the streamlining of the Bizonal administration in May 1947 fuelled these suspicions and was one of the main factors contributing to the Russians setting up the German Economic Commission (DWK) in their zone on 4 June 1947. This was intended to coordinate economic policy and, after due consultation with SMAD, to draw up a zonal economic plan. The Commission was composed of the presidents of the zone's central ministries, created by the Russians in 1945, and the chairmen of the FDGB and the Association for Farmers' Mutual Help (VdgB). As with the Bizone, it too was the 'germ cell' of a future German state – the GDR – although, like the British and the Americans, the Russians tried to play down the political and economic significance of their initiative by stressing that it was firmly under the control of SMAD [35; 53].

THE IMPACT OF THE MARSHALL PLAN AND THE SOVIET RESPONSE

While the emergence of Bizonia began to anticipate the creation of a West German state, the Marshall Plan (see *pp. 70–1*) created the international context in which the new state would eventually have to function. The US Secretary of State, George Marshall, announced the European Recovery Programme (ERP) at Harvard University in June 1947 and offered American aid to rehabilitate Europe's economies provided that the recipients agreed on a common economic programme and a liberal free trade system. The Western European nations responded enthusiastically. By early 1948 Congress had approved the funding for the Marshall Plan and ERP funds began to be channelled to Europe. When the Organization for European Economic Cooperation (OEEC) was set up in April 1948 to coordinate the ERP, sixteen West European states joined and significantly both Bizonia and the French Zone were represented on it. This was, as Pulzer has observed, 'the first entry of the western zones into those supra-national European linkages that were to become their defining characteristic' [27 *p. 41*].

Soviet suspicions that Britain and America were aiming to integrate Western Germany into a liberal, capitalist bloc dominated by America were naturally increased by the ERP programme. Initially, the Soviet government was not sure how to react, but by September Stalin had decided on all out opposition and had set up the Cominform, 'a new coordinating agency for the international Communist movement' which would mastermind the fight against the Marshall Plan [120 *p. 46*]. The hardline stance taken by Stalin was backed by the SED leadership, which was only too aware that the economic misery within the Soviet Zone made the Marshall Plan potentially attractive to the East Germans [49; 53].

THE MOMENTUM TO PARTITION ACCELERATES, NOVEMBER 1947–JUNE 1948

When in late November 1947 the Foreign Ministers of the occupying powers met in London, 'partition seem[ed]', as General Robertson, the British Military Governor, observed, 'to be in the air' [67 *p. 114*]. The London Conference was a disaster and showed how deeply divided the Western powers and Russia had become. The Russians recited a long litany of complaints in which they accused Britain and America of violating the Potsdam Agreement by setting up Bizonia and denying them their share of reparations, while Bevin and Marshall rejected Soviet proposals for the formation of a central German government on the grounds that they would merely lead to the creation of an unrepresentative Communist puppet regime. The Conference broke up on 17 December amid bitter recriminations. A day later, during bilateral Anglo-American discussions, there was agreement that the Bizone should be given more political responsibilities and, failing a quadripartite understanding, that a new currency should be introduced into the whole of Western Germany. It was also becoming increasingly obvious that the French Zone would have to be integrated into what would shortly become a West German state. Bevin was, however, careful to stress that the door should be left open for free elections for an all-German government 'so that any irredentist German movement should be based on the west rather than the east' [67 *p. 115*]. In other words, West Germany would, it was hoped, ultimately act as a 'magnet' for the Eastern Zone, rather than the other way round.

The Russians and the SED attempted to exploit the mixed feelings that many West Germans had about the impending partition of their country. Urged on by SMAD, Ulbricht called a 'German People's Congress [*Volkskongress*] for Unity and a Just Peace'. Party delegates from all over Germany were invited to attend sessions on 6–7 December in Berlin, the aim of which was to send a delegation of Germans to the London Conference to support the Soviet demand for a German central government. Out of some 2,225 delegates, roughly one-third came from the West, but these were for the most part representatives of the KPD strongholds in the Ruhr [49]. There were hardly any members of the Western middle-class parties there, and it was quite clear that the Congress was in reality a 'charade of political unity' [53 *p. 57*]. An important secondary objective of the whole exercise was to bring pressure to bear upon the leaders of the 'bourgeois parties' in the Soviet Zone. Thus Jakob Kaiser and Ernst Lemmer of the Eastern Zone Christian Democrats (CDUD), who were sceptical about the Peoples Congress, were summarily removed by SMAD and replaced by the more pliant Otto Nuschke. Wilhelm Külz of the LDPD attended, but at the cost of alienating Heuss and the Western Liberals (see *p. 23*). It was hardly surprising that the British authorities refused to allow the delegation to come to London [35; 49; 53].

Over the next six months the impetus to partition continued. First, in February, Bizonia gained further attributes of an independent state. The representation of the Economic Council was doubled and it was given the power to raise taxation while a second house was created to represent the *Länder*. A high court and a central bank were also set up. In the Soviet Zone SMAD reacted to these reforms by giving the German Economic Commission greater scope to coordinate and plan the economy. In April its power was significantly strengthened when it was permitted to issue ordinances which were binding on the population. Like its counterpart in Bizonia, it was rapidly evolving into a prototype government [53; 59].

On 23 February 1948, the USA, Britain, France and the Benelux states met in London where, over the next four months, a whole number of crucial decisions was taken. French cooperation was assured by Anglo-American endorsement of French plans, which were already far advanced, for integrating the Saar into the French economy. On 6 March, the Conference recommended the creation of a West German state and the formation of an international Ruhr Authority on which the USSR would not have a seat. These decisions were taken against the background of steadily escalating East–West tension. The Communist seizure of power in Czechoslovakia at the end of February was answered by the creation of a Western European security system at the Brussels Conference on 17 March.

In response to these decisions the Russians withdrew their representative from the Control Council and sporadically began to block rail freight traffic between the Western Zones and West Berlin. They also attempted to exploit the German desire for unity by calling another People's Congress in Berlin and set out to evoke for propaganda purposes the spirit of the 1848 revolutions. A 'German Peoples' Council' (*Volksrat*) of 400 delegates, a quarter of whom were from the Western zones, was set up as a permanent body to continue the political work of the Congress when it was not sitting. The *Volksrat* was entrusted both with preparing a referendum on German unity and with drawing up a constitution for a united centralized German state. In the event of the SED's almost certain failure to unite Germany, the draft constitution for the whole of Germany would then have to become the basis for an East German constitution. In May, Wilhelm Pieck, the Chairman of the SED, told its leadership cadres that once a West German state was created the Soviet Zone would inevitably have to 'develop its own independent state structure'. It was immaterial whether the Western powers 'tore Germany apart ... a month earlier or a month later. The important thing was to be prepared for every eventuality' [64 *pp. 121–2*].

The moment of decision for the West Germans came in early June. At the conclusion of the second part of the London Conference the Western Allies announced that they intended to authorize the West Germans to convene a constituent assembly, whose delegates would be selected by a procedure to be determined by the *Land* parliaments. The constitution would then have to be approved by the (Western) Military Governors and ratified by referendum in the *Länder*. The West Germans would also have to accept an Occupation Statute, reserving for their former occupiers far-reaching powers in the spheres of foreign relations, trade, reparations, economic questions and disarmament, and above all the right to 'resume the exercise of their full powers in an emergency threatening security' [52 *p. 51*].

CURRENCY REFORM AND THE BERLIN BLOCKADE

Nearly three weeks later the intention of America and her Allies to create a West German state was underpinned by the introduction of a new currency, the *Deutschmark* (DM), in both Bizonia and the French Zone on 20 June, and then three days later in West Berlin (see *pp. 68–9*). The introduction of the *Deutschmark* was a crucial step in the division of Germany. 'It touched', as Klessmann observed, 'the main nerve affecting any form of national unity' [46 *p. 188*]. The Russians were caught by surprise, but on 23 June introduced their own currency reform (see *p. 95*). They had no time to print fresh notes and had to improvise by sticking coupons on existing notes.

The immediate consequence of the currency reform in the Western zones was the Berlin Blockade. East German historians used to describe it as a defensive and temporary measure to stop the Soviet Zone being swamped with devalued *Reichsmarks*. In reality, however, it was a desperate, but not unexpected, attempt to block the creation of a West German state. The full blockade did not begin until the night of 23–24 June when the *Deutschmark* was introduced into the western sectors of Berlin after Britain and America had rejected a Soviet proposal for the exclusive circulation of the new East Mark within the city. For the next six months both currencies circulated within the Western zones. The rail and road links to the West were cut, as was the supply of electricty from East Berlin to the Western sectors. The blockade rapidly became a great symbolic struggle which America and its Allies could not afford to lose if their plans for the construction of a West German state were not to unravel. The immediate response of the Western

Allies was to begin an airlift which, contrary to the pessimistic forecasts of the British Military Governor, was able to supply West Berlin throughout the very mild winter of 1948–49 with food and fuel. The Americans also moved 60 B29 planes to Britain, which, in fact inaccurately, it was assumed were capable of carrying atomic bombs. Negotiations lasting from the end of July to early September explored the possibility of allowing the East Mark to become the sole currency for the whole of Berlin, subject only to the control of a four-power financial commission, but they broke down when it became clear that Stalin and Molotov really wanted to use an East Mark monopoly to weaken the Western powers in Berlin and force them to give up their plans for a West German state. Consequently, despite efforts by the United Nations to find a solution to the Berlin crisis, the blockade continued until 12 May 1949 when Stalin belatedly realized that it had been counter-productive. Not only did it accelerate the integration of the Western zones into an American-dominated Western Europe, but it also split Berlin and ensured that the Western part of the city eventually became an outpost of West Germany with its own city government and *Deutschmark* currency [12; 59; 67].

THE EMERGENCE OF THE TWO GERMANIES

Against the threatening background of the Berlin crisis the Germans in both the Eastern and Western zones began to draw up constitutions for separate states. Superficially, the predicament of both German political elites was similar. They were not free agents and their respective occupying powers could, if international circumstances changed, simply consign their work to the rubbish bin. The founding fathers of the two German states were resigned to what they hoped would only be a temporary partition. In June 1947 an all-German Minister-President Conference had met in Munich to discuss German unity, but progress was made impossible by the demands of the East Germans for a centralized administration which the West Germans, and of course their occupiers, feared would lead to Soviet domination [26; 41].

In varying degrees, both the East and West German political elites distrusted the people. In the West there was the desire to create a democratic system of checks and balances, which would ensure stability and consensus. In Merkl's words 'the framers of the Basic Law were motivated by a deep distrust of the common man' [52 *p. 176*]. In the East much was made of the power of the 'people', but in reality this was propaganda aimed to give the regime moral authority. The position of the West German politicians was undoubtedly stronger than their counterparts in the SED. There was a broad consensus on both the left and on the right for a democratic constitution, and skilled operators like Adenauer were able to exploit the differences between the Western Allies themselves to achieve concessions and modifications. The SED leaders, on the other hand, were entirely dependent on Stalin for their survival, and had no means at that stage of bringing pressure to bear upon him [35; 49; 53].

The Federal Republic

In July the Minister-Presidents and the party leaders, sometimes meeting independently and sometimes with the Military Governors, decided that a parliamentary council comprising 65 members elected by the *Länder* parliaments should draw up a provisional constitution 'for the uniform administration of the occupation zones outside the iron curtain' [52 *p. 54*], which would last only until the unification of Germany. They were critical of the proposed Occupation Statute, and were also, in principle, opposed to the American demand that the new West German constitution should be ratified by a referendum. They feared that public opinion might be encouraged by the KPD to reject it in favour of unification with the Soviet Zone. The Western Allies accepted the provisional nature of the constitution and the Minister-Presidents' objections to a referendum.

The outline of the new constitution was initially drafted by a committee of constitutional and political experts delegated by the *Länder* in August and then discussed in depth for the next six months at Bonn by the 65 delegates of the Parliamentary Council. The political issues and manoeuvring of the rival politicians and groups were in many ways a curtain-raiser to the politics of the early FRG. The CDU/CSU and the SPD were finely balanced, each with 27 seats. However, in social economic issues the former could count on the backing of the five Liberal (FDP), two Centre Party and two DP (a regional Lower Saxony party) representatives, while the SPD could only occasionally rely on the backing of the two KPD members. The SPD made a decisive mistake when it decided not to oppose Adenauer's nomination as president of the Parliamentary Council in return for allowing Carlo Schmid to chair the main committee. Adenauer was able to exploit this position to become a national figure which was to help him later in winning the election. He was helped, too, by the absence through illness of his principle opponent, Schumacher [20 Vol. 1].

Essentially, the founding fathers were, to quote Pulzer, 'burnt children who knew what fire was like. Their vision was one of disaster-avoidance, not a new heaven and a new earth' [27 *p. 47*]. Eschenburg has described the Basic Law as a 'hybrid' or 'mixture of Weimar traditionalism and a determination to reform' [41 *p. 511*]. Some twenty years later, revisionist historians in the FRG attacked the Basic Law as a betrayal of the working classes which was almost as great as the victory of Fascism in 1933. Under Western Allied pressure, so ran the line of argument, 'a late capitalist system' was restored which was much to the detriment of the workers [38;

60]. Certainly there were elements of 'restoration' in the constitution and no dramatic new deal for the workers, but then the founding fathers were deliberately avoiding grand and arguably empty gestures. They were more intent on creating a workable constitution which, while drawing on the Weimar model, improved it. One of General Clay's advisors, Carl J. Friedrich, observed that the Basic Law was an example of 'the negative revolutions' of the post-war era, which he characterized as an attempt to find a middle way between revolution and counter-revolution [52 p. 176]. Article 67, for instance, aimed to prevent a repetition of the unstable coalition government of the Weimar period by insisting that a Chancellor could only be forced to resign if there was already a majority in the lower house (*Bundestag*) for his successor. Similarly, Article 68 laid down that the President could only dissolve the *Bundestag* if, after 21 days, it had failed to choose a new Chancellor. Except for local *Länder* matters, there were to be no popular referenda and the president was to be elected by the Federal Convention, a body made up equally of *Bundestag* and *Länder* representatives (Article 54). Basic human rights, such as freedom of conscience and speech and the right to property, were safeguarded in the first nineteen articles of the constitution and a federal constitutional court was set up to watch over the workings of the constitution. As the Basic Law was a compromise, there was little in it defining in detail the future socio-economic shape of the West German state. The churches were pleased to see that in Article 6 'marriage and family' were 'under the special protection of the state' [52 p. 214], but there was nothing specifically about denominational schools. Similarly, contrary to the demands of the trade unions, there was no mention of co-determination or nationalization [27; 30 Vol. 1; 41].

The most divisive and complex issue debated in the Parliamentary Council was the form of the federal state to be created. It was a question, too, of vital importance to both America and France, for whom 'strong *Länder* were an essential aspect of the constitutional deliberations' [20 Vol. 1, p. 416]. Initially, the centralizers, the SPD and Adenauer's wing of the CDU, favoured an elected senate, because they did not want a *Bundesrat* (an upper house) composed of *Länder* representatives who would be able to block policies decided in the *Bundestag*. The SPD then accepted a proposal from the Bavarian CSU for a weakened *Bundesrat* in which individual *Länder* delegations would sit. To avoid conceding to the SPD, which controlled most of the smaller *Länder*, a built-in majority in the *Bundesrat*, Adenauer eventually agreed to a compromise whereby votes were given to the *Länder* delegations on the basis of their population. When the Parliamentary Council came to discuss taxation and revenue, they were again confronted with the issue of federalism. After lengthy negotiations a 'grand compromise' [52 p. 79] was agreed, whereby the South German federalists accepted a centralized fiscal administration in return for increasing the powers of the *Bundesrat*.

On 10 February the Parliamentary Council submitted the final draft of the Basic Law to the Military Governors who, after consulting with their governments, forced the Germans to modify the law in two key areas: West Berlin was not for the time being to be part of the Federation, although it was permitted to send representatives to sit in the *Bundestag* and *Bundesrat* (but they would have no voting rights), and the fiscal administration was to be further devolved to the *Länder*. In the latter question, the Council compromised by creating a 'joint fiscal administration' [*52 p. 79*] run by both the Federation and *Länder*. Taxes would be fixed centrally, but where they concerned the interests of the *Länder*, the approval of the Upper House was needed. Also, the money raised by taxation would be divided between the *Länder* and the federal government [27].

On 8 May the Parliamentary Council finally approved the Basic Law [*Doc. 14*] and two days later it decided that Bonn, then a sleepy Rhineland city, rather than the great city of Frankfurt in the American Zone, should be the seat of government. A mixture of motives inspired this decision: the desire to stress the provisional nature of the new republic; the avoidance of too direct a dependence on the Americans; and finally, in the case of Adenauer, personal convenience and the wish to locate the new capital in the heartland of the middle-class Catholic Rhineland [32]. Between 16 and 22 May the *Länder* legislatures, with the single exception of Bavaria, ratified the Basic Law, but in reality even the Bavarians were 'whisper[ing] "yes" in the same breath as shouting "no"' [*52 p. 160*], as they agreed in a second vote to accept the Law if two-thirds of the *Länder* had already approved it [29 Vol. 1; 32; 52].

The date for the election of the *Bundestag* was then set for 14 August. The electoral law was a compromise. Half the deputies were to be elected by a direct constituency vote, while the other half were to be chosen from party lists compiled on the basis of the *Länder*. The election campaign rapidly became a duel between Schumacher and Adenauer, who had outmanoeuvred the left wing of his party and made the main theme of his campaign, as he announced in Heidelberg in July, a crusade against 'the birth of a Socialist economy' [*20 Vol. 1, p. 428*]. His campaign was strengthened by his alliance with Erhard, the Economics Director of the Bizone, whose vigorous social market economic policy (see *p. 70*) was at last beginning to bear fruit. Adenauer successfully pulled strings behind the scenes to have Erhard elected Chairman of the Bavarian CSU. His campaign was also helped by Schumacher's intemperate attack on the Catholic Church as the 'fifth occupying power', which alienated many moderate Catholic voters [*Doc. 15*]. On 14 August the CDU/ CSU won 139 seats and the SPD 131, while the FDP gained 52 [*Doc. 21*]. When the *Bundestag* met in September [*Doc. 18*], Adenauer was elected the first Chancellor of the FRG (see *p. 33*).

The German Democratic Republic

While the West German politicians were deliberating in Bonn, the SED weighed up possible responses. In the winter of 1948–49 the Russians were reluctant to commit themselves irrevocably to creating a separate East German state if there was still the slightest chance of a return to four-power control leading ultimately to a neutral Germany, potentially friendly to Russia. Consequently, in December 1948, Pieck, Grotewohl and Ulbricht found that Stalin still thought that the entry of East Germany into the Cominform was premature. He was ready to concede the Soviet Zone greater administrative independence, but for the moment this was to be seen as a holding operation which should not exclude eventual German unity. As Pieck observed, 'the way to Socialism' was a 'zig-zag course' ... one must 'camouflage oneself in battle...' [64 *p. 127*].

Throughout the spring and summer of 1949 the SED leadership pursued three interrelated aims: to convert the *Volkskongress* movement into the National Front which, in deference to the 'double strategy' [64 *p. 128*] of Stalin, would allow the SED to claim the role of 'the genuine defender of national unity in contrast to the "splitters" in the West' [53 *p. 58*]; to form an East German state which would guarantee the dominating position of the SED), while attracting Communists in West Germany; and finally the leadership sought to persuade the SMAD to withdraw into the background and allow it greater independence. This, it was hoped would 'lift the burden of guilt by association – for the rape, plunder, repression and economic exploitation by Soviet forces' which had weighed on the party since 1945 [53 *p. 58*].

In March 1949 the *Volksrat* approved the constitution of the future German Democratic Republic. As the GDR would be still in its 'bourgeois democratic stage of development' [28 *p. 53*], its constitution, on paper at least, was not to be so very different from the Basic Law, yet in reality, as events were to show, it was to be but a 'make-believe constitution' [52 *p. 175*] camouflaging a one-party dictatorship. Theoretically, its citizens were guaranteed the fundamental rights of a democracy – freedom of the press, freedom of speech, the right to strike and even the right to emigrate. Parliament also appeared very similar to the model adopted in the FRG. There was a Lower House, the *Volkskammer* (People's Chamber), which was elected for a four-year term under a system of proportional representation, while the Upper House, the Chamber of States, was a weaker version of the *Bundesrat*. Legislation was not dependent on its consent, although it possessed a veto which could, however, be overridden by the Lower House [35].

In May a third *Volkskongress* was elected. The voters had been presented with just one list of candidates representing the mass organizations and the bloc parties, which included the CDUD and LDPD, whose leaders still optimistically hoped that by cooperating with the SED they could form a bridge to their sister parties in the West. The voters were simultaneously asked whether they were 'for or against German unity and a just peace treaty'. In reality, as the voters knew, this was an appeal for a vote for an East German state. Despite a massive campaign and manipulation of the voting results, some four million, one-third of the electorate, registered a negative vote, an embarrassing fact which led the SED leadership in October to delay any further elections for at least a year [35; 49].

At the end of May the Congress met and endorsed the draft constitution already approved by the *Volksrat* in March, but Moscow's double strategy kept the SED in suspense. The Russians still believed that there was an outside chance of stopping the setting up of the FRG. They hoped to negotiate a compromise at the Foreign Ministers' Conference, which met in Paris in May 1949, but it broke up without any agreement. Once the West German elections, in which the KPD won a mere 5.7 per cent of the votes, had taken place in August, it was clear that there was little alternative to setting up the GDR, even if for the Russians it was an exercise in damage limitation. Thus, in September, the SED leaders once more went to Moscow to finalize dates, procedures and the list of ministers. On 7 October the *Volkskongress* announced the creation of the German Democratic Republic as 'a powerful bulwark in the struggle for the accomplishment of the National Front of Democratic Germany' [53 *p. 59*]. SMAD was dissolved and a Soviet Control Commission was created which tranferred all administrative responsibilities to the new GDR. The *Volksrat* transformed itself into a provisional parliament (*Volkskammer*) and the new government, headed by Grotewohl with Ulbricht as one of his deputies, was formed on 12 October (see *p. 84*). Gerhart Eisler, the Director of the Information Department of the Economic Commission, remarked prophetically at a meeting on 4 October that 'once we have set up a government, we will never give it up, neither through elections or other methods'. Ulbricht then added: 'A few still have not understood this' [64 *p. 143*].

CHAPTER FOUR

TWO RIVAL STATES

The two German states owed their existence to the Cold War and were from the beginning locked into a struggle to re-unite Germany in their image. Both were increasingly integrated into the rival Cold War blocs. The Federal Republic posed as the legitimate and sole heir to the German Reich founded in 1871 and laid claim to the former German territory beyond the Oder–Neisse line, while the GDR traced its legitimacy to the 'popular revolution' which purged the Soviet Zone of Nazism in the immediate post-war years. It consequently argued that it had an historical mission to set up a united German workers' state and rid the West of both capitalism and the considerable remnants of Nazism [124].

WESTERN INTEGRATION: THE ECSC AND EDC

In 1949 the infant Federal Republic was distrusted by its neighbours, who were apprehensive of the emergence of a potentially powerful West Germany. The Saar was in the process of becoming a French satellite state, while the International Ruhr Authority supervised the exports of the Ruhr's heavy industries. For Adenauer, integration was the 'great hope of the 1950's' [20 Vol. 1, *p. 459*], as it offered the prospect of partnership with the Western European democracies and security within the international community. It could also be a lever for revising the Ruhr and Occupation Statutes and eventually for producing an acceptable solution to the Saar question. Integration was powerfully backed by the Americans who saw in it not only the means for containing Soviet Russia, but also a way of indirectly controlling West Germany itself [61]. Adenauer's first foreign policy success came with the Petersberg Agreement in November 1949, which has been called 'the basic charter of West German foreign policy in its opening phase' [29 Vol. 1, *p. 258*]. By permitting Bonn to join the Council of Europe and the OEEC, to open consulates in other countries and take a seat on the board of the International Ruhr Authority, it enabled the FRG, in Adenauer's words, to 're-enter the international sphere' [9 *p. 221*]. Yet when the French set up an autonomous Saar in March 1950, Adenauer's policy seemed momentarily to be forced back into the mould of an old-fashioned and discredited German nationalism. He even threatened not to join the Council of Europe, but this was just a demonstration for domestic consumption and he continued to signal through numerous channels his desire for closer economic and political integration with Western Europe. The French were becoming more receptive to Adenauer's signals. Faced with the inevitable prospect of West Germany's economic revival, which in turn would lead to its re-emergence as a formidable competitor, Schuman, the French Foreign Minister, and the businessman and civil servant, Jean Monnet, made a daring bid to achieve 'a long-term control of Germany ... through an entirely modern concept designed to lead to partnership' [20 Vol. 1, *p. 510*]. They put forward a plan for the pooling of the European coal and steel industries under supra-national control to create a European Coal and Steel Community. Adenauer realized of course that the Schuman Plan was a subtle instrument for ensuring that France retained more influence over the Ruhr than was commensurate with its economic strength, yet to him these concessions were worth while. The ECSC Treaty of 18 April 1951, which was signed by France, the FRG, the Benelux states and Italy, not only replaced the Ruhr Statute but, by removing the threat of Franco-German economic rivalry, broke out of the vicious circle of Franco-German hostility. In this sense it can be argued that the Plan 'fulfilled many of the functions of a peace treaty' between the two powers [29 Vol. 1, *p. 270*; 121].

European integration was again the means Adenauer employed to defuse the emotive issue of German rearmament. As early as the spring of 1950 he was floating the idea of an armed security police and a West German contribution to 'an international legion' [20 Vol. 1, *p. 526*]. The outbreak of the Korean War in June, which initially seemed to be the prelude to a new global war, strengthened the demand for a West German defence contribution and put Adenauer in a potentially strong position to demand concessions from the Western Allies in return. First, in Strassburg in August, Churchill called for a European army and then at the NATO meeting in New York in September the Americans put forward concrete proposals for a German army to serve under an integrated command in Western Europe. To reconcile the urgent need for West German troops with fears of German militarism, in October the French Prime Minister, Pleven, seized on a plan produced once again by Monnet 'to make control of Germany into a European virtue' [20 Vol. 1, *p. 591*]. The subsequent Pleven Plan envisaged a European Defence Community directed by a defence minister answerable to a European Commission of Control. All German troops would be committed to the EDC, but the other European powers, particularly the French, would reserve some of their forces for colonial and national purposes. Adenauer readily agreed in principle to the EDC, but also seized his chance to couple German rearmament with the demand for the abolition of the Occupation Statute and the restoration of German sovereignty.

For the next eighteen months Adenauer's foreign policy was dominated by two complex and interrelated sets of negotiations. In Paris the nuts and bolts of the EDC were painstakingly assembled, while in Bonn Adenauer, advised by the formidable Professor Hallstein, who was State-Secretary in the West German Foreign Office, which was set up in January 1951, negotiated 'the General Treaty' with the High Commissioners. By this, the Western powers abolished the Occupation Statute and recognized both the Federal Republic's sovereignty in international affairs and its membership of the EDC. They also committed themselves to work for a unified democratic Germany which, provided it accepted the obligations of the FRG, would ultimately be integrated into the European community. The three Western powers retained their rights to negotiate at some future date a peace treaty with a united Germany and thus the question of the eastern frontiers was left open. There were further articles covering the rights and security of the Allied troops still stationed in the FRG [20 Vol. 1; 32].

In early 1952 discussions also took place in London on the payment of German debts. By agreeing to pay an annual sum of DM 567 million rising to DM 765 million in 1958 to cover Marshall Plan credits (see *p. 70*) and the repayment of pre-war loans under the Dawes Plan, West Germany was able both to avoid being saddled with any further reparation demands and to legitimize itself in a practical way as the heir to the Reich. In separate negotiations Adenauer also agreed that the FRG should pay DM 3 billion's worth of reparations in kind to Israel. The General Treaty was signed in Bonn on 26 May 1952 and the EDC Treaty in Paris a day later. The two treaties had a difficult passage through the *Bundestag* (see *p. 58*), but were ratified a year later. When the French Chamber refused to ratify the EDC Treaty on 30 August 1954, it appeared as if the whole West German settlement had collapsed like a house of cards [20 Vol. 2].

THE FRG ACHIEVES SOVEREIGNTY AND ENTERS NATO

Such a rebuff would certainly have had far more serious repercussions for Adenauer if it had occurred two years earlier when Schumacher menacingly declared that anyone signing the treaties could not call themselves a German. It might well have destroyed the Adenauer government and plunged Bonn into bitter political conflict reminiscent of the Weimar period [*Doc. 17*] and been the catalyst to renewed Franco-German rivalry. By 1954, however, Adenauer's position was immeasurably stronger. The CDU/CSU had increased its vote in the elections of 1953, the FRG enjoyed a booming economy (see *p. 72*) and Adenauer had excellent relations with the new American Secretary of State, John Foster Dulles. The French, on the other hand, were weakened by their defeat in Indo-China and dependent on Anglo-American diplomatic assistance [20 Vol. 2; 32].

Adenauer's immediate priorities were to save the General Treaty and secure the FRG's entry into NATO. To achieve this he had to overcome latent French fears of a rearmed Germany. Thus he agreed to limit the Federal army to the size envisaged in the EDC Treaty and voluntarily to renounce nuclear weapons. He also consented to the Saar's new status as an autonomous territory economically united to France, subject only to a plebiscite of the inhabitants, whom it was universally assumed would approve this arrangement. In October the outline of a new settlement emerged in the London negotiations. A new General or German Treaty was negotiated which recognized the sovereignty of the Federal Republic and its membership of NATO. The Western Allies again bound themselves to work towards a united federal Germany integrated into the European community. In the meantime their troops would remain in the FRG and Berlin would still be under four-power control. On 5 May 1955 the Treaty came into force [*Doc. 25*] and four days later the FRG joined NATO [20 Vol. 2; 32].

The only problem that now remained was the Saar. In October, much to the surprise of both Bonn and Paris, the population of the Saar rejected their autonomous status and in subsequent elections pro-German parties were returned. Thanks to the progress already made in economic integration and the decline of the Saar's heavy industries the French readily agreed to its return to the FRG in 1957. This painless solution to the Saar problem is eloquent testimony to the new stability created in Western Europe by the 1955 treaties, which Schwarz has compared favourably with the Vienna Settlement of 1815 [79 Vol. 2]. Yet this success did have its price. While theoretically the door was kept open for German unification, in reality the integration of the FRG into NATO, the ECSC and the Council of Europe made unity in the foreseeable future unlikely. The very success of Western integration intensified what Klessmann has called 'the reactive mechanism' [46 *p. 177*] of the Cold War and in the end led to a deeper integration of the GDR into the Soviet bloc. Schumacher had recognized this danger when he declared in 1950 that the SPD would oppose any agreements that did not 'leave open and even strengthen the possibilities of German unity' [16 *p. 172*]. Adenauer's *Westpolitik* was supported by the majority of the West Germans, but it was nevertheless, as Graml had put it, 'constantly subjected to furious detailed criticism and anxious attempts to apply the brakes' [30 Vol. 1, *p. 355*], as it inevitably intensified the division of Germany.

THE REACTION OF THE GDR AND THE USSR TO WESTERN
INTEGRATION

It was exactly this disquiet and alarm at the consequences of Western integration that Moscow and the GDR tried to exploit in an increasingly
desperate attempt to stop West German rearmament. From the autumn of
1950 until the autumn of 1954 the Russians orchestrated either at international level or through the GDR a series of initiatives aimed at achieving
a united but neutral Germany. Whether these initiatives were genuine offers
which would have created an independent, albeit neutral Germany, or
merely attempts to slow up Western integration and to destabilize the
Adenauer regime is a matter of considerable historical controversy. For the
GDR these moves were potentially fraught with danger as any scheme
acceptable to the West would involve the wholesale rejection of the SED.
Recent research, however, has shown that there were some members of the
GDR Politbureau who welcomed unity and were even ready to sacrifice the
SED [49; 82].

In November 1950 the GDR called for an 'all German constituent
council' and followed this up in January with more detailed proposals for
elections. Behind the scenes the SED's leadership was bitterly divided over
the wisdom of this policy. Ulbricht, who could only contemplate unity at
that stage if it resulted in a Stalinist Germany, was forced to take a back
seat while Grotwohl, supported by Herrnstadt and Ackermann, seized the
initiative. Indeed, Herrnstadt had even declared in a speech to the plenary
meeting of the Central Committee of the SED on 26–27 October 1950 that
his colleagues should disabuse themselves of the idea that 'the coming unified democratic Germany would simply be an enlarged copy of the present
GDR' [82 *p. 97*]. Ulbricht, as on other occasions, was saved by the determination of Adenauer and the Western Allies to persist with West German
rearmament. A three-month meeting of the Foreign Ministers' Deputies in
Paris (March–June 1951) failed to produce an agenda for a four-power
conference on Germany. In 1952 and 1953 there were further potentially
far-reaching Soviet initiatives. In March 1952 Stalin proposed in two notes
plans for an independent Germany and free elections supervised by a commission of the four great powers. This new Germany was not to be allowed
to make alliances against former enemies, and so could hardly join the
EDC, but on the other hand it would not be burdened with demands for
reparations, denazification and for the socialization of the economy. It
would also be allowed to have its own armed forces for defensive purposes
only [49]. In Schwarz's words, a 'certain mythology' [79 Vol. 2, *p. 159*] grew
up around the history of this note, reminiscent of the old stab-in-the-back
legend of 1918. To many Germans, among whom were included Schumacher,
Kaiser, the Minister for All German Affairs, and Paul Sethe, the influential

editor of the *Frankfurter Allgemeine* newspaper, Adenauer should have responded more positively to Stalin's initiative [*Doc. 22*]. They were convinced that it was a 'missed opportunity' on a grand scale, an opinion that has been echoed by more recent historians, of whom Loth and Steininger are the most persuasive [49; 128]. Adenauer, however, like the Americans, was reluctant to see the whole complex structure of the proposed EDC unravel and be replaced with the high-risk policy of a unified neutral Germany, in which his own government would most likely be succeeded by a left of centre coalition [*Docs 22* and *28*]. Besides, he simply did not believe that Stalin could risk the potential domino effect which the granting of independence to East Germany would have on the other European satellites. Thus the initiative was allowed to peter out into what Anthony Eden called a 'battle of notes' [120 *p. 126*] concerned with electoral details and Stalin resigned himself to the fact that 'Adenauer was in the pocket of the Americans' [120 *p. 128*]. It may well be that Stalin intended 'to mobilize the German masses, particularly in the Federal Republic ... to oust Adenauer's government and to force the western powers out' [130 *p. 418*], but certainly the less Stalinist members of the East German Politbureau, such as Grotewohl and Herrnstadt, were ready to see the GDR subsumed into a democratic Germany in which the SED, if it was lucky, would enjoy a position comparable to the Italian or French Communist parties [82].

After Stalin's death in March 1953 it looked briefly, much to Adenauer's alarm, as if the log jam over the German question might break up. Churchill proposed a four-power summit in which plans for German unification and possible neutralization might be discussed, while Soviet Russia, to Ulbricht's consternation, toyed with a similar plan. Beria, the Soviet Deputy Prime Minister, in the weeks before his arrest in June was urging his colleagues to abandon the GDR for $10 billion, 'as it was only kept in being by Soviet troops' [82 *p. 111*]. Despite Beria's fall, the riots of 17 June in the GDR and Ulbricht's survival (see *pp. 87–9*), the Russians continued to play with plans for all-German elections. At the end of August Grotewohl, Ulbricht and Honecker were invited to the Kremlin and told that they were to prepare for unification. Malenkov added that 'the GDR was a temporary entity born to create a new large peace-loving Germany to guarantee peace and security in Europe and the world as a whole' [82 *p. 151*]. These words probably did not exclude the ultimate Soviet aim of creating a Communist Germany, but to realists within the GDR it was obvious that such was the unpopularity and weakness of the SED in the aftermath of the June riots that any form of election acceptable to the West would lead to its virtual annihilation. Erich Glückauf, the head of the Department for All German Affairs, for instance, believed that the West 'would be complete fools not to accept such an offer' [82 *p. 152*; 49].

However, before the Russians had time to formulate their proposals,

Adenauer himself, largely for electoral reasons, suggested a four-power conference of Foreign Ministers after the West German elections. This met
without result in Berlin in early 1954, but it did effectively delay the con-
vening of the summit conference until after Churchill's retirement. By the
time the summit finally took place in Geneva in July 1955, the Federal
Republic had been recognized as a sovereign state and had become a
member of NATO, while the GDR had joined the new Warsaw Pact, which
had been created to counter NATO, and the question of German unification
had been pushed firmly into the background. When Khrushchev visited
East Berlin on his way home he effectively ruled out unification by observing that Russia would not tolerate any threat to the 'political and social
achievements' of the GDR. He followed this up on 20 September with a
treaty granting sovereignty to the GDR [*Doc. 26*]. The division of Germany
and the foreign policies of the two German states now entered a new phase
[20 Vol. 2; 120; 128].

THE FRG AS A SOVEREIGN STATE, 1955–58

Its western priorities

In October 1954 Adenauer boasted that Germany, as represented by the
FRG, was 'once more about to become a great power' [20 Vol. 2, *p. 125*].
At the time the claim was an exaggeration, but over the next few years it
rapidly gained some substance. Bonn soon became a pivotal member of
NATO and the European Economic Community (EEC), and enjoyed some
scope within these groupings to defend its interests by exploiting the
growing friction between France and the Anglo-Saxon powers. Burgeoning
economic power also enabled it to profit from the vacuum caused by the
decline in British power in the Mediterranean where state visits by
Adenauer to Iran, Turkey and Greece opened up the way for increased
trade and political influence [20 Vol. 2].

Yet in essentials Adenauer's priorities still remained what they had been
in 1949. He wanted a strongly rearmed FRG within NATO and an integrated Western Europe, which from a position of strength would eventually
attract the GDR. Despite the siren voices urging *détente*, he saw no real evidence of any weakening in Russia's determination to undermine the West.
Thus, for Adenauer, military security remained the essential precondition
for the existence of the FRG and 'the special relationship' with America of
overriding importance. Although his relations with Dulles, Eisenhower's
Secretary of State, were for the most part excellent, by the late 1950s nothing could mask the fact that American interests did not always coincide
with Bonn's [20 Vol. 2].

The second pillar of his foreign policy remained Western integration, the core of which was Franco-German cooperation. He regarded the Treaty of Rome, which set up the EEC in March 1957, as an historic event almost comparable to the unification of Germany. It was, as he told Erhard, 'a vital springboard for us to get back once again into foreign affairs' and a means for committing the Americans to the defence of Europe since they 'regard it as the starting point of all their policies in Germany' [20 Vol. 2, *p. 233*]. On the other hand, it provided West Germany, and by extension Western Europe, with a potential insurance against the very event which Adenauer most feared: the departure of American troops from Europe. The more Adenauer became disillusioned with American policy, the closer to France he drew. In November 1956, for instance, alarmed by both the Radford Plan for thinning down American conventional forces in Germany and the emergence of what seemed to be a potential American–Soviet axis in the Security Council of the United Nations, when both states used their veto to halt the Anglo-French attack on Egypt, he used the occasion of an official visit to Paris to give significant moral help to the beleaguered French government, thereby laying the basis for 'a remarkable intensification of Franco-German cooperation' [20 Vol. 2, *p. 245*].

The Franco-German entente survived the change of regime in Paris in 1958 and de Gaulle, the new President, continued to seek closer links with Bonn. Adenauer was even paid the great compliment of being invited to the General's chateau at Colomby-Les-Deux-Eglises in September 1958. Both leaders needed the support of each other, but their visions of Europe were contradictory. Adenauer wanted an ever more integrated community and a close alliance with America, while de Gaulle hoped for a loosely federated Europe based on the nation states and completely independent of the United States. Their ambiguous relationship has been characterized variously as a 'masked conflict' or as a 'senile friendship based on a misunderstanding' [73 *p. 76*]. Essentially, however, it was Adenauer's growing disillusionment with American and British policy that drove him into the arms of Gaullist France.

Its policy towards Russia and the GDR

Although Adenauer remained convinced that negotiations with the USSR on German unification could only be conducted from a position of overwhelming strength, he visited Moscow in September 1955 and agreed to the exchange of ambassadors in return for the repatriation of the remaining German prisoners of war in Russia. The resumption of diplomatic relations certainly opened the way up for a direct dialogue between Bonn and Moscow, but Russia's recognition of the GDR as an independent state a few days after Adenauer's visit confronted the FRG with a considerable dilemma. It was axiomatic in Bonn that recognition of the GDR as an independent German state would fatally undermine the claims of the FRG to be the legal heir to the old Reich. Thus, to ensure that diplomatic relations with the USSR did not imply a recognition of the GDR, Adenauer announced in the *Bundestag* on 22 September the policy which became known as the Hallstein Doctrine (named after Professor Hallstein who had helped to formulate it) [Doc 27]. According to this, Bonn would consider the recognition of the GDR by any state other than the USSR as an unfriendly act, which would result in the rupture of diplomatic relations [20 Vol. 2].

The Doctrine was rigorously enforced up to 1969. Throughout the developing world in Asia, Africa and Latin America, Bonn made financial assistance and development aid dependent on the non-recognition of the GDR. Nasser in Egypt was kept in line by generous grants, as was Nehru in India by the building and financing of an ultra modern steel plant at Rourkehla. The most significant challenge to the Hallstein Doctrine came when Yugoslavia recognized the GDR in 1957, but further generous offers of West German aid to the neutral third-world states managed to deter their governments from following Belgrade and by 1963 only Cuba had recognized the GDR.

The intention behind the Hallstein Doctrine was to isolate the Soviet 'puppet state', the GDR, and to prevent the division of Germany from becoming an accepted diplomatic fact, but the more permanent the division of Germany appeared, the less satisfactory the policy became. Increasingly it was seen as a quixotic attempt to 'overcome the status quo by ignoring it' [73 *p. 85*]. Although it cut off the GDR from the Western and developing worlds, it inevitably strengthened its integration into the Soviet bloc. By 1957 officials like Blankenhorn and Pfleiderer, the West German Ambassador in Yugoslavia, were beginning to argue for the 'acceptance of the two state doctrine to help the East bloc to disintegrate internally' [20 Vol. 2, *p. 299*]. The essence of their argument was that exposure of the Eastern satellite states to the dynamic economy of the FRG would create a magnetic force that would 'slowly draw them step by step into the direction of the West and as a consequence towards liberty' [20 Vol. 2, *p. 299*].

In the spring of 1958 West German public opinion was becoming more alarmed by the escalating arms race and the decision by the Americans and the British to equip their forces in Germany with tactical nuclear weapons. Adenauer was also subjected to bitter attacks in the *Bundestag* about the 'missed opportunities' for German unification (see *p. 60*). He therefore took the initiative to sound out the Russians as to whether the GDR could be neutralized and allowed internal autonomy along the lines conceded by them to Austria in 1955. Clearly then, Adenauer was capable of being more flexible than his enemies gave him credit for, although Klessmann [73] has argued that even this and the subsequent Globke Plans (see *p. 49*) of 1959 and 1960 did not offer the USSR any real concessions in return for the radical changes they were invited to make to the status of the GDR [20 Vol. 2; 125].

THE BERLIN CRISIS, 1958–61

Moscow's recognition of the GDR's sovereignty in September 1955 brought to an end a period when Russia hovered on the verge of sacrificing the GDR to prevent the integration of the FRG into NATO. The GDR, however, remained a fragile, isolated and artificial state dependent on Moscow and the presence of twenty divisions of Russian troops stationed within its frontiers. The central thrust of its foreign policy throughout the 1950s was to draw ever closer to Russia and its allies. In 1950 it joined the COMECON, the Committee for Mutual Economic Assistance, which was set up in Moscow in 1949. It also signed the Görlitz Treaty with Poland in 1950, which recognized the Oder–Neisse frontier. This was a significant step towards an East German–Polish *rapprochement* and prepared the way for further East bloc integration. The relationship was not, however, completely one-sided. For the USSR the GDR was beginning to become a valuable ally. In 1956, at the time of the Hungarian uprising and the 'Polish October' (see *p. 92*), Ulbricht displayed exemplary loyalty to Moscow and the GDR was perceived by the Russians to be a 'clamp' which kept Poland and the East European satellite states in place [35; 73; 124].

The most effective weapon Moscow had at its disposal to force the Western powers to recognize the GDR was to reactivate the still unsolved problem of Berlin. Khrushchev himself graphically observed: 'Berlin is the testicles of the West ... every time I want to make the West scream, I squeeze on Berlin' [120 *p. 140*]. By the autumn of 1958 impressive developments in its nuclear and missile capabilities gave Russia an apparent immunity from an American attack, which had not existed ten years earlier. Khrushchev thus decided to take a dramatic initiative to liquidate the Berlin problem and so strengthen the GDR. On 10 November he called for a peace treaty with the two German states; then on 27 November he issued a six-month ultimatum in which he demanded the demilitarization of West Berlin, which would involve the withdrawal of Western troops and its metamorphosis into a 'free city' [*Doc. 29*]. If the Western Allies refused to sign a peace treaty with the two German states, Khrushchev threatened to conclude a peace agreement unilaterally with the GDR and to recognize its sovereignty over East Berlin. This would then enable it to control access to West Berlin. The Western Allies would thus be compelled to deal with East German rather than Russian officials and so, in effect, recognize the sovereignty of the GDR [120].

Although the NATO powers firmly rejected the ultimatum, they did declare their willingness to discuss the German question as a whole and in February proposed a Foreign Ministers' Conference, which met in Geneva in the summer of 1959. In the preceding months Adenauer viewed with increasing alarm statements from London and Washington signalling the desire for compromise and concession, and inevitably drew closer to de Gaulle, who urged a much tougher line against the Russians. In an attempt to pre-empt damaging concessions, Bonn drew up in early 1959 an intricate package, the Globke Plan, which ambitiously contained proposals both for a provisional and a comprehensive solution to the German problem. In essence the two German states would recognize each other and Berlin would become a free city. Within five years a referendum on unification would take place and if a majority voted for reunification, free elections would follow. The escalating Berlin crisis, however, effectively stopped both this plan and a revised version in 1960 from ever being discussed [20 Vol. 2; 73; 79 Vol. 3].

The Geneva Conference brought the Western Allies time, but not even an interim solution. Over the next two years Khrushchev alternated periods of *détente*, when he either extended the time scale of the ultimatum or let it lapse, with spells of acute crisis during which further threats were devised to force the West into making concessions. His actions were not without success. Behind the scenes in London and Washington, and at times even in Paris, various schemes for creating a nuclear free zone in Central Europe, recognizing Poland's western frontiers and the *de facto* recognition of the GDR jostled with each other. To prevent any of these schemes reducing the FRG to a disarmed, subordinate status, Adenauer used every diplomatic ploy at his disposal, but by May 1960, when a further conference opened in Paris, he had no idea what Eisenhower and Macmillan might be ready to concede. Thus it was 'a gift from heaven' [73 *p. 89*] for him when Khrushchev used the shooting down of an American spy plane, a U2, over Russia as an excuse to torpedo the summit. This temporarily eased the pressure on Bonn by discrediting the summit politics of Macmillan and Eisenhower, and Khrushchev himself announced that he would not negotiate again with the West until the spring of 1961, by which time there would be a new American president [20 Vol. 2; 120].

Until the autumn of 1960 it was Khrushchev who determined the course of the Berlin crisis. Ulbricht, who certainly stood to benefit from a successful outcome, was little more than a spectator. However, in desperation as the numbers of refugees to the West dramatically increased during the years 1960–61 (*see p. 93*), Ulbricht began to urge Khrushchev to sign a separate peace treaty with the GDR, at one juncture sarcastically observing: 'You only *talk* about a peace treaty, but don't *do* anything about it' [120 *p. 144*].

Khrushchev's hopes that Kennedy, the new American President, would make the concessions that Eisenhower had refused, proved unfounded. Nevertheless Kennedy's response to Russian threats to sign a separate peace treaty with the GDR hinted at a possible solution to the Berlin problem. While he dramatically built up American forces in Europe, he also urged negotiations and began significantly to emphasize that the West was primarily interested in free access to West Berlin rather than to Berlin as a whole. Up to this point Khrushchev had consistently rejected the option of closing the frontier with West Berlin. He had hoped rather to uncouple West Berlin from the FRG than to cut it off from East Germany. However, the growing unrest in the GDR and the ever-increasing number of refugees to the West finally persuaded him to agree to East German demands for sealing off the GDR's borders in Berlin. Without this measure the GDR faced certain collapse [*Docs 30* and *31*] [120; 124].

THE CONSEQUENCES

The prolonged crisis over Berlin effectively ended with the construction of the Berlin Wall on 13 August 1961, although this was not immediately obvious to contemporaries. The crisis marked a turning point in the German question. The United States had made it brutally clear that it had dropped the ritual incantation of German unification for a more realistic acceptance of the *status quo*. From now on it was only ready to defend the FRG, West Berlin and the Allied rights of access to it. The existence of the GDR was assured for the foreseeable future, and ultimately there would be little option for Bonn but to recognize it and seek, in the words of Egon Bahr, the SPD politician and father of *Ostpolitik*, 'change through rapprochement' [73 *p. 93*]. For Ulbricht, the Wall was a pyrrhic victory that emphasized the inhumanity and the deep unpopularity of his regime. It fell far short of Khrushchev's original plans announced in November 1958. Ulbricht was also further disappointed by Moscow's failure to carry out its promise to sign a separate peace treaty with the GDR [120].

Britain's and America's evident desire for a *détente* with the USSR, even during the height of the crisis, confirmed Adenauer's determination to strengthen his links with France, although de Gaulle had very different conceptions of the future of the EEC. Thus, despite the objections of Walther Hallstein, who was now President of the European Commission, he did not protest at de Gaulle's dramatic veto of Britain's application to join the EEC on 14 January 1963, and on 23 January he signed the Franco-German Treaty of Friendship. The treaty's impact was greatly weakened by the preamble that was added by the *Bundestag* during the ratification debate. This emphasized that the treaty did not entail a new anti-American and British shift in the FRG's foreign policy. Nevertheless, it marked the beginning of bitter divisions in the CDU/CSU between the Atlanticists, like Erhard and Schröder who looked primarily to Washington and wanted Britain in the EEC, and the Gaullists, like Strauss and Adenauer himself who looked to Paris and wanted an EEC increasingly independent of the USA [20 Vol. 2; 32; 79 Vol. 3].

PART FOUR

RECONSTRUCTION AND
CONSOLIDATION:
THE FRG, 1949–63

CHAPTER FIVE

POLITICS: DEVELOPING A DEMOCRACY

THE FORMATION OF THE ADENAUER GOVERNMENT AND ITS INITIAL PROSPECTS

Although the CDU/CSU emerged as the strongest party in the elections of 14 August 1949, it had no overall majority and could only form a government in coalition with other parties [*Doc. 21*]. Adenauer rejected a 'grand' coalition with the SPD since it opposed the social market economy, which had been the main plank of the CSU/CDU's electoral programme. He felt that a fudged coalition, as had so often been negotiated in the Weimar Republic, would only discredit democracy and drive the opposition into extra-parliamentary channels. Yet this view was not shared by many on the left-wing of his party such as Karl Arnold, who believed that the complex problems facing the new government could only be solved by the greatest possible consensus. Nevertheless at a specially convened meeting of leading members of the CDU/CSU at his house in Rhöndorf on 21 August, Adenauer managed to win the arguments for a 'small' coalition with the Free Democratic Party (FDP) and the German Party (DP). His case was strengthened by Schumacher's insistance that the SPD could only join a coalition if it controlled the Economics Ministry, which would in practice mean the end of the social market economy [*Doc. 15*]. When the *Bundestag* met, the supporters of a grand coalition made a last-ditch attempt to secure their aim by ensuring that candidates sympathetic to it were elected to the influential position of Leader of the *Bundesrat*, President of the FRG and the Chancellorship itself. They succeeded in securing Arnold's election in the *Bundesrat*, but their efforts to find a suitable coalition candidate on the right of the SPD for the presidency were blocked by Shumacher, who himself stood as a candidate. In the second ballot Adenauer's preferred candidate, Theodor Heuss of the FDP, won by a majority of thirteen votes. Three days later Adenauer won the vote for the Chancellorship with a majority of one [9; 20 Vol. 1; 79 Vol. 2].

Adenauer's first Cabinet, of fourteen members, inevitably reflected the limited independence of the FRG, while the portfolios given to ministers indicated the problems with which it would have to grapple. There were Ministries of Housing and Refugee Affairs, a Ministry for All German Affairs was set up under Jakob Kaiser, the former CDUD leader (see *p. 22*) and Erhard became Economics Minister. Adenauer also insisted on a Ministry for *Bundesrat* Affairs to emphasize the importance of the states. The CDU/CSU managed to secure all the key positions except for the Ministry of Justice. The strong South German Catholic wing of the Union dominated the Cabinet, while the North German Protestant wing was represented only by Gustav Heinemann, the Minister of the Interior. This failure to integrate the Protestants more effectively into the party was later to cause Adenauer considerable problems. As both foreign and military affairs were in the hands of the High Commissioners, there were no Foreign and Defence Ministries, but Adenauer set up a secretariat for foreign affairs in the Chancellor's Office, and when the question of building up a West German army arose in 1950, he also ensured that military matters came within the Chancellor's remit. He also appointed Hans Globke, an 'administrative genius' [79 Vol. 1, *p. 38*] who had written the commentary on the Nuremberg laws in 1935, to run his own office. It rapidly became a sophisticated and efficient political machine, which carefully monitored developments within the party and vetted senior appointments to the civil service to ensure that only politically 'reliable' candidates occupied the key posts.

By the mid-1950s the FRG had made such an impressive recovery under Adenauer that, as C. Grant Robertson observed about Bismarck, it is tempting for historians to reconstruct 'a marvellous march of events, in which each stage seems to slip into its pre-appointed place' (Grant Robertson, *Bismarck* (Constable, London, 1918), p. 128). In reality, in the winter of 1949–50 'success', as Mary Fulbrook has observed, 'could not be predicted with any certainty' [24 *p. 16*]. It was by no means clear that Adenauer possessed sufficient power to govern effectively. The Occupation Statute, which replaced the Military Government with a civilian High Commission, gave the Western Allies a pivotal position in West Germany and in effect made them a 'superior government' [*Doc. 16*]. They were still ultimately responsible for foreign policy, security, the export trade, the Ruhr and a whole raft of measures for controlling German industry and air traffic. The *Länder*, in Adenauer's eyes at any rate, seemed to be a further impediment to effective government. Through their position in the *Bundesrat* they were able to put the central government under considerable pressure. They were not, as Kopf, the Minister of Lower-Saxony, remarked, there 'to sing the Horst-Wesel song and to say yes' [79 Vol. 2, *p. 178*]. Within the *Bundestag* Adenauer initially faced a situation which was more reminiscent of the *Reichstag* during the Weimar Republic. Despite the electoral law banning small parties from gaining seats in parliament (unless they won a minimum of 5 per cent of the total votes cast), there were still twelve parties in the *Bundestag*. As in the 1920s many of these, such as the Bavarian Party (BP) or the South Schleswig Voters League (SSW), represented regional or group interests or else were mainly parties of protest. The CDU itself was also a potentially fragile centrifugal organization. It was only at the party conference at Goslar in October 1950 that a decision was taken to build up an effective national organization. There was, above all, the pressing problem of the 9.5 million refugees and expellees from the East, which was 'ticking like a time bomb in the framework of the fledgling state' [79 Vol. 2, *p. 120*].

THE ADENAUER–SCHUMACHER DUEL

Biding his time in opposition was Schumacher, who was convinced that the government's economic policies would fail and that the disillusioned electors would then turn to the SPD. With hindsight it can be seen that Schumacher's strategy was flawed, but that was not clear in the first two years of Adenauer's premiership. Compared with the more loosely organized CDU/CSU, which in its early years could still have unravelled, the SPD was a centralized, homogeneous, largely working-class party. Despite being cut off from its heartlands in central Germany, it had still managed to secure 131 seats – the same number as it had secured in the whole Reich in December 1924 [16; 74].

The gladiatorial combat between Schumacher and Adenauer obscured the fact that there was in certain areas considerable common ground between them. The SPD supported the government's decision to apply to the Constitutional Court to ban both the KPD and the extreme right-wing SRP in November 1951, and it also refused to recognize the GDR. The SPD worked constructively with the CDU/CSU on major legislation covering housing, trade unions' rights and compensation for expellees. In their different ways both Adenauer and Schumacher were also determined not to allow the extreme right to monopolize German patriotism as it did in the inter-war period. Indeed, Schumacher's nationalism was so strident that François-Ponçet, the French High Commissioner, called him the 'Hitler on the left' [79 Vol. 2, *p. 59*].

Like all Germans, both politicians wished to see an end to the occupation and a restoration of German independence. Yet they disagreed deeply on how this should be achieved. Schumacher rejected Adenauer's policy of close cooperation with the High Commissioners and ultimately of integration into a capitalist Western Europe. He maintained that only a united Germany could integrate with its neighbours, provided that they were prepared to construct a social democratic Europe. He therefore opposed Adenauer's *Westpolitik* at every step. He was furious when Adenauer accepted the Petersberg Agreement and agreed to participate in the International

Ruhr Authority in return for major concessions over dismantling, and was suspended temporarily from the *Bundestag* for calling Adenauer the 'Chancellor of the Allies' during an all-night debate on 24–25 November [*Doc. 17*]. Similarly, six months later, he criticized the Schuman Plan because it was essentially a capitalist solution which would create a Europe 'in the shape of a joint-stock company' [20 Vol. 1, *p. 507*] and prevent any future SPD government from nationalizing the coal and steel industries.

Given Schumacher's vitriolic criticism, it is not surprising that the Allies preferred Adenauer, but the High Commissioners were quickly ready to distance themselves from him in the event of economic failure. This became evident in the winter of 1949–50 as the economy began to stagnate and unemployment began to rise (see *p. 71*). Both the trade unions and the SPD pressed for a programme of massive public investment to create jobs and the nationalization of the basic industries and the banks. To a certain extent they were supported by the left wing of the CDU, which again began to agitate for the creation of a grand coalition. More dangerous still for Adenauer was that the High Commissioners began to press for action and had to be rapidly appeased by a work creation project costing some DM 2 billion (see *p. 71*).

With the outbreak of the Korean War the economy immediately picked up, but the war plunged the FRG into political turmoil as it brought to the fore the controversial question of German rearmament (see *p. 40*). Opposition to Adenauer's plans for the formation of German fighting units was widespread in the Churches, the trade unions and the SPD. This led to a sharp drop in the government's popularity in the autumn elections in Württemberg-Baden, Hesse and Bavaria. The SPD vote increased by slightly under 2 per cent, but Schumacher was able to claim a psychological victory for the party. Although he was no passivist and in essence shared Adenauer's belief that the Western Allies' need for German troops could be used as a tool to wrest concessions from them, he rejected a bipartisan approach to rearmament, and decided to exploit the widespread revulsion against war in the FRG to topple Adenauer. He was prepared to work with Pastor Niemöller, the leader of the passivist wing of the Evangelical Church, and on the strength of the autumn elections they both issued a statement demanding a dissolution of the *Bundestag* and a general election on the issue of rearmament [79 Vol. 2].

The Schumacher–Niemöller axis was a considerable threat to the coalition. Adenauer feared that it would appeal to the traditional Lutherans not only in the FDP but also in the North German Protestant wing of the CDU. His fears seemed to be confirmed when Heinemann, who was also the Chairman of the Synod of the German Evangelical Church, resigned from the Cabinet in October 1950 in protest against Adenauer's defence policy on the grounds that it would provoke Soviet retaliation. Heinemann failed, however, to strike while the situation favoured him. He waited until 1952 to set up his own party by which time he had lost most of his support. The threat from Niemöller also subsided when it became clear that the more conservative majority of the Evangelical Church distanced itself from his root-and-branch attack on West German rearmament. After this greater care was taken by Adenauer to give the Protestant wing of the party more influence [79 Vol. 2].

Despite the acute balance of payments problem in the winter of 1950–51 (see *p. 72*), Schumacher's chances of forcing Adenauer to call a crisis election slowly receded. In January Adenauer was faced with the threat of a political strike in the Ruhr. The unions were determined to preserve and extend the element of co-determination which the British Military Government had introduced into the iron and steel industries in 1947 on the basis of parity between labour and capital on the supervisory boards of the larger companies. By 1950 this agreement was due to lapse and the FDP and the industrial wing of the CDU/CSU, which was grouped around Erhard, were opposed both to the parity principle and to its extension to the coal industry. To emphasize their demands, the DGB called a political strike for 1 February. Adenauer could not afford to alienate the Ruhr workers, who were a prime target for Communist infiltration. Besides, he also saw an opportunity for driving a wedge between the unions and Schumacher by winning their support for the ECSC. He persuaded Hans Böckler, the Chairman of the DGB, to call off the strike, and brokered a compromise between the employers and unions which he persuaded the Cabinet to accept. Co-determination was recognized in the iron and steel industries and even extended to the coal industry, yet Adenauer craftily lived up to his reputation as 'the machievellian representative of the German bourgeois' [20 Vol. 1, *p. 455*] by carefully avoiding giving parity to the unions. On the supervisory boards five representatives were to be shareholders, five were to be employees and the eleventh was to be nominated by the directors. Nevertheless, the agreement was greeted by the DGB as an important victory and came to be regarded as one of the guarantees of domestic stability in the FRG [32]. In the *Bundestag* the bill was opposed by the FDP, the DP and the BP and was only passed on 10 April 1951 with the support of the SPD. Ironically, the SPD provided the votes which Adenauer needed in order to win the unions' backing for his future domestic and foreign policy.

This brief display of bipartisanship between the SPD and CDU/CSU was quickly terminated. Schumacher resumed his attacks on Adenauer when the latter signed the ECSC Treaty a few days later on 18 April, dismissing it as 'an agreement ... to tie German industry to France' (61 *p. 199*). He was also fiercely critical of the Pleven Plan and argued that German unity must have priority over Western integration. Momentarily it seemed as though the Stalin note of March 1952 (see *p. 43*) would give him the oppportunity to swing public opinion behind this approach, but Adenauer and the Western Allies were more in tune with West German public opinion when they refused to abandon their plans for Western integration and the European Army. A public opinion poll in July 1952, asking which was the more important, national unity or protection against the Russians, showed that over half the population preferred the latter [20 Vol. 1; 79 Vol. 2].

ADENAUER'S RE-ELECTION, SEPTEMBER 1953

The signature of the General Treaty in Bonn on 26 May 1952 and the EDC Treaty in Paris a day later (see *p. 41*) marked a turning point for Adenauer. He was now perceived as a man who could get things done [*Doc. 18*]. His popularity began to rise and public opinion swung behind his European policy. The West Germans became increasingly bored with the protracted battle through the winter of 1952–53 in both houses of parliament to ratify the treaty and were critical of the SPD's unsuccessful attempt to have the treaties declared unconstitutional by the Federal Constitutional Court [79 Vol. 2].

The Coalition's electoral prospects were also strengthened by the strong showing of the economy from the second half of 1952 through into 1953 and by the impressive progress made in housing construction (see *p. 72*). This made Adenauer's efforts to integrate the 9.5 million expellees and refugees so much easier. The potential danger of an extremist backlash among the expellees was indicated when the newly formed 'Bloc of Expellees and Disfranchised' (BHE), whose three leaders were all ex-Nazis, won 23.4 per cent of the vote in Schleswig-Holstein in July 1950 [*Doc. 5*]. Adenauer attempted with some success to establish contacts with the Bloc, which was drawn into a coalition with the CDU and FDP in Schleswig-Holstein in September 1950. It was accepted right across the political spectrum that those like the expellees, who had suffered particular hardship in the war, needed to be compensated at the expense of those whose assets had survived. The SPD wanted to ensure that this compensation would, in effect, become a 'second Basic Law' [46 *p. 242*], as Ollenhauer expressed it, which would create a more just and equal society, while the CDU and FDP were interested in using it to buttress a more traditional property-owning society. In practice, a compromise was achieved. The Equalization of Burdens Law (*Lastenausgleich*) was theoretically the 'greatest tax' on wealth in the history of Germany [46 *p. 242*]. There was to be a levy on 50 per cent of the wealth of all real assets, that is land, buildings and capital goods, within West German territory, as measured by the values current on 21 June 1948. The tax would be paid over 30 years and would be redistributed in the form of grants and pensions to expellees and other casualties of war after their claims had been carefully sifted by special committees. However, as the value of property and land rapidly appreciated in the 1950s and 1960s as a result of economic growth and creeping inflation, 'an originally daring venture became a quite marginal affair' [101 *p. 80*]. Nevertheless, by the end of 1978 the tax had raised DM110.4 billion, and together with the expanding economy was one of the key measures in integrating the expellees successfully into the FRG. Not surprisingly, large numbers voted directly for the CDU in September 1953 [29 Vol. 1; 74].

Adenauer began the election campaign in a strong position. Not only was the economy booming, but his patient policy of disarming potential enemies of the new state by generous and adroit concessions won widespread support for the new regime. The government had, for example, appeased the right by passing a law in May 1951 reinstating 150,000 officials who had been sacked as a result of the Allied denazification programme. Adenauer was also seen to have restored the prestige of the German state – his successful visit to Washington in April 1953 was visible evidence of this. Soviet intervention to crush the East German uprising in June 1953 (see *p. 88*) fuelled the hatred and mistrust of the USSR in the FRG and acted as an endorsement of his policy of Western integration [20 Vol. 1].

Meanwhile the SPD had been marginalized by both events and Adenauer's skill. Schumacher, who died on 20 August 1952, had gambled on the collapse of the market economy and on becoming the patriotic voice for Germany. Once it became clear that this was not going to happen the SPD had little to offer. He left the SPD politically isolated and in an electoral ghetto [74]. The new leader, Ollenhauer, was no match for Adenauer. It was no wonder, then, that Adenauer won a decisive victory at the polls. The CDU/CSU won a clear 45.2 per cent of the vote, while the SPD remained stuck at 28.8 per cent and the FDP declined to 9.5 per cent [*Doc. 21*] [74].

COALITION POLITICS, SEPTEMBER 1953–FEBRUARY 1956

The election of 1953 was a turning point in West German politics. The scale of Adenauer's victory confirmed that neither the policy of Western integration nor of the social market economy could now be easily reversed. To ensure maximum support for his foreign and defence policies he renewed the coalition with the FDP and DP and also brought in the League of Expellees. He combined the post of Foreign Minister with Chancellor, while Erhard and Schäffer held the key Ministries of Economics and Finance. To give the Cabinet a fresh face he appointed two younger men, representing the front generation: Strauss (Minister without Portfolio) and Schröder (Interior), while Lübke became Minister for Agriculture.

Among the left-wing journalists and intelligentsia there was some fear of what Adenauer would do with his power, but essentially to hold his coalition together Adenauer had to pursue a policy of compromise and balance. His domestic policy aims were to consolidate the social market economy and develop a programme for the comprehensive reform of social security, yet for the first year his government achieved very little in this area. Preoccupied with foreign policy, Adenauer was unable to give any clear lead on social reform. Within the Cabinet the tensions between the more clerical wing of the CDU/CSU and Protestant FDP were enflamed by an element of Catholic triumphalism which sought to give the government's social policy a specifically Catholic stamp. Thus there were demands for generous financial allowances to be given to mothers with three or more children, for increased censorship of the cinema and even for modifying civil marriage in favour of church ceremonies. Such demands were in turn met with fierce opposition from the FDP. When, in the autumn of 1954, a family allowance bill granting an extra DM25 per child, starting with the third child, came before the *Bundestag*, the coalition temporarily disintegrated and it was opposed by both the FDP and SDP, albeit for different reasons. The former saw it as too generous, while the latter wanted to extend the benefits to all children.

The main battleground between Catholicism and Liberalism was education and the question of secular or denominational schools, but this was fought out at *Land* level. By the end of 1954 the high tide of political Catholicism had begun to ebb. In Lower Saxony an FDP–SPD and left-wing CDU majority abolished state denominational schools, a decision which Adenauer unsuccessfully tried to challenge in the Constitutional Court. Then, in December, as a result of a bitter conflict over the education of teachers in Bavaria, the CSU, despite winning 38 per cent of the vote in the *Land* elections, were left out of the new ruling coalition composed of the SPD, the BP, the FDP and BHE [79 Vol. 2].

What had originally held Adenauer's Conservative-Liberal coalition together was common support for the social market economy. Now that this seemed secure there was a danger that the two groups would drift apart. Increasingly, major differences over foreign policy between the BHE and FDP on one side and Adenauer on the other began to surface. The decisions taken at Messina in June 1955 (see *p. 46*) to press on further with Western integration made the prospect of German reunification even less likely. In October, the BHE withdrew from the coalition, although its leaders, Kraft and Oberländer, split from their party and remained in the coalition. More serious for Adenauer was the critical attitude of Dehler, the parliamentary party leader of the FDP. In an increasingly acrimonious exchange of letters over the summer, Dehler informed Adenauer that it was his patriotic duty 'to develop a concept for "German policy", which included the preconditions for reunification, a status for Germany as a united country' [20 Vol. 2, *pp. 201–2*]. Adenauer attempted to force the Liberals to drop Dehler, even if this meant splitting the party. To achieve this he threatened to reform the electoral law so that the number of directly elected seats would be increased. As in Britain, this would favour the large parties at the cost of the smaller ones. In February 1956 this prospect galvanized the FDP in Düsseldorf to open negotiations with the SPD and to the subsequent formation of an SPD/FDP coalition in North Rhine-Westphalia, which strengthened the anti-government forces in the *Bundesrat*. Adenauer only managed to stop similar coalitions being formed in some of the other *Länder* by rapidly dropping his plans for electoral reform. At the same time the FDP in Bonn split. Sixteen Liberals continued to support the government while the remaining 38 withdrew with Dehler into opposition. One of the key pillars of the 1949 coalition had collapsed. The Swiss newspaper, the *Neue Zürcher Zeitung*, even called this the most decisive point in the seven years of the FRG's history. Initially there was optimistic talk of an FDP–SPD coalition should the electoral arithmetic in the next election be favourable, but this was shown to be premature when Adenauer again won a landslide victory in 1957. Nevertheless, as Schwarz has stressed, 'irrevocable forces were let loose by this event ... which ventured into new directions, and gained a majority in the 1960's' [79 Vol. 2, *p. 210*].

THE CREATION OF THE *BUNDESWEHR*: A CITIZENS' ARMY

The most important task facing Adenauer in his second term was the formation of a West German army. Historically, the question of integrating the armed forces into the constitutional state was one of the 'classic problems facing German parliamentary history' [79 Vol. 2, *p. 289*]. Both the government and the *Bundestag* remembered the sceptical, if not hostile, attitude of the *Reichswehr* towards the Weimar Republic, and the part played by some of its officers in bringing Hitler to power. They were therefore determined to ensure that history did not repeat itself. Their mood was voiced by Dr Richard Jaeger, a member of the Parliamentary Security Committee when he observed that: 'Germany had in the past a good army. Today we doubtless have the start and development of a good democracy. But we in Germany have never had at the same time, a good army, a good democracy, and a balanced relationship between the two' [71 *pp. 122–3*].

When it seemed that the FRG might be required to make a contribution to a European defence force, Adenauer set up an office in October 1950 under Theodor Blank to begin, in cooperation with a panel of former *Wehrmacht* generals, to make preparations for a defence force of twelve armoured divisions or 250,000 men. The protracted delay caused by the French failure to ratify the Pleven Plan was a blessing in disguise. It was not until September 1954 that the FRG was invited to join NATO. By that time a considerable amount of constructive thought had gone into the problem of the ethos of the new German army and how it should be integrated into a democratic society. A department was set up in Blank's office under Wolf Graf Baudissin to deal with 'moral matters'. He set out to create the image of the new German soldier as a 'citizen in uniform'. No longer would the soldier blindly obey orders without thinking. Instead, as a democrat, he would fight willingly in defence of a free and pluralistic society. The army would be humanized and reflect the values of the society of which it was a part. This new military philosophy was summed up by the term *innere Führung* or 'moral leadership'. It made the creation of the army acceptable to the SPD and to a public that was deeply anti-militarist [71].

In the summer of 1955 Adenauer began to move quickly to obtain parliamentary consent. A brief bill was submitted in July to enable Blank to recruit staff officers and training personnel. It immediately ran into stiff parliamentary opposition. Adenauer had originally hoped to place the army fully under the control of the Cabinet, but a cross-party majority quickly seized the initiative and forced him to concede parliament a far greater say in military affairs. A parliamentary special commissioner was to be appointed with far-ranging investigative powers into the armed forces and a Personnel Advisory Committee was to be set up by parliament to review the appointments of senior officers. Parliament also insisted on calling the new army the *Bundeswehr* rather than reviving the *Wehrmacht*, the term which was used in the Third Reich. Having made these concessions, Adenauer was able to amend the Basic Law in March 1956 with the requisite two-thirds majority so as to allow the creation of an army. In December a conscription law was passed permitting the call-up of young males for a period of twelve months. The lengthy process of ethical reform and parliamentary debate at last laid the ghost of the *Wehrmacht* and ultimately produced a citizen army subject to effective democratic controls [32; 71; 79 Vol. 2].

ADENAUER RE-ASSERTS HIS AUTHORITY

Between January and May 1956 Adenauer's popularity, as measured by the opinion polls, fell by 18 per cent. Not only in the left-wing press were demands for his resignation growing, but within the CDU/CSU there was a feeling that his days were numbered. Strauss, for instance, had been indiscreet enough to tell foreign journalists that 'that worn out guy should be on the gallows' [20 Vol. 2, *p. 213*]. The secession of the Liberals, the mounting evidence that despite the long debate over the *Bundeswehr* Blank's office was not up to the complex task of building barracks and equipping an army of 500,000 men, and then the somewhat exaggerated fears about the economy overheating (see *p. 72*) had adversely affected Adenauer's popularity. There was also growing friction between Adenauer and Erhard. The latter, a global free trader, did not hide his belief that a protectionist EEC, which was beginning to be hammered out in inter-governmental negotiations in 1956–57, was 'an economic nonsense' [79 Vol. 2, *p. 346*]. At the annual conference of the Federal Association of German Industry in May 1956 Adenauer publicly criticized both Erhard's attempts to cut tariffs and the Central Bank's raising of the interest rate. In October Adenauer managed to strengthen his government by a long over-due Cabinet re-shuffle, which involved the promotion of Strauss to the Defence Ministry and the axing of Blank and two other ministers, Neumayer and Kraft. This purge disciplined the Cabinet and stopped the squabbling. Now, despite Erhard's and Schäffer's opposition, Adenauer was able to embark on a major policy of tax concessions and social reform which prepared the way for the general election in September 1957. In January 1957 he intro-duced index-linked state pensions, accompanied by a massive one-off rise of 60–75 per cent, which enabled him to pre-empt any attempts by the SPD to exploit the pension issue. The act was enormously popular and played an important part in his electoral victory, but it did bequeath serious problems to future generations when the growth rate slowed and the percentage of elderly people in the population increased [79 Vol. 2].

In June Adenauer skilfully prevented the SPD from exploiting the pot-entially controversial decision to arm the *Bundeswehr* with tactical nuclear weapons by stressing that this was a medium-term plan that would be imple-mented only if disarmament talks between the great powers failed. The election was again dominated by foreign affairs, an area in which SPD policy was unclear. Despite having voted for the Treaty of Rome in July 1957, it still clung to its plans for making Germany a nuclear-free area and eventually withdrawing the FRG from NATO. Fighting the election cam-paign under the slogan of 'Safety – No experiments', Adenauer had little difficulty in showing the risks inherent in these stategies. Yet in the end the voters turned towards the CDU/CSU, probably more because of its great economic achievements, and gave Adenauer an absolute majority in the *Bundestag* with 50.2 per cent of the vote [20 Vol. 2; 32; 79 Vol. 2].

THE LAST YEARS OF THE ADENAUER ERA, 1958–63

Adenauer's landslide victory, which enabled the CDU/CSU Union to govern alone, did not change the essential nature of consensual government in the FRG. The Union was 'a microcosm of the differing economic interests in contemporary Germany' [79 Vol. 3, *p. 156*], as was shown when it took virtually six weeks of haggling between the CDU and the CSU before Adenauer was able to finalize his Cabinet. He did, however, manage to move Schäffer, who had become increasingly unpopular with the industrialists, to the Ministry of Justice and replace him with Franz Etzel, an industrial lawyer [79 Vol. 3].

For most of Adenauer's third term the government's attention was distracted by the outbreak of the Berlin crisis in November 1958. A start was made with implementing Erhard's concept of 'people's capitalism' by the partial privatization of *Volkswagen*, and the outdated 40-year-old system of rent control was abolished. An attempt to reform the administration of the West German health system foundered on the opposition of the SPD and the doctors. Adenauer also suffered 'one of the most spectacular defeats in the whole of his chancellorship' [79 Vol.3, *p. 361*] when he tried to introduce commercial television into the FRG during the years 1958–61. In cavalier disregard for the constitution, he challenged the monopoly of the *Länder*, which according to the Basic Law [*Doc. 14*] were supposed to be the custodians of a politically unbiased radio and television network, by setting up the commercial television company, Deutschland-Fernsehn GmbH, in which the Federal Government would have a controlling interest. Adenauer had quickly grasped the powerful role television would increasingly play in election campaigns and wanted to ensure that he could guarantee at least one channel favourable to the government. 'His motives', as Schwarz observed, 'were as impure as the motives of a party leader could possibly be' [20 Vol. 2, *p. 506*] and he suffered a major defeat when the *Länder* appealed to the Constitutional Court, which on 25 February 1961 ruled against the government.

Adenauer's prestige suffered a further blow. In 1959 Heuss was due to retire from the presidency. Adenauer, who had a very poor opinion of Erhard's political skills, at first suggested that he should stand as the next president. When Erhard refused, he himself decided to stand. He wanted to defeat the SPD candidate, Carlo Schmid, but he also believed, wrongly, that he could exploit the position to appoint a successor of his own choice to the Chancellorship while continuing, like General de Gaulle, to conduct foreign affairs. When it became clear that this would be unconstitutional, Adenauer quickly retreated and pushed the rather colourless Minister of Agriculture, Heinrich Lübke, whom he disliked, into standing for the post. The latter was duly elected in July 1960. Both within the CDU/CSU and in the country at large these machinations, which were aimed at stopping the popular architect of the 'economic miracle' from succeeding to the Chancellorship, were viewed with considerable scepticism [20 Vol. 2; 32].

Inevitably, Adenauer's approval ratings in the public opinion polls again began to sink. He also faced the challenge of a more effective and modernized SPD. In reaction to their defeat in 1957 the party had at last come to terms with the Adenauer–Erhard revolution. In the Godesberg Programme of 1959 the SPD embraced much of the philosophy of the social market economy. In the words of Professor Schiller, it would combine 'as much competition as possible' with 'as much planning as necessary' [32 *p. 157*]. In June the party endorsed the FRG's membership of NATO. In

August it nominated Willy Brandt, the young and popular *Bürgermeister* of West Berlin as the Chancellor candidate to challenge Adenauer [32; 79 Vol. 3].

By November 1960 opinion polls were showing that 40 per cent of those asked preferred Brandt, as opposed to 30 per cent for Adenauer. To avoid awkward questions about his future as party leader, Adenauer reluctantly agreed to the slogan: 'Adenauer, Erhard and the Team' [79 Vol. 3, *p. 219*]. By July 1961 support for the CDU/CSU had climbed back to 50 per cent. As the Berlin crisis intensified (see *pp.* 48–9), Adenauer seemed a much safer bet than the young, inexperienced Brandt. The election campaign was dominated by the building of the Berlin Wall. Adenauer made a serious mistake when he delayed his visit to West Berlin until 22 August [*Doc. 31*], which allowed Brandt to accuse him of indifference towards both West Berlin and the whole question of German unity. Even so, the CDU/CSU managed to retain 45.3 per cent of the vote, while the SPD vote rose by only 4.4 per cent. The FDP, however, increased its share of the poll to 12.8 per cent, thereby holding the balance of power between the SPD and the Union [*Doc. 21*].

Erich Mende, the FDP leader, was ready to form a coalition with the CDU/CSU, but he wanted it led by Erhard. After nearly seven weeks of negotiations Adenauer managed to cobble together a CDU/CSU–FDP coalition still under his leadership, but he was only able to do this at a considerable price. He had to head off challenges from Erhard and Gerstenmaier, the President of the *Bundestag*, by promising that he would stand down in time for a new leader to take the party into the next election. He also had to defeat Erich Mende's attempt to insist on his immediate resignation by holding discussions on a possible coalition with the SPD. This forced Mende to climb down and agree to work with Adenauer. The Adenauer administration of 1961–63 appeared to be a transitional government beset with problems. Adenauer was no longer capable of effectively bridging the divisions between the Rhineland, Westphalian and South German Catholics and the Protestant, *laissez-faire* wing led by Erhard and Schröder. His party, particularly the Catholic core, which since 1949 had defined itself in opposition to the SPD, was also confused and disorientated by his apparent readiness to form a coalition with the Social Democrats [20 Vol. 2; 32; 79 Vol. 3].

The event that brought forward Adenauer's retirement was the *Spiegel* Affair. Rudolph Augstein, the editor of the *Spiegel* news magazine, was determined to destroy Strauss's political career on the grounds that he was a dangerously undemocratic politician who was prepared, if necessary, to unleash a pre-emptive nuclear strike against the USSR once the *Bundeswehr* was armed with nuclear weapons. The magazine led a protracted campaign against Strauss, accusing him, among other things, of making illegal profits out of awarding contracts for the building of barracks for American troops to the FIBAG Construction Company. Then, on 10 October 1962, in the midst of the Cuban crisis, it ran an article, which was clearly using classified information, on the inefficiencies exhibited by the *Bundeswehr* in the latest NATO manoeuvres. Strauss was persuaded by his civil servants that the article was treasonable and that Augstein and his deputy editor, Ahlers, should be arrested. The *Spiegel's* offices were raided by the police and Ahlers, who was on holiday in Spain, was arrested by the Spanish authorities at the request of the Bonn Defence Ministry. Inevitably, this awakened memories of the arbitrary actions of the Third Reich and, once the Cuban crisis had been resolved, public opinion swung round against Strauss. The press was overwhelmingly critical, many writers and academics openly supported Augstein and there were student demonstrations and sit-ins at several universities [*Doc. 32*]. Adenauer badly mishandled the situation in the *Bundestag* on 7 November when he launched a bitter attack against Augstein, claiming that the country faced an 'abyss of treason' [*32 p. 174*].

Adenauer could no doubt have ridden out the storm, if the FDP had not also withdrawn from the coalition in protest against the failure of the Defence Ministry to consult the FDP Minister of Justice, Wolfgang Stamberger. The Ministry, aware of the *Spiegel's* close links with the FDP, had, with some justification, feared that news of its intended action would be leaked. Adenauer, however, as in the autumn of 1961, again exerted pressure on the FDP by opening negotiations with the SPD for a possible coalition. Although the CDU/CSU was tainted by the *Spiegel* Affair, a 'black–red' coalition would have enabled the SPD to escape from thirteen years of opposition and gain some practical experience of government. A deadly threat aimed at the FDP was the revival of the controversial proposal to introduce a majority voting system along British lines, which was remarkably effective in forcing Mende back to the negotiating table. Thus, as Strauss had resigned on 30 November, the way was open for the reconstruction of the original coalition, which Adenauer had all along desired.

The *Spiegel* Affair was an important chapter in German history. For the first time a government in Germany had been forced constitutionally to give way over the question of civil liberties [32]. Adenauer never recovered. His approval ratings dropped dramatically and the CDU did particularly badly in the Rhineland–Palatinate *Land* election in March 1963. Finally, on 22 April, the party decided in a secret ballot by 159 to 47 (with 19 abstentions) to vote for Erhard as Adenauer's successor. Erhard was still widely popular in the FRG and it was thought that only under his leadership could the Union win back lost voters. Adenauer resigned on 15 October, although he was able to retain the chairmanship of the CDU, a position from which he continued to snipe at Erhard until his death in 1967 [20 Vol. 2; 32; 79 Vol. 3].

CHAPTER SIX

THE WEST GERMAN 'ECONOMIC MIRACLE', 1948–63

The West German economy developed so spectacularly during the 1950s that to describe it as an 'economic miracle' seems to be no exaggeration. A mythology, too, has grown up about the causes of this miracle: social market theories, the currency reform and Marshall Aid have all in their turn been seen as the magical key to growth. However, the West German economic recovery was, as Overy has stressed, 'not a miracle in the sense that defied explanation' [105 p. 34]. Before the war the German economy was the second strongest in the world, and even in 1945 the total value of factory buildings and plant in the Western zones that had survived the bombing was greater than in 1936. There was also an abundance of cheap and skilled labour. Thus, given the right circumstances, there was no reason why the West German economy should not recover rapidly. It was the FRG's good fortune that a favourable conjunction of domestic and international factors enabled this to happen [103; 104; 105].

THE SOCIAL MARKET ECONOMY

The 'social market economy' rapidly became the 'brand name' [101 p. 31] for the West German economic system. The concept of the social market economy originated in the 1930s with a group of scholars, politicians and journalists, of whom Eucken, Böhm and Röpke were the leading members. They aimed at a middle way between the old and discredited *laissez-faire* capitalism of the nineteenth century and the rigidly state-controlled economies of the 1930s which appeared to be strangling all entrepreneurial initiative. Convinced that uncontrolled capitalism eventually degenerated into the setting-up of cartels, they believed, as Röpke put it, that the state must defend 'capitalism against the capitalists' [41 p. 424]. In other words, the state must play the role of 'market policeman': it must enforce fair competition, prohibit the formation of cartels and, above all, ensure a sound currency by creating an independent national bank, the main task of which was to stop politicians inflating the currency. The state would control public transport and the main public utilities, such as water and gas, and in times of depression would intervene to stimulate the economy. The Ordo-Liberals were criticized by both the SPD and the Christian-Socialist wing of the CDU for their hostility towards a fully developed welfare state. They were, however, confident that the market economy would create wealth which would enable individuals to make their own welfare provision. The state should only provide the barest safety net [32; 41; 104].

In the immediate post-war period of rationing and scarcity it seemed inconceivable that central government, be it Allied or German, could ever relax its grip on the economy, yet by 1948 there was, as Erik Nölting, the SPD Economic Minister of North Rhine-Westphalia, reluctantly conceded, a 'renaissance of economic liberalism' [41 *p. 427*] helped by both American influence and the very obvious failures of Allied attempts to regulate the German economy. When an independent Advisory Council to the Bizonal Economic Administration was set up in January 1948 the Ordo-Liberals were strongly represented, and three months later Ludwig Erhard, who was influenced by their views, was elected with combined FDP/CDU support to the post of Economic Director of the Bizone [*Doc. 33*].

On 21 April, in his inaugural speech to the Bizonal Economic Council, he outlined a radical economic programme for abolishing rationing and controls on consumption and production, which would be implemented with assistance from the Marshall Plan funds as soon as the Western Allies had carried out a currency reform in their zones. In the meantime, until the new currency was introduced, Erhard tacitly encouraged firms and businesses to hoard raw materials and goods [103].

CURRENCY AND ECONOMIC REFORM, JUNE–DECEMBER 1948

The currency reform introduced by the three Western Military Governors on 20 June 1948 was 'the central political event in the experience of the German people in the post-war period' [103 *p. 134*]. The reform consisted of three major parts. First, it introduced the *Deutschmark* to replace the *Reichsmark*. Everybody was immediately allowed to change RM 40 at a 1:1 rate and then, two months later, they could exchange a further RM 20. Businesses were given an allowance of DM 60 per worker towards their wage costs. Wages, salaries, pensions and share dividends were protected and converted into *Deutschmarks* at the rate of 1:1. The swingeing measures adopted to cut down the number of notes in circulation hit the small saver as opposed to owners of shares or real estate. For those with money on deposit in the banks the old currency had to be exhanged for the new at a rate that worked out to be a ratio of RM 100 to DM 6.50. Secondly, the banks were granted generous deposits of *Deutschmarks*, which would enable them to grant credit to businesses. Thirdly, the Western Allies protected the new currency by making the *Bank Deutscher Länder* into an independent central bank with full powers to manage the currency. They also laid down that public authorities must not run up debts unless they were covered by current income. To encourage the building up of capital reserves the Military Governors cut personal income tax by about one-third and reduced corporate income tax by 15 per cent. They also introduced a scheme for tax exemptions on savings and investments [101; 103].

Currency reform was a necessary but 'brutal deflation' [103 *p.135*]. For the second time in 25 years small savers saw their savings wiped out while material assets and shares were untouched. Originally, the reform was to be accompanied by measures aimed at compensating the small savers and those who had lost their property and their means of livelihood in the war, but the Allies left this task to the new West German government. This provided some limited help in housing, education, job creation and pensions in 1949, but it was only in 1952 that a more comprehensive package of aid was granted (see *pp. 58–9*).

On the same day as the currency reform Erhard took a significant step towards freeing the Bizonal economy. Without consulting the Military Governors, he announced on the radio the lifting of price controls on virtually all manufactured goods as well as on a limited range of foodstuffs, and at the end of the month did not renew the Bizonal directives covering rationing and the central allocation of resources. Eschenburg has called this a 'coup' [41 *p. 434*], but it was less radical than it seemed since the prices for basic foodstuffs, rents, raw materials such as iron, coal, steel and oil as well as wages, rents and rates were controlled and food rationing was also still in force [32].

These reforms destroyed the black market and released hoarded goods of all kinds. In the shops 'everything from salami to saucepans miraculously re-appeared' [103 *p. 136*]. To satisfy the pent-up demand for consumer goods industrial production increased from the second quarter to the third quarter by 30 per cent. On balance, most economic historians regard the currency and economic reforms of June 1948 as the vital catalyst for economic growth, despite Abelshauser's argument that this overlooks the strong upturn in production in September 1947, which, as much of it was hoarded, was not accurately recorded in official statistics [92]. Comparisons, however, with growth rates in East Germany and the French Zone, which initially kept the controlled economy, point to the significance of Erhard's policy of deregulation [32; 101].

The six months after the currency reform were 'one of the most dramatic in German economic history' [41 *p. 439*]. The great demand for consumer goods, the continued conversion of *Reichsmarks* into *Deutschmarks* and the willingness of banks to grant credit to their customers led, by the autumn, to inflationary pressures which seriously threatened Erhard's policies. Between the end of July and December the amount of new money in circulation more than doubled and the cost of living index rocketed up by 31 per cent. Wages were still pegged at their 1938 level although the Military Governors allowed increases of up to 15 per cent. In the autumn there were even signs that the black market was re-emerging. Erhard came under pressure from the left wing of the CDU, the SPD and the trade unions, which demanded the declaration of a 'state of economic emergency' [101 *p. 43*], the appointment of a price commissioner with powers to control prices and the re-introduction of rationing and raw material controls. On 12 November there was a one-day general strike against Erhard's policy, which was the biggest labour demonstration since the strike against the Kapp Putsch in 1920. Apart from setting up 'a toothless independent price council' [101 *p. 43*] to appease the Military Governors, Erhard kept his nerve and allowed the central bank to defeat inflation by tightening up its monetary policy. By December the economy was cooling off and increases in both monetary supply and the cost of living were sharply declining.

THE ROLE OF MARSHALL AID

To many West Germans in the 1950s it was axiomatic that the Marshall Plan triggered the West German boom. Yet in strictly *economic* terms, it played a relatively small role in the economic recovery. In February 1948 Erhard had optimistically predicted that the Plan would provide the investments and imports necessary for rebuilding the industrial infrastructure of the Bizone. The reality was very different. By December 1948, out of $99 million worth of aid, only $22 millon was in the form of industrial goods, the majority of which was cotton. At its peak in the last quarter of 1949 Marshall Aid accounted for 37 per cent of West Germany's imports, but by 1952 this had declined to 3 per cent. As part of the Marshall Plan, America also loaned the FRG dollars to pay for imports, which German consumers then purchased with Deutschmarks. These marks were called 'counter-part' funds and were paid into a special account. Erhard had hoped that they would be made available to invest in the consumer goods industries, but the Marshall Plan administrators in Germany insisted they could only be used to buy vital equipment to break bottlenecks in key sectors of the economy. Although the funds only amounted to about 6.7 per cent of the total investment in West German industry, they were used with considerable effect to expand the capacity of the railways, the electrical, iron and steel industries and above all coal mining, for which they provided in 1949 47 per cent of the total investment [103]. The real significance of the Marshall Plan lay in creating a stable environment in which the West German economy could expand. Generous Marshall Aid grants to Britain and France, which were double the size of those given to the FRG, were a substitute for German reparation deliveries and made it easier for France to accept the emergence of a strong West German economy. Also, the fact that through the Marshall Plan the USA was granting medium-term aid for economic reconstruction rather than emergency short-term relief was seen as evidence by German businessmen and investors that the Americans were not going to abandon Western Europe [103].

STRUCTURAL PROBLEMS, 1949–51

The collapse of the consumer boom in the autumn of 1948 slowed down the growth of the West German economy. Although industrial production still grew by an overall 24 per cent in 1949, in the winter of 1949–50 it began to falter. There was a shortage of investment capital, which inevitably slowed up the rebuilding of industrial plant, as well as both an adverse balance of trade with the Western European states – made temporarily worse by the devaluation of their currencies in September 1949 – and insufficient funds to purchase all the raw materials needed if Germany was to resume its traditional role as an exporter of machinery and finished goods. Denied access to the former Eastern territories across the Oder, the FRG had to import nearly 49 per cent of its foodstuffs, while in 1936 the Reich had imported only 35 per cent.

Rapid structural readjustments to the economy also affected the labour market. Employment in the iron, steel, metal and vehicle manufacturing industries grew, while agriculture, forestry and many small rural industries rapidly shed labour. During the period June 1948–December 1949 in agriculture and forestry 350,000 jobs were lost. There was also a regional imbalance in unemployment. In Schleswig-Holstein, Lower Saxony and Northern Bavaria, where a large number of refugees and expellees had found temporary work on the land, there was a very high rate of unemployment. In Schleswig-Holstein, for instance, unemployment stood at 26.3 per cent [*Doc. 5*]. Overall, the expellees accounted for 16 per cent of the population but 40 per cent of the unemployed. By February 1950 there were two million unemployed in the FRG [92; 101; 103].

To Erhard's opponents it seemed that the social market economy had failed. The administrators of the Marshall Plan in February 1950 openly criticized him for ignoring the problem of mass unemployment and pressed for a series of public works programmes and a loosening of credit policy. Erhard made a few concessions by announcing work creation and house construction programmes totalling about DM 2 billion but he again refused to be panicked into any major change of course. This policy could have been blown off course by trade union militancy, but the unions were still recovering from their destruction by Hitler and, under Böckler, the DGB pursued what Kramer has called a policy of 'wage renunciation' [103 *p. 212*], both in the interests of the economy and in the hope that in return the unions would be granted the right of co-determination (see *p. 57*). Subsidies to farmers, which kept the price of food low, rent control, social welfare for the millions of the destitute and the resettlement of some 300,000 expellees from Schleswig-Holstein, Lower Saxony and Bavaria to some extent softened the impact of Erhard's measures. Nevertheless his economic policy was 'a race against time' [79 Vol. 2, *p. 8*].

Erhard's refusal to be panicked into emergency measures was initially vindicated when the outbreak of the Korean War in June 1950 led to a sharp increase in industrial production – between March and December 1950 it rose by 32.3 per cent. Yet by early 1951 the West German economy was again faced with a serious balance of payments deficit caused by the importation of raw materials, particularly coal. The situation was made worse by the renewed consumer boom which the government's work creation projects had encouraged. Ironically, Erhard was put under pressure by the Americans, who were the champions of the free market, to ration raw materials to ensure that heavy industry would have priority [61]. The SPD jumped to the conclusion that the social market economy had failed but Erhard skilfully avoided state intervention by entrusting the industrialists to allocate raw materials to the manufacturing industries through their own trade associations [92; 104].

ECONOMIC RECONSTRUCTION AND MODERNIZATION, 1951–63

By the autumn of 1951 the global economic boom triggered by the Korean War began to operate in favour of the FRG. There was an insatiable demand for machine tools, cars and vehicles, steel and high-quality manufactured goods, all of which the FRG was in a strong position to provide. The export of vehicles, the great majority of which were cars, reached its pre-war level in 1950 and by 1955 was five times higher than had been achieved for the whole Reich in 1938. The mechanical engineering industry did particularly well and by 1958 40 per cent of its output was exported. Those sections of the economy not involved in exporting were given a considerable stimulus by the house-building programme. Between 1949 and 1959 some five million new dwelling units were constructed. The first half of the 1950s was a golden age for the West German economy with a rapid and sustained growth [*Docs. 34* and *35*]. In 1955, for example, the gross domestic product grew by 12 per cent. Nor were there any serious economic problems in the second half of the decade. In the spring of 1956 inflation rose to 2 per cent, but the central bank increased the discount rate, much to the annoyance of Adenauer, who feared that it might impede economic growth in the run up to the election (see *p. 63*). In 1958 there was a minor recession in which the GDP rose by a mere 4.4 per cent. The bank then eased the monetary brakes and in 1960 there was another boom year in which the economy grew by an annual rate of 8.6 per cent [101].

What were the reasons for this phenomenal success? Liberalization of world trade under American pressure, coupled with a tight monetary policy carried out by the central bank, ensured that manufacturers made their profits in the export market. They could only do this initially because so many machines and industrial plant had survived the war intact or at least in a reparable condition. They thus had the spare industrial capacity to respond to world demand for German products. The work force remained moderate in its wage demands, even though Viktor Agartz, the Chairman of the DGB's Economic Research Institute, constantly called for steep wage increases. Yet, with the exception of a three-week engineering strike in Bavaria in 1954, the unions were receptive to warnings from Erhard and the liberal press about the threat of inflation [79 Vol. 2]. There was, too, a high degree of labour mobility, which helped funnel labour away from the decaying heavy industries in the Ruhr to the new industries growing up in southern Germany. In any one year in the 1950s, three million Germans moved house [103]. The labour force was constantly being boosted by the flow of refugees from the GDR. Between 1950 and 1962 3.6 million predominantly young and highly-trained refugees left the GDR [*Doc. 23*]. It was, as Kramer has observed, 'ironic that it was not the Marshall Plan and its contribution of $1.5 billion spread over four years, but Stalin's – and Stalinism's – annual gift of DM 2.6 billion worth of trained labour that provided the greatest capital input to the West German economy' [103 *p. 213*]. Unlike its competitors, the FRG was also initially spared the huge expense of rearmament, although from 1952 onwards the Finance Ministry began to put aside money into a contingency fund in preparation for setting up the new army [32].

Until the late 1950s there is a case to be made that 'West German economic growth reflected by and large not the modernization of the economy but the extremely rapid restoration of the pre-war sectoral structure of German industry' [103 *p. 178*]. The FRG's main export successes were in those areas where Germany had been pre-eminent before the war: mechanical engineering, the electrical and chemical industries and motor manufacturing [*Doc. 35*]. Inevitably, too, many of the industrialists and managers in heavy industry tried to cling to the highly-organized cartel system that had flourished in Germany since the 1890s. In the early 1950s, as Berghahn has observed, 'powerful, older traditions and attitudes now came to enjoy an "after-life"' [106 *p. 71*]. Yet it is misleading to describe West Germany's industrial renaissance simply as a restoration of former economic patterns. The European and global context in which the FRG's economy functioned had altered radically since 1945. Before 1939 some 15 per cent of Germany's exports had gone to eastern and south-eastern Europe, while by the early 1950s this had shrunk to 2 per cent for the FRG at the most. The bulk of its exports went to Western Europe, whose markets were opened up by the ECSC and the EEC.

The influence of America on both the organization and culture of post-war West German industry was also profound in the medium term. Under American and British pressure the Frankfurt Economic Council had produced a draft law to outlaw trusts and to break up monopolies which dominated any particular market. Although Erhard had delayed introducing an anti-cartel bill until 1953 as he suspected that the Allies were more interested in weakening than in reforming German industrial organization, he fully shared the American belief in competition. He claimed that his bill was the 'Economic Basic Law', which complemented the political Basic Law of 1949 [106 *p. 71*]. It met with bitter opposition from the Ruhr industrialists, several ministers, including Adenauer, and most of the industrial associations. It was not until 1957 that it eventually became law. In principle it outlawed cartels, set up the Federal Cartel Office to supervise the functioning of the Act and provided a structure for the liberalization of West German industry, even though there were still some considerable loopholes in the legislation [92; 93]. The younger managers and industrialists also began to copy American management techniques, factory rationalization and the standardization of production and, like the Americans, to link 'mass production with the notion of mass consumption and prosperity for all' [94 *p. 97*; 93].

By the end of the 1950s the period of restoration was over and industrialists were beginning to face new challenges which were typical of a 'mature' industrial economy [105 *p. 10*]. The once-dominant coal industry was in decline as industry switched to cheap oil. Full employment was reached in 1958 and until 1973 labour shortages became a major problem, which was partly solved by recruiting foreign workers or '*Gastarbeiter*'. By 1963 3.7 per cent of the labour force was made up of foreigners mainly from southern Europe. Full employment encouraged greater wage demands and between 1958 and 1962 wage levels actually rose faster than productivity. In the first half of the 1960s the growth rates in Italy and France actually overtook the FRG. In 1963, for instance, the economy grew by only 2.8 per cent. 'The miracle years had passed' [101 *p. 141*].

Erhard had engineered a brilliant capitalist restoration, but the FRG's economy was only in a limited sense a social market economy. He had tamed the cartels, encouraged free enterprise and nearly halved the FRG's protective tariffs. Yet farming was still heavily subsidized, as it had been under Hitler, and the index-linking of the 1957 Pension Act was driving the cost of social welfare steadily upwards. Social market economists were also critical of Germany's membership of the EEC, which they perceived to be a potentially dirigiste and bureaucratic organization. Erhard preferred a larger and looser free trade bloc with Britain as a member. However, whatever reservations the neo-liberals had about the federal economy, there is no doubt that stable prices, impressive export growth and high levels of internal investment 'turned the German economy in ten years back to the trajectory of high growth interrupted in 1914' [105 *p. 9*]. By 1963 the FRG was, in economic terms, the strongest state in Europe.

CHAPTER SEVEN

SOCIAL AND CULTURAL DEVELOPMENTS, 1949–63

From the perspective of the late 1960s the Adenauer era was often seen to be a period of 'barrenness, stagnation and a considerable degree of tedium' [*79 Vol. 3, p. 430*]. Yet the 1950s was a more complex period than this. They were, as Schwarz has observed, 'one of the most elusive decades of recent German history in which reconstruction shades imperceptively into modernization' [*107 p. 5*]. Initially, the energies of the West German people were devoted to reconstruction. Only in the second half of the decade did the FRG begin to move into the consumer age and the rigid conservativism of the early 1950s began to fade and gradually be replaced by more relaxed and liberal attitudes.

THE CONDITION OF THE PEOPLE

In 1950 the West Germans were still haunted by the traumatic experiences of the Second World War and its aftermath. About one-third of the population had been directly affected by bombing, the death of relatives or the loss of position and wealth as a consequence of the forced flight from the East [*Doc. 4*]. Unemployment stood at 2 million and housing conditions were still inadequate. For each room (including the kitchen) in the FRG there were on average 1.2 people – in the big cities more. It is not surprising, then, that these factors led to a feeling of intense insecurity among the population. In 1956 F.R. Allemann characterized the ethos of the West Germans as being 'post revolutionary' [70]. By this he meant that they had decisively rejected the patriotic bombast of the past, viewed politics and public affairs somewhat sceptically and had withdrawn into a private world of work and family. Their desire to distance themselves from politics gave rise to the term *ohne mich* or the 'without me' attitude [95].

In the early 1950s affluence was still a dream for most West Germans. Both industrial and office workers worked long hours for modest wages. Steel workers, for instance, worked on average 48 hours per week (54 if overtime is included). In 1955 a turning point was reached when the five-day week was introduced. Any spare money that individuals could save went into improving housing and living conditions [*Doc. 37*]. In 1953 there were still only one million private cars on the road as compared to 15 million bicycles [79 Vol. 2]. Over the period 1949–59 wages for industrial workers rose by 79 per cent, and by the end of the decade social historians argue that a 'qualitative jump' [107 *p. 8*] into the 'consumer age' had taken place. The West Germans began to spend more on cars, new furniture and holidays. For example, the amount spent on furniture, kitchen equipment, etc., nearly doubled. West Germany society was in the throes of a profound change. The cities with their new skyscrapers became increasingly Americanized, while the spread of car ownership led to the growth of satellite towns, again on the American model. The period can be compared with the 'Roaring Twenties' in America in that 'a mass comfort-loving civilization was firmly established, the hedonism of which was beginning deeply to penetrate all the traditional values and patterns of life' [79 Vol. 2, *p. 388*].

CHANGING SOCIAL STRUCTURES

The Adenauer era was a paradoxical period. In it were inevitably considerable elements of 'restoration', yet it was also a period of accelerated economic and social change comparable to the years 1870–1914. The remaining pre-industrial and mostly rural businesses that had survived the Third Reich and its defeat were swept away. Farming was mechanized and in the period 1950–60 lost half its work force. An upwardly mobile society with a large middle class was created. The 'economic conquest of the countryside' [103 *p. 219*] gradually weakened the grip of both the Catholic and Protestant Churches on the peasantry. On the other hand, the 1950s also witnessed the survival or at least partial restoration of many of the pre-war elites. In the Catholic Church, for instance, there was an unbroken continuity. Faulhaber, the Archbishop of Munich, who had been appointed Cardinal in 1921, led the Church until his death in 1952. In the universities there was a return to the traditional teaching and syllabuses of the pre-Hitler period and a considerable number of the dons, like the historians Franz Schnabel and Hans Herzfeld or the scientists Werner Heisenberg and Carl Friedrich von Weizsäcker, had already been eminent in the 1920s. In big business and industry, superficially it looked as if there had been a complete restoration. In the industrial heartlands of the Ruhr, the flagships of German industry – Klöckner, Thyssen, Otto Wolff and Mannesmann – had survived, but within these industries power slowly shifted away from the original founding families to professional managers and shareholders. The one traditional elite that was destroyed by the war was the old Prussian ruling class that had dominated the army and the bureaucracy. This enabled the FRG to create a new bureaucratic elite of southern and western German middle-class officials.

Only in the Foreign Office and *Bundeswehr* was there a scattering of Prussians. The composition of the Federal Cabinets in the 1950s also reflected this shift to new middle-class Germany. In Adenauer's Cabinets only three ministers were connected with the traditional ruling classes – Seebohm, von Brentano and von Merkatz [79 Vol. 3].

The role of women in the period 1949–63 highlights the uneasy balance between restoration and change that characterizes the Adenauer era. Women played a leading role in the fight for survival in the immediate post-war period [*Docs 2 and 36*]. In Article 3 of the 1949 Basic Law they were formally given equal rights and the government was supposed to amend, by 1953, the Civil Code dating from the Wilhelmine period, which relegated them to second-class citizens. Yet it became clear by the early 1950s that the immediate post-war period had 'only disrupted, not transformed' the position of women [102 *p. 31*]. The retreat into the family that so characterized the 1950s inevitably emphasized the role of women as home-makers and mothers. Indeed, the Catholic Church demanded that the family should become 'the building block of the new German democratic order' [106 *p. 173*] and appealed to the government to protect it. Far from amending the Civil Code, the government attempted to ignore the whole question of civil rights. In the revised Civil Service Law of 1950 married women could be dismissed from the Civil Service provided their husbands earned enough to support them [102]. In December 1953, however, the Federal Constitutional Court insisted that the government should revise the legal code to bring it in line with Article 3 of the Basic Law, although it stressed that 'the man will normally serve the family by employment outside the home..., while the woman will serve the family by looking after the household and caring for the children' [102 *p. 48*]. The relevant sections of the Code were suspended and over the next five years the courts made several judgments of importance. Women, for instance, could now work outside the home without the permission of their husbands and, in the event of divorce, they retained control over their children. In 1958 these rulings were included in the Code, as was the stipulation that the property and possessions acquired by a couple would from now on be regarded as jointly owned rather than just the husband's [102].

Despite these modifications 'the expectations that a woman should marry, raise a family and build her life around the private sphere remained in force' [102 *p. 79*] [*Doc. 36b*]. Yet, as a consequence of the war, there were a large number of women who had no prospect of finding a man to marry. Inevitably, they developed a new and independent lifestyle. They worked, went to theatres and cinemas and on holidays without a man. 'Unwittingly', in Eva Kolinsky's words, 'the non-married women of the "lost generation" were trailblazers of change' [102 *p. 80*].

THE PARTIAL AMERICANIZATION OF WEST GERMAN CULTURE

In the 1950s the availability of international drama, fiction and films became the symbol of the end of Nazi censorship and tyranny. In the book-shops, while the great pre-war German writers, like Thomas Mann and Brecht, were far from forgotten, there was an impressive cosmopolitan choice of classics, contemporary literature and poetry from both Germany, Western Europe and the USA. American literature was particularly sought after. Hemingway, for instance, was by far the best-selling author in Germany. In the decade after 1945 over 1,400 American books were translated into German. American influence played an important part in creating a popular Westernized culture in the FRG. Through films, jazz, fashions (blue jeans, for instance), modern design and not least advertising, particularly for such well-known and popular products as *Coca-Cola* and *Lucky Strike* cigar-ettes, American cultural influence was all pervasive [100; 109].

Michael Geyer perceives in the fascination of the West Germans in the 1950s for all things American a desire to forget the violent origins of their society and 'to disguise its present appearance in foreign images' [106 *p. 116*]. Up to a point that was true, but there were plenty of attempts by West German intellectuals and writers to view the FRG critically and to explore such difficult moral questions as the legacy of Nazism. The influ-ence of *Die Grüppe 47*, a group of left-wing writers which included Heinrich Böll and Günter Grass, steadily grew in the 1950s. Even though it was highly critical of big business and was 'an influential pre-cursor of the New Left of the 1960s' [29 Vol. 1, *p. 416*], it met with little hostility from the ruling elites, who were 'good to their critical intellectuals' [79 Vol. 2, *p. 425*], if only because they felt so secure in their wealth and influence.

It was the influence of the cinema and the impact of American role models on German youth that was to be the real cultural battlefield of the 1950s. 'At stake', according to Heide Fehrenbach, 'was the issue of who would define the nature of the new German nation' [106 *p. 168*]. The dec-isive battle was fought over the German film, *Die Sünderin* ('The Sinful Woman') by Willi Forst. Not only did the film show a female nude scene, but its story of the love of a high-class call girl for a dying man 'resonated with wartime dislocations in social and gender relations' [106 *p. 169*]. The outrage caused by *Die Sünderin* led to tighter film censorship and a policy of generous tax concessions to culturally 'valuable' films. The Catholic Church set up its own Christian film societies, which in 1954 had nearly four million members, to put pressure on local cinemas not to show what the Church judged to be unsuitable films. These measures had a consider-able effect and led to the production of the *Heimat* films, the reassuring message of which was of central importance for the spiritual and moral reconstruction of the FRG: the Germans were themselves the victims rather than the accomplices of Nazism. In the uncertainties of the early 1950s the *Heimat* films did respond to the contemporary mood. In the more confident period after 1956 they began to loose their audience appeal [106].

In the mid-1950s 'rock 'n' roll' and the emergence of the *Halbstarken* or 'teddy-boys' triggered another cultural battle. The *Halbstarken* were seen by the West (and East) German authorities as yet another negative product of American popular culture. Moreover, their flamboyant fashions and ill-disciplined behaviour undermined the image of the new young male who would shortly be required to join the *Bundeswehr* as a 'citizen in uniform'. After the disturbances in many cities in September 1956, caused by the showing of *Rock Around the Clock*, some influential newspaper commentators compared the *Halbstarken* to the SA in the Third Reich, thereby specifically linking American popular culture with Nazism. Adenauer himself joined in the attack and dismissed attacks on the *Bundeswehr* as the work of the *Halbstarken*.

Essentially, what was at stake was what Uta Poiger has called 'the complicated processes of reconstructing Germanness' [106 *p. 116*]. The West German conservative elites fully supported Adenauer's efforts to integrate the FRG politically and militarily into the Western European–American world, but they were far more sceptical about cultural integration. Fehrenbach has even argued that they 'pushed instead in the direction of a cultural *Sonderweg*, or special path' [106 *p. 174*]. By the end of the 1950s it was clear, however, that the attraction of American consumerism and popular culture for the West German youth made this path an almost impossible one to follow [100; 106].

PART FIVE

THE GDR FROM ITS FOUNDATION TO THE BERLIN WALL, 1949–61

CHAPTER EIGHT

POLITICAL DEVELOPMENTS IN THE GDR, 1949–61

THE CREATION OF THE SED DICTATORSHIP

Theoretically the party system in the GDR was pluralist, but in reality it was dominated by the SED and firmly under Soviet supervision. In 1948 two satellite parties had been created, the German Democratic Farmers' Party (DBD) and the National Democratic Party of Germany (NDPD). Their task was to present 'socialist policies to their target groups' [80 *p. 396*], the peasantry and the former Nazis and Conservative Nationalists. Both parties, together with the CDUD and LDPD, were brought into the Democratic Bloc where they were forced to follow the party line by the SED and the Russians [35; 80].

The SED modelled itself on the Communist Party of the Soviet Union. Shortly before the first Party Conference of January 1949 it elected that 'classic model of the executive committee of the Communist Party, the Politbureau' [36 *p. 52*], which was composed of four former Communist members – Pieck, Ulbricht, Merker and Dahlem – and three former Social Democrats – Grotewohl, Meier and Ebert. A key organ was its Small Secretariat, under the chairmanship of Ulbricht, which not only prepared the agenda of the Politbureau, but in reality anticipated its decisions and then monitored their execution. The decisions of the Politbureau were referred usually for automatic endorsement to the Central Committee composed of 80 members elected at the annual Party Congress. These three organs formed a formidable machine which was increasingly able to control not only the SED, but the bloc parties, the mass organizations like the trade unions and the Free German Youth Movement, and the state. In October 1949 Ulbricht's committee issued secret instructions that any 'laws and ordinances of significance' should first 'be directed either to the Politburo or the Secretariat of the Politburo' [49 *p. 125*]. Decisions, as one dissident member of the Politbureau, Paul Merker, was later to observe, were taken by a small core of members in the Politbureau's Secretariat, 'the Party Chairman, General Secretary (Ulbricht) and a few other confidants' [82 *p. 58*]. In essence, a vertical system was created in which the line of command ran from the top to the bottom. Ultimately, this hierarchical pattern of democratic centralism was extended right across the GDR so that all subordinate party committees at whatever level received their instructions from the committee immediately superior to them [*Doc. 13*].

Ulbricht was the most influential politician within the GDR, but he was a bureaucrat not a charismatic leader like Hitler or Lenin [*Doc. 20*]. The main political battles in the GDR were fought out within the Politbureau and the Central Committee. The ex-Social Democrats like Grotewohl and the former KPD members, Merker and Dahlem, who had spent the war in exile in the West or in Nazi concentration camps, gave a higher priority to German unity than did Ulbricht. Merker was seen as a possible 'liberal' successor to Ulbricht in 1949 and was expelled from the Party in 1950 and arrested two years later. Ulbricht also faced persistent criticism for repressing free debate within the Party but, as General Secretary, he was able to brush it aside. Essentially, as long as the Soviet Control Commission and Stalin continued to back him, Ulbricht could ride out criticism from within the Party, but he would become vulnerable once he lost Moscow's confidence, as was to happen in the spring of 1953.

Constitutionally, the GDR appeared to be a parliamentary democracy. There was a parliament, a prime minister and cabinet, but in reality these were just a camouflage for a one-party government. The one force which the SED could not yet completely control, as the third *Volkskongress* elections showed in May 1949 (see *p. 35*), was the electorate. Private soundings by the SED a few months later had indicated that the middle-class parties, the CDUD and the LDPD, were confidently expecting a landslide victory in the coming election. Therefore, to give the SED more time to consolidate its position, the parties of the Democratic Bloc were manipulated under Soviet pressure into agreeing to delay elections for another year shortly before the new provisional government was announced. The leaders of the middle-class parties were also promised positions in the Cabinet. On 12 October the Cabinet, headed by Otto Grotewohl, was confirmed in power by the Provisional Parliament. Theoretically it was a coalition. His deputies were Ulbricht, Nuschke (CDUD) and Kastner (LDPD). Although only five of the fourteen departmental ministers were members of the SED, the key posts of the Interior, Education, Planning, Justice and Industry, were all in the hands of the SED, while three other ministries (Agriculture, Health and Reconstruction) were in the control of former Communists. The Ministry for Foreign Affairs was given to the General Secretary of the CDUD, Georg Dertinger, but any hope that the two bourgeois parties entertained of influencing government policy was illusory. The Cabinet's independence was severely circumscribed both by the SED and the Soviet Control Commission, which replaced SMAD on 10 October and became 'the real centre of power in the GDR' [88 *p. 100*]. Like the Allied High Commission in the

FRG, not only could it suspend laws, issue ordinances, investigate and control government policies, but it also had ultimate responsibility for reparations, occupation costs, the development of agriculture, industry and education policy [35; 37; 80].

In the year before the elections the SED systematically consolidated its position. Its grip on the state was strengthened by the creation in December 1949 of the Supreme Court and the Department of Public Prosecutions. By April 1950 over half the judges and 86 per cent of the public prosecutors in the GDR were members of the SED. In February 1950 the Ministry of State Security, the *Stasi*, which was accountable to the Politbureau, was set up. Its personnel were trained by Soviet experts and it was organized along the lines of the NKVD, the Russian Commissariat or Ministry of Internal Affairs. Its duty was to detect internal opposition to the SED regime and to spy on the mass organizations and bloc parties. During the hysterical atmosphere heightened by the outbreak of the Korean War, witch-hunts were carried out against alleged 'Titoists' and other dissident Socialists. In September 1950, in Waldheim, 157 Social Democrats and 55 veterans of the KPD were sentenced, together with nearly 3,000 former Nazis, to imprisonment. The Central Committee of the SED was responsible for choosing the judges and indicating in advance what the verdicts should be. When Nuschke questioned the legality of this, Helmut Brand, the CDUD State Secretary in the Ministry of Justice, who had supplied him with information, was arrested and imprisoned for fourteen years [83; 88].

After a campaign of intimidation orchestrated by the SED, the CDUD and the LDPD reluctantly agreed in May 1950 that in the election the voters should again be presented with one, united list of candidates [*Doc. 19*]. Although this would deprive the people of the chance of effectively voting against the SED and camouflage its dictatorship, both parties were determined to remain in the government to salvage what little influence they still possessed. Pressure was also exerted on the bloc parties through a mixture of veiled threats and altruistic appeals for unity in the face of the grave problems facing the GDR, to join the National Front, a huge umbrella organization which developed from the *Volkskongress* movement and claimed to be a comprehensive all-German organization representing all parties and organizations interested in national unity. Within the GDR the Front's role was to facilitate the control of the SED over the other parties and the mass organizations. It was entrusted with drawing up the single unified lists of candidates, all offering the same policies, which were to be presented to the voters in the elections on 15 October. The SED was only allotted 25 per cent of the vote, but thanks to the 30 per cent given to the mass organizations and a further 7.5 per cent each to the DBD and the NDPD there was never any chance of the two bourgeois parties being in a position to form a government. The elections were held in an atmosphere of psychological and at times physical intimidation which effectively 'widened rather than reduced the regime's deficit in legitimacy' [36 *p. 65*]. The Party was able to claim that 99.72 per cent of the voters had voted for the unity list.

The election was the last stage of what Loth has called 'a *coup d'état*' against the GDR constitution [49 *p. 125*]. The SED was now able to start on the process of transforming the GDR into a socialist society. In the first six months of 1951 it expelled over 150,000 Party members who were seen as either unreliable or inefficient and the remainder were forced to keep up to date with the basics of Marxism-Leninism and the current party line once a month in night schools. In January 1951 a new department was established under the Central Committee both to control more effectively and to gather information about the bourgeois parties and the mass organizations at state, *Land* and district levels. The Free German Youth Movement (FDJ), which had originally been intended to be independent of the Party, also became a training ground for future leaders of the SED.

At the Second Party Conference in July 1952 it was announced that the primary task of the Party was the 'construction of socialism' in the GDR [46 *p. 263*]. In practical terms this meant increases in productivity at the expense of consumer goods, collectivization and confiscation of private industries (see *p. 97*). To implement this, the power of the state was to be still further increased. All five of the GDR *Länder*, the separate parliaments and administrations of which had been seen as 'obstructive' by the SED [88 *p. 105*], were abolished and replaced by fourteen counties (*Bezirke*). The frontier police had already been placed under the control of the *Stasi* in May, and in an effort to stem the flood of refugees westwards a depopulated frontier zone, five kilometres deep, was created. The state, like the Party, was now organized according to the principle of 'democratic centralism' [35; 36; 87].

The speed with which Ulbricht attempted to introduce the socialist revolution needs to be viewed in the context of the international situation. The future of the GDR, as the Stalin note of March 1952 indicated, was by no means assured (see *p. 43*). Ulbricht hoped that the socialization of the GDR along Stalinist lines would make reunification impossible on anything but the SED's terms, a policy which has been described by Schroeder as 'a disguised opposition to the keeping open of the German question by the Soviet Union' [88 *p. 116;* 49].

17 JUNE 1953 AND ITS CONSEQUENCES

The priorities of the Five Year Plan and the decision to create an armed frontier force as a prototype army put an immense strain on the finances of the GDR, which could only be alleviated by a rigid control of wages, higher taxation and rising food prices. The situation was exacerbated by the increasing food shortages caused by the growing exodus of farmers to the West in protest against the government's hostility towards capitalist agriculture (see *p. 97*). The number of refugees fleeing to the West increased to 'somewhere between 225,000 and 426,000' [112 *p. 180*] in the first six months of 1953. Tension was further heightened by a purge of leading politicians in the bloc parties – both the LDPD Minister for Trade, Karl Hamann, and the CDUD Foreign Minister, Georg Dertinger, were sentenced to long periods of imprisonment. In February 1953 the situation was so tense that the bishops of the German Evangelical Church in the GDR urged the government to take note 'of the distress which threatened to lead to a catastrophe of major proportions' [85 *p. 45*]. Within the Party, too, there were warnings that 'the limits of the burden on the population ... [had been] breached' [49 *p. 149*].

Ulbricht dismissed these warnings as politically motivated attempts to destroy his policy and sought to negotiate a loan and extra deliveries of raw materials from the USSR, but with Stalin's death in March 1953 he was ultimately forced to modify his policies. The new Soviet Prime Minister, Malenkov, and his deputy, Beria, refused to grant any aid package and embarked on a 'new course' which not only encouraged political decentralization and an increased production of consumer goods within the Soviet Union, but also a *détente* with the Western powers, that once again appeared to place the whole future of the GDR in jeopardy (see *p. 44*). This dramatic change of direction inevitably strengthened the opposition against Ulbricht. At first, however, he attempted to persist with his grandiose plans for a socialist transformation. In May, in an effort to cut costs, he defiantly announced a 10 per cent increase in the work norms which were to come into effect on 30 June, and some two million farmers, traders and landowners in the private sector were told that they would no longer be issued with ration cards for food supplies [88; 94; 134]. In early June Malenkov summoned Ulbricht, Grotewohl and Oelssner to Moscow and warned them that if the situation in the GDR was not corrected there would be 'a catastrophe' [123 *p. 472*]. The East Germans were then given a plan with detailed proposals for radical reform: the move towards the collectivization of agriculture was to be halted, independent businesses and the middle classes were to be encouraged rather than economically harried and the Churches were to be left alone [*Doc. 23*]. In Loth's words 'war had been declared on the solidification of the provisional arrangement which was the GDR as it had been emerging since the spring and summer of 1952' [49 *p. 155*].

On 9 June the Politbureau stunned the people of the GDR by announcing this dramatic U-turn imposed upon it by Moscow. Wild rumours began to spread that Ulbricht had been arrested or that the Americans were about to invade. One important policy, however, remained in place. Much to the bitter frustration of the workers, the 10 per cent increase in the norms was not cancelled. Some contemporaries saw this as a deeply machiavellian attempt by Ulbricht to provoke an uprising which would inevitably lead to Soviet intervention and the subsequent collapse of the threatening attempts by the USSR to find a solution to the German problem that would almost certainly entail the demise of the GDR. In reality, however, it is more likely that the norms remained simply as a result of an oversight by the Soviet government [85].

By mid-June the GDR was in the midst of a potentially revolutionary crisis. The change, of course, had badly shaken the morale of the leadership, while it had not appeased the hostility of the workers. On 15 June this hostility began to make itself forcefully felt in East Berlin. On 16 June a crowd of building workers marched first to the trade union headquarters and then to the 'House of Ministries' to demand the abolition of the new norms. There, after a considerable delay, which naturally increased their impatience and anger, they were informed that the 10 per cent increase would be withdrawn. On the way back to their building sites this apparently unambiguous statement was thrown into doubt when workers were met by SED officials in loud-speaker vans who 'in the legalistic and ambiguous jargon employed by the politbureau' [81 *p. 46*] appeared to put the whole concession in doubt. The workers then began to call for a general strike and 'butter instead of cannons' [112 *p. 182*], the restoration of works councils and re-legalization of the SPD. In some ways the strikes were reminiscent of the stoppages in 1919–20 except that the employer was the state rather than the individual capitalist [87]. By the following day waves of spontaneous and uncoordinated strikes and demonstrations had erupted across the whole of the GDR. Crowds collected outside prisons, state and Party offices and called for the resignation of the government, but only in Görlitz and Bitterfeld were there determined efforts to form democratic local governments. Elsewhere there were no plans to control radio stations and transport networks or to seize arms. In East Berlin alone there were 100,000 people on the streets. The government, distrusting the loyalty of its own police forces, appealed to the Russians to intervene. By 18 June a combination of Soviet military intervention and the withdrawal of the work norms restored order, although sporadic strikes, protests and demonstrations continued for a few more days [85; 87; 112].

The events of 16–17 June were a complex phenomenon which, under the impact of the Cold War, were interpreted in diametrically opposed ways in the two Germanies. In the GDR they were, officially at any rate, dismissed as a reactionary Fascist *putsch* inspired by the capitalist powers [*Doc. 17*], while initially in the FRG 17 June was seen as a popular uprising against Stalinist tyranny and a demand for German unity. In 1965 Arnulf Baring modified this latter view in his seminal study of the revolt [81]. He argued that the first stage of the uprising consisted of strikes and demonstrations by the workers, who 'were interested primarily in lower quotas and lower prices, especially food prices. The demand for free elections was far less urgent'. Then in the afternoon (of 17 June) the second stage was reached when these 'orderly demonstrations' were 'transformed into a popular revolt' but the intervention of Soviet troops did not mark a turning point as the 'revolutionary wave had already begun to ebb' since it lacked both leaders and a coherent programme [81 *pp. 73–6*]. In the West, Baring's arguments were broadly accepted until the early 1990s when historians had access to the GDR archives. Then, Mitter and Wolle, after analysing the relevant files, claimed that 17 June was after all a revolutionary event which could well have led to German unity had it not been for Russian intervention. They interpret the uprising as a forerunner of the events of 1989, since there were demands for lifting the frontier, free elections and the resignation of the government. Probably without the demonstration of Soviet power, these demands would have created an unstoppable momentum for unity. Yet both of these explanations are to a certain extent simplifications of complex events. The GDR was a deeply divided society and, as Pritchard has shown [87], many of those who demonstrated on 16 and 17 June had their own agendas, which do not easily conform to a uniform explanation. There were many different strands in the revolt. It was partly a recrudescence of Nazism and a youth protest, as well as a struggle for Westernization and a violent but last spasm of the German socialist tradition of the 1920s [87].

The uprising at first strengthened Ulbricht's critics. The Organizational Commission of the Central Committee struck a major blow at his power base by proposing the abolition of the Party Secretariat and the position of General Secretary. Ulbricht's downfall seemed inevitable, but he was given a unique opportunity to save himself when Beria was arrested in Moscow on 26 June. Inevitably, this changed the balance of power in Moscow to Ulbricht's advantage as Beria had been anxious to break the deadlock in Germany and create a neutral and independent German state. He was therefore an ally of Ulbricht's enemies and a powerful advocate of the new course. Ulbricht was able brilliantly to exploit the mood of fear and uncertainty that now prevailed. On 4 July he was able to persuade the Politbureau to revise the draft resolution for the 'New Course' on Party reorganization and the development of a more consensual domestic policy, warning his colleagues of the dangers of betrayal, treason and division. Even so, in a meeting on 7 July in the Politbureau he had only two supporters, Honecker and Matern, but the majority now lacked the courage to strike without explicit Kremlin backing, which was no longer forthcoming. The following day Grotewohl and Ulbricht flew to Moscow to be briefed on Beria's fall. When they returned with the official communiqué,

Oelssner and Jendretzky swung round to support Ulbricht and on 18 July Zaisser and Herrnstadt were expelled from the Central Committee and Fechner, who had dared to defend the workers' right to strike, was arrested. Ulbricht, through a mixture of good luck and political skill, had defeated a major political challenge. The New Course was not formally dropped, but Ulbricht made clear his reservations about it. On 26 July the Central Committee announced that '[i]t was indeed correct that our party led Germany on the path to socialism and began to errect the foundations of socialism. This general line of the party was and remains correct' [49 *p. 166*; 85; 112].

Nevertheless, the Party could not go on as if nothing had happened. The restoration of order by Russian troops illustrated with embarrassing clarity that 'the power of the SED rested on Russian bayonets' [85 *p. 162*]. It was this painful fact that made the 17 June so traumatic for the SED elite and spurred them on to prevent its repetition. Thus some 6,000 people were immediately arrested and held in conditions reminiscent of 'the torture chambers of the SA ... during the Hitler period' [85 *p. 107*] and thousands were purged from the SED, the trade unions and the bloc parties. The SED also sought to strengthen and build up the security apparatus of the state. The police were increased by nearly 16,000 and the *Stasi* was placed more effectively under Party control. From now on it had to compile daily reports, which would be processed by information groups in each county administration (*Bezirksverwaltung*). Under Soviet supervision the police and the paramilitary plant defence groups were re-equipped and made more effective. At the same time the SED, under pressure from Moscow, took steps to appease the population through a series of economic concessions. Pensions were increased, more consumer goods were to be produced, food prices lowered and, as a gesture of good will, the USSR agreed to return the last 33 SAGs to German ownership. The persecution of the Church was stopped and the heavy taxes and demands on independent farmers and businessmen were eased [35; 85; 112].

Temporarily at least, these measures took the pressure off Ulbricht. At the Fourth Party Congress in 1954, in line with the new emphasis in Moscow on collective leadership, he was re-elected First Secretary, rather than General Secretary, but in reality he remained the most powerful man in the GDR. In January he had Zaisser and Herrnstadt expelled from the Party and another voluble critic, Ackermann, removed from the Central Committee. While Ulbricht conceded at the Congress that temporarily both the private and state economic sectors could co-exist, he nevertheless reiterated that the GDR had 'now begun to create the foundations for socialism' [49 *p. 168*]. In the election of October 1954 the voters were again presented with a single list of candidates, and in the new government 20 out of 28 ministers belonged to the SED.

Over the course of the next year the future of the GDR appeared to become much more secure. In response to the FRG joining NATO, the GDR joined the Warsaw Pact and in the following January began to build up the NVA – the National People's Army. In September 1955 Russia recognized the GDR as a sovereign state [*Doc. 26*] and Khrushchev specifically declared that 'the German question cannot be solved at the expense of the interests of the German Democratic Republic ... eliminating all its political and social achievements'[49 *p. 170*]. Yet within six months the GDR was again faced with a serious crisis.

THE CRISIS OF DE-STALINIZATION, 1956

Khrushchev's dramatic revelation of Stalin's crimes at the 20th Party Congress in Moscow in February 1956 plunged the Communist world into a crisis from which the GDR was not immune. The radical break with the Stalinist personality cult and regime of terror appeared to pave the way for a more democratic form of socialism by conceding that even the Communist Party in the USSR could make mistakes. It was no wonder that Ulbricht, in the words of one of the Politbureau members, Karl Schirdewan, was 'terribly frightened about the consequences of the speech' [82 *p. 169*]. Yet with consummate political skill he managed to survive the crisis which swept away his Polish and Hungarian colleagues. Initially he took great care to minimize the impact of the speech in the GDR by cryptically announcing in the Party newspaper, *Neues Deutschland*, on 4 March, the day before the third anniversary of Stalin's death, that Stalin could not be regarded 'as one of the all time greats of Marxism-Leninism' [35 *p. 79*], but, as a result of broadcasts from Western radio stations, the news of Khrushchev's speech inevitably became common knowledge and unleashed a wave of criticism against Ulbricht and the Party. At the Third Party Conference in March he denied that Khrushchev's speech had any relevance for the GDR since there had been no personality cult or mass purges, and insisted that the Conference devote its time to discussing the second Five Year Plan.

Nevertheless, he could not isolate the GDR from the crisis sweeping Eastern Europe in the summer and autumn of 1956. There was considerable sympathy with the Polish uprising in Posen in June. In August and September there was a rash of strikes throughout the GDR. The Hungarian uprising and the Suez Crisis at the end of October led to futher unrest in both the universities and the large industrial centres such as Rostock, Magdeburg and East Berlin. In the words of one miner in Saxony, it seemed that 'a small spark would be sufficient to begin an uprising' [85 *p. 256*]. However, a repetition of 17 June was avoided, partly by political and economic concessions such as the shortening of the working day, the release of 20,000 political prisoners and the political rehabilitation of such party figures as Dahlem and Ackermann, but also by the effective deployment of plant defence forces. The brutal defeat of the Hungarian revolt by Soviet troops in November also acted as a powerful deterrent to the population of the GDR [88; 112].

Although the events of 1956 were 'a flashpoint that failed to ignite' [112 *p. 187*], Ulbricht's position remained insecure until 1958. There were several groups hoping to replace him with a more moderate figure, a 'German Gomulka'. In the autumn of 1956 one group crystallized around the philosopher Wolfgang Harich, the publisher Walter Janka and the former dissidents Merker and Dahlem. Their aim was to rid the GDR of Stalinism, end the dictatorial position of the SED and develop a uniquely German road to socialism, which could appeal to the SPD in the FRG. Within the Politbureau and the Central Committee, Schirdewan, Oelssner, Selbmann and Wollweber also wanted a less centralist approach to government and to allow more independence and competition in the economy. In early 1956 Schirdewan was actually being 'groomed' [82 *p. 211*] by Moscow as Ulbricht's replacement, but the revolts in Poland and Hungary distracted Khrushchev at the critical moment from the domestic politics of the GDR, and of course at the same time Ulbricht's prestige and value to Moscow were enhanced by the relative stability of the GDR. This gave Ulbricht the necessary freedom to defeat his reformist rivals. He had the Harich group arrested in early 1957 and by skilfully exploiting the divisions among his other opponents he managed, at the 35th Plenary Meeting of the Central Committee in February 1958, to destroy his political enemies. Schirdewan and Wollweber were expelled from the Central Committee and Oelssner from the Politbureau, while the Central Committee's Secretary, Gerhart Ziller, who had in vain tried to unite the anti-Ulbricht faction, committed suicide. There were further purges at the Fifth Party Conference later in the year when another 21 members lost their places on the Central Committee [82; 112].

Ulbricht reacted to these challenges to his authority by further developing, over the next three years, the dictatorship of the SED and the effectiveness of the security apparatus. Armed militias, for instance, were now to be formed in the universities, polytechnics and machine tractor stations in the countryside. Political sections responsible only to the SED were set up in the Frontier Police, in the factories and in the army. The criminal code was also amended in December 1957 so that the state could more easily proceed against its critics. Anti-state propaganda, which could include political jokes, became a crime, as did helping somebody to leave the GDR or passing information to the representatives of a hostile state. In the legal process, as elsewhere, the Party's wishes were paramount. The Director of Public Prosecutions formulated this principle with considerable lucidity when he observed that 'judges' decisions must reflect the willingness to implement decisions taken by the party of the working class and the government' [88 *p. 142*].

By the summer of 1958 Ulbricht had not only defeated his enemies but consolidated his position. The programme of the Fifth Party Congress reflected this. It set the ambitious aim of completing the victory of socialism in the GDR and of economically overtaking the FRG [35; 36; 88].

THE CONSTRUCTION OF THE BERLIN WALL

In 1958–59 the GDR's economy grew by the rate of nearly 12 per cent per annum (see *p. 98*) and in the following year the number of refugees declined dramatically. Briefly, it looked as if the GDR might be beginning to establish some claims to legitimacy in the eyes of its population. Weber has argued that by this date the old Western cliché that 'a handful of fanatical communists were repressing in the GDR a consistently anti-communist population which was conspiring with the West, no longer corresponded to reality' [37 *p. 47*]. However, the prolonged crisis triggered by Khrushchev's Berlin ultimatum of November 1958 [*Doc. 29*] and the forced collectivization of agriculture in 1960 showed how fragile the foundations of the state still were (see *pp. 48–9*). The immediate economic impact of collectivization was disastrous and there was consequently a massive rise in the number of refugees fleeing westwards through the open frontier in Berlin. In 1960, 199,000 fled and in the six months up to June 1961 a further 103,000. By June 1961 reports were pouring into government offices from the *Stasi* of unrest and discontent in the factories. Ulbricht, however, refused to make any concessions. It is possible, as Staritz and Klessmann have conjectured, that he embarked upon such a radical course in order to push Khrushchev into sanctioning the construction of the Berlin Wall, but it is just as likely that the Party went ahead with collectivization because socialization in the countryside was lagging behind the rest of the economy (see *p. 100*) [36; 73; 85].

The torrent of refugees this policy caused made the closure of the frontier in Berlin inevitable if the GDR was not to collapse. Ulbricht finally achieved the go-ahead for this at the meeting of the Warsaw Pact states on 3–5 August 1961 [*Doc. 30*]. The operation was well planned by Honecker, the minister in charge of security, and was carried out in the early hours of 13 August. Initially, 'the anti-Fascist protective wall' [36 *p. 138*] consisted mainly of barbed wire, but this was rapidly replaced by a more permanent concrete structure. Although it was deeply unpopular in the GDR, the security forces prevented any repetition of 17 June and protests were reduced to sporadic and ineffective individual actions which could easily be contained [112].

The closing of the frontier in Berlin was a major turning point in the history of the GDR. The Party faithful were to look back on 13 August 1961 and to regard it as the 'secret foundation day of the GDR' [37 *p. 138*]. It at last guaranteed that factory managers would be able to retain their work forces, while it enabled Ulbricht, in 1963, to develop the 'New Economic System' that was supposed to revolutionize the GDR's economy and gain enthusiastic acceptance for socialism.

1. Helped by a mild winter British and American planes were able to fly in by January 1949 a daily average of 5,620 tons of supplies to Berlin. By April this had risen to 8000 per day. The planes became known as 'candy bombers' as the pilots often dropped sweets out of the windows for the watching children.

2. In an attempt to stop the FRG's integration into NATO Molotov pleaded at the Moscow Security Conference on 19 November 1954 for all-German elections. Here on 4 December Grotewohl and Ulbricht are delivering the same message.

3. Big four leaders at Western summit, 19 December 1959. Harold Macmillan, Charles De Gaulle, Konrad Adenauer and Dwight D. Eisenhower. Here the decision was taken to invite Khrushchev to a summit meeting in Paris in the Spring of 1960.

4. On 17 August 1962 GDR frontier troops fatally shot 18-year-old Peter Fechter, a building worker, just as he was trying to climb over the Berlin Wall near Checkpoint Charlie. He was left to bleed to death for well over an hour before his body was carried away.

CHAPTER NINE

THE ECONOMY IN THE GDR, 1948–61

The Cold War and the SED's determination to introduce a Stalinist system of centralized planning ensured that radical structural changes had to be rapidly made to the East German economy. In 1947 two-thirds of the Soviet Zone's trade was still with Western Germany, but in 1948 in retaliation against the Berlin blockade, the British stopped all coal and steel deliveries, while the Bizonal Economic Commission progressively restricted inter-zonal trade. The Soviet Zone had consequently little option but to look towards the Socialist states of Central and Eastern Europe for its vital supplies of coal, iron and steel. In turn, this meant that East German industry would have to offer its new trading partners what they needed, which was mainly the products of heavy engineering. The East German economy had therefore to switch from its traditional textile and light industries and to build up a new economy based on heavy engineering [118].

The private sector was progressively weakened. In the currency reform of June 1948, which introduced the new East German Mark (see *p. 29*), the remaining independent industrialists and businessmen were severely penalized. Their financial assets were converted at a rate varying from 3 to 10 *Reichsmarks* to one East Mark, while money belonging to state-owned factories (VEBs), *Land* governments, trade unions and the SED was converted at the rate of 1:1. In effect, the currency reform became 'a partial confiscation of savings and investments' in the private sector [54 *p. 253*]. By 1950 the VEBs, together with the SAGs, accounted for some 76 per cent of the total industrial production, while the banking and insurance sectors were completely in the state's hands. Independent retail trade also faced fierce competition from the shops run by the State Trade Organization (HO), and the larger farmers and independent artisans were harried by punitive taxation.

THE PLANNED ECONOMY, 1948–61

Between 1948 and 1950 the socialist planned economy was introduced into the GDR in two main stages. First, in 1948, came the Two Year Plan which aimed to increase productivity to 80 per cent of the GDP of the whole German Reich in 1936. Two years later, the Five Year Plan was launched with the intention of doubling the output of 1936, while living standards were 'to exceed significantly the pre-war level' [35 p. 54]. The Plan's main targets were the metallurgical and machine-building sectors, which were to expand by 153.6 per cent and 114.8 per cent respectively. The technical organization of these Plans was based on the Stalinist model. A centralized planning system presided over by the State Planning Commission gave detailed production plans, determined initially in outline by the SED, to the factories. There was no room for managerial initiative. In the words of the Deputy Chief of the DWK, the intention was 'to plan down to the last machine, down to the last production unit of state-owned industry' [118 p. 48]. All this had to be done without any Marshall Aid, while reparations and occupation costs paid to the USSR in 1949 accounted for 16.9 per cent of the national income of the GDR.

To implement the Five Year Plans the industrial work force had to be increased by one million. This target was in fact more than met. Through retraining programmes, recruiting of redundant land workers and the 'carrot' of higher wages, labour was attracted to the new heavy industries. Overall, in the ten years 1945–55, the number of people in the GDR in work increased by two million, despite the flight of 1.4 million, of whom many were young skilled workers, to the West. This was achieved largely by recruiting women and keeping on pensioners in work [116].

The SED further developed the policies introduced by SMAD in Order 234, issued in October 1947 (see p. 20), in an attempt to increase output. The workers were set norms (targets) and were encouraged to compete against each other in order to raise their productivity. The winners became an 'Activist' elite with higher pay and other privileges. On the factory floor, however, there was immense hostility to competitive piece rates, while the managers had little idea of how to initiate 'socialist competitions' [117 p. 32]. To appease their workers and to stop them from moving to other factories or indeed fleeing to the West, they set low norms which in practice amounted to giving them wage rises. Wages then began to rise faster than productivity and, in the words of a Soviet official, 'threaten the normal monetary circulation and financial system of the Zone' [117 p. 32]. Not surprisingly, the Russians intervened and ordered the East Germans to tighten up on norms and wage rates and expand the Activist movement. In imitation of the way the Russians had built up the coal miner Alexei Stakhanov in the 1930s into a 'hero of socialist labour', Adolf Hennecke, a 51-year-old coal miner from Zwickau, was carefully groomed to exceed his norm of coal mined during one shift by at least 250 per cent. When he achieved this by 387 per cent in October 1948, he was turned into a popular hero. Despite scepticism and often fierce opposition on the factory floor, the system was extended throughout the GDR. The replacement of the works councils, which had sprung up in 1945, by SED-dominated trade union councils in November 1948, and the conversion of trade unions to a mere arm of the Party, strengthened the state's grip on the work force and made the transition to piece rates and the acceptance of norms easier to enforce. By 1951 some 65 per cent of the work force were paid according to piece work [53; 117].

Despite supply bottlenecks, the problem of Western migration and labour hostility to work norms, by 1952–53 it was clear that the Five Year Plan was already achieving some impressive successes in the production of iron, steel and chemicals. For instance, raw steel production in 1953 was already double that of 1936. On the basis of these optimistic figures the SED, ignoring Soviet reservations, announced at the Party Conference in July 1952 its intention to accelerate the planned construction of Socialism and to overcome the 'last traces of capitalist thought' [36 *p. 76*]. The economic implications of this were that the construction of heavy industry would be speeded up, while there would be a new campaign to collectivize agriculture and take over private firms. Above all, there would be yet more pressure on the workers to increase productivity. The introduction of the new 10 per cent work norm, accompanied by increases in food prices, health care and public transport fares, led to renewed worker unrest, culminating in the uprising of 16–18 June 1953 (see *p. 88*). Despite the purges and strengthening of the security apparatus in the aftermath of these events, Kopstein has argued that the 'uprising effectively crippled the regime on the shop floor' [117 *p. 37*]. The attempt to enforce a vigorous norm policy was quietly shelved and throughout the 1950s wages rose more quickly than productivity, which in turn led to growing budget deficits.

By 1955 the standard of living in the GDR was the highest in the COMECON. Economic growth had averaged 13.7 per cent per year between 1951 and 1955. Consumption of butter, meat and eggs had at last caught up with pre-war levels, while wages had overtaken them. Yet as far as the availability of consumer goods went, the GDR was still lagging far behind the FRG. The financial capacity of the population to buy more consumer goods than the regime could in fact supply was a constant source of frustration that led to many GDR citizens voting with their feet and fleeing westwards [118].

In the next two industrial plans the SED attempted to address this problem. The second Five Year Plan was delayed by the turmoil in Eastern Europe in 1956, and was not effectively launched until March 1958. At the Fifth Party Conference in the summer of 1958 Ulbricht stated unambiguously that the 'main economic task' was to overtake the FRG 'within a few years ... in per capita consumption of all important food items and consumer goods' [73 *p. 309*]. This was, as Klessmann has observed, 'aiming for the stars' [73 *p. 310*], since the GDR lacked the resources and global backing which the FRG enjoyed. Yet Ulbricht had little alternative but, as he put it, 'to square off' against West Germany [117 *p. 43*]. Only by raising the standard of living in the GDR could he finally defeat the magnet-like pull of the FRG and effectively counter the claims of the Hallstein Doctrine [*Doc. 27*].

Although the main emphasis of the Five Year Plan was placed on raw materials and the development of the machine tool industry, an increase of 40 per cent was envisaged for consumer goods. Initially it looked as if Ulbricht's gamble would pay off. In 1958–59 the GDR's economy grew by the rate of nearly 12 per cent per annum which enabled the SED to abolish ration cards and raise wages for most of the working population. The USSR also made a significant concession when it brought to an end the GDR's liability for occupation costs [35; 37].

In 1959, to bring the GDR into line with the USSR, the second Five Year Plan was replaced by a new Seven Year Plan. Its emphasis was on energy, chemicals and electrical engineering, and it was designed to complement the output of the other Eastern European states and so tie the GDR ever more closely to the Eastern Bloc. The development of plastics and modern synthetic fibres was to be made possible by the supply of petroleum from the USSR. By 1965 industrial production was scheduled to increase by 188 per cent and consumer production by 177 per cent, but by 1960 it was clear that these targets were a mirage. In July 1960, in a letter to Khrushchev, Ulbricht conceded that the GDR was unable to compete against the FRG without extra steel deliveries from the USSR and hard currency loans to buy equipment from the West [117]. On purely economic terms the interaction of high labour costs in the GDR, the low quality of output, the lack of foreign exchange and the domination by the Western powers of the global economy indicated that the GDR would fall ever further behind the FRG [119]. This in turn meant that the GDR would fail to 'craft an appealing socialist modernity' [117 *p. 46*] and so continue to lose skilled personnel to the West through the open frontier in Berlin. In January 1961 Ulbricht succinctly told Khrushchev: 'the booming economy in West Germany, which is visible to every citizen of the GDR, is the main reason that over ten years about two million people have left our Republic' [117 *p. 44*]. The ultimate solution to this dilemma was, as we have seen, the construction of the Berlin Wall, which brutally solved the border question until 1989 and allowed the GDR a second chance to engineer a miracle of its own [35; 117].

AGRICULTURE AND COLLECTIVIZATION

Post-war land reform had seriously weakened the agricultural sector. As a result of the break-up of farms of over 100 hectares to provide land for the expellees, it was dominated by small and middle-sized holdings which were economically much less efficient. Many of the new farmers who had been settled on the old estates had not been provided with the necessary equipment for cultivating their land, and the ruthless Soviet policy of requisitioning crops and livestock for the army of occupation had merely made the situation worse [*Doc. 11*]. By the winter of 1947–48 agriculture in the Soviet Zone was in a state of deep crisis. The harvest had been poor and much of the potato crop had been destroyed by a plague of bugs. Well over 10,000 of the new farmers had simply abandoned their plots and either moved to the towns or to the West, and meat and fat consumption had slipped to a mere 50 per cent of their 1934–38 level [53].

Within the SED there was pressure for collectivizing the farms in line with what was happening in other Soviet bloc states, but as long as Stalin was still undecided about the future of the GDR, this was not a practical policy [115]. A move towards collectivization only became politically possible when the West rejected Stalin's note of March 1952 and Adenauer signed the European Defence Community Treaty in May (see *p. 44*). To Ulbricht, who announced the programme at the Second Party Conference, it seemed the best way to bring back into cultivation the land abandoned by the peasants who had fled to the West or into the towns, to increase production and to mobilize the rural population for Socialism. Collectivization was voluntary, but the small peasants were offered considerable incentives, such as tax relief and preferential treatment in the delivery of fertilizers, to form collectives as soon as possible. The larger farms, on the other hand, were declared to be the class enemy and discrimination against them intensified to the point where many fled to the FRG. Inevitably, this caused yet more land to lie fallow and by early 1953 some 13 per cent of the total cultivated area in the GDR was no longer farmed [115].

With the acceptance of the 'New Course' (see *p. 89*) under Russian pressure in June 1953 both the persecution of the larger farmers and the pressure on the peasantry to enter collectives ceased. The official line was now that the German peasantry was not yet ready for collectivization, and peasants were even allowed to move out of the collectives. While this change of policy benefited the private sector, the collectives faced growing economic problems. They had neither sufficient labour nor resources to farm effectively. The state therefore continued to subsidize them and attempted with only partial success to persuade industrial workers to work on the land. In the autumn of 1956 much of this financial help had to be cut when the crises in Poland and Hungary disrupted the delivery of vital raw materials to the GDR. To some members of the SED this was seen as an opportunity for the GDR to re-think its agrarian policy. Kurt Viehweg, for instance, suggested that there should be an element of competition allowed between private farms and collectives, but this heretical idea was rapidly dismissed by Ulbricht as 'counter-revolutionary' and Viehweg was dismissed from the Central Committee in March 1957 [35; 115].

One of the aims of the second Five Year Plan was to overtake the FRG in agricultural production. Once again new efforts were made to attract peasants into the collectives, while renewed pressure was exerted on the private sector, but by the autumn of 1958 it was clear that the deep reservations that many peasants still had about collectivization had not been dispelled. The decision was therefore taken at the Plenary Meeting of the Central Committee in December 1959 to force the remaining independent farmers into collectives in time for the spring sowing. It was a radical 'leap forward', prompted by the belief that only through total collectivization would the GDR be able to fulfil the Plan. In January 1960 large numbers of SED agitators were drafted into the countryside to persuade the peasants of the benefits of collectivization. Their efforts were supplemented by coercive pressure from the *Stasi* and special brigades recruited from Party zealots and the *Volkspolizei* [85]. By mid-April the operation was accomplished, but the immediate economic impact of collectivization was disastrous: yields plummeted and serious shortages in bread, butter and meat were reported. Only in 1963, after the investment of a further billion Marks was the agricultural sector at last stabilized [115].

CHAPTER TEN

SOCIALISM AND THE EAST GERMAN PEOPLE

Whereas there was a considerable element of 'restoration' in West German society, in the GDR 'almost the whole of the old society' [36 *p. 77*], with the exception of the Churches, the medical profession and a few small businesses, was deconstructed over the decade 1950–60. Although the speed and timing of the introduction of Socialism was a matter of debate, Ulbricht and the other leading Communist politicians within the SED never doubted the apparently scientifically proven truth of Marxism-Leninism and its applicability to the German situation. Convinced that capitalism was the seed-bed of Nazism, they were determined to eradicate both it and the attitudes associated with it from East German society. Having constructed through democratic centralism a party dictatorship, the SED sought to penetrate society at every level [80; 112; 116].

EDUCATION, CULTURE AND THE CREATION OF A NEW ELITE

Crucial to this process was the removal of the old traditional elites and their replacement by new personnel loyal to the regime and its aims. By the early 1960s, to quote Kocka, 'an exchange of elites had taken place which was unique in modern German history' [116 *p. 548*]. Only in a few professions, such as the Church and Medicine, did the educated bourgeoisie manage to survive. By 1948, over half a million people had been removed from teaching, the legal profession, public administration and industrial management. The top Party posts, the key ministries and administrative positions were for the most part occupied by former KPD members who had gained their political experience in the Weimar Republic. Below them a new elite had hastily to be trained to fill the middle management posts in the mass organizations and Party, as well as those positions vacated by the old managerial and business elite in the public services and the economy. The SED looked for their successors among the generation which had joined the Free German Youth (FDJ), just after the war. These were usually children of workers and peasants and were given the chance to study at university through generous grants and preliminary crash courses at special 'Worker and Peasants faculties' [46 *p. 287*].

The FDJ, which was open to young people between 14 and 25 years old, was an important instrument for educating youth in the principles of Socialism. In 1950 it was given the right to represent all young people at work, even if they did not belong to the organization, and it was admitted into the Democratic Bloc as a mass organization [111]. In May 1952 its role as a recruiting ground for the Party was confirmed in a new constitution which pledged it to support the SED and to help build a socialist society [35; 46; 111].

In 1950 the SED had hoped that over 70 per cent of the GDR's youth would join in the FDJ, but this target was not achieved for another 25 years. Thus the key role of the educational system both in moulding a collective socialist identity among the GDR citizens and in producing the future socialist elite was not diminished. The new Ministry for People's Education sought to break the old elite traditions of German scholarship and make education more 'work related'. Great efforts were made to ensure that as many children of workers and peasants as possible attended the academic high schools (*Oberschulen*) so that they would be then eligible for university places, but by 1953 children from working-class backgrounds still made up only 43.6 per cent of the total number of pupils at these high schools.

The task of schools, as defined by the Politbureau in 1952, was primarily to 'build socialism and defend the achievements of the workers to the last' [46 *p. 283*]. The teachers, supervised by 'pedagogic councils' on which the secretary of the local FDJ usually sat, were forced to become activists and in the newly introduced current affairs lessons exhort their pupils to be 'democratic and socialist patriots' ready to defend the GDR against the 'imperialism' and 'fascism' of NATO and the FRG. The New Course forced on Ulbricht by the Russians in June 1953 delayed further reforms, but the dismissal of the education minister, Paul Wandel, in October 1957 signalled a new phase of educational reform. Two years later the high schools, which the SED viewed as being too academic and middle class, were abolished, and integrated with the elementary schools (*Grundschulen*) into a single 'general polytechnical ten-class higher school'. There was now to be a uniform curriculum, heavily biased towards the sciences and technical subjects for all children, who, during their last four years, would spend one day a week doing practical work in industry or agriculture. Those going on to university would have to spend a further two years at an 'expanded high school' where there would be a further mix of work experience and academic subjects [35; 46; 73].

The universities, too, had to be converted into 'socialist seats of learning' [35 *p. 93*]. No longer were they to be institutions where pure research and 'objectivity' were at a premium. Instead, they were to provide the necessary expertise and research for a scientific back-up to the Five Year Plan. As with the high schools, great efforts were also made to broaden their intake so that a new working-class socialist intelligentsia could be educated (see *p. 15*). In 1951 the teaching curriculum of the universities was subjected to detailed supervision by a new department of the state specially set up for the purpose. Through seminar groups run by the FDJ, the supervisory role of the Party was strengthened. The content of syllabuses was carefully checked and obligatory courses on Russian and the social sciences, which provided the vehicle for Marxism-Leninism studies, were introduced. Between 1951 and 1955 the number of universities and institutes of technology increased from 21 to 46 and the number of students more than doubled from 27,822 to 60,148. Initially the universities still retained some vestiges of their former independence and for all the efforts to create a new socialist intelligentsia, care was taken to appease the traditional professorate, particularly in the natural science and technical departments, with good pay and extra 'perks', as their contributions were vital to the Five Year Plan. However, in 1958, the Party mounted a fresh campaign against the remnants of bourgeois influence in the universities. By taking a harder line against the universities, the SED precipitated the flight of the very teachers whose services were needed for scientific research. Their dilemma was not solved until the closing of the Berlin frontier [35; 73; 88].

Literature, art, the mass media and all other cultural activities also played a vital part in the attempt to create a working class and socialist identity. In 1951 a tight system of censorship was introduced when the Bureau for Literature and Publishing and the State Commission for Artistic Affairs were set up. 'The official state aesthetic' [25 p. 443] in literature and the arts was, as in Russia, socialist realism. Modern art was dismissed as decadent, deeply pessimistic and as obsessed with insignificance. Instead, according to official guidelines, artists were to produce work that was lifelike, comprehensible to the people, depicting typical everyday events and, above all, optimistic. Similarly, the 'literature of reconstruction', as the contemporary novels and poetry were called, was 'socially therapeutic' in character and consequently often bland and boring in content [46 p. 289]. An important part of the GDR's cultural policy was also to lay claim to the classical heritage of Bach, Beethoven, Goethe and Schiller, in its attempt to project itself as the legitimate nucleus of a future united socialist Germany [25; 35].

The New Course led to some relaxation of pressure on writers and artists, but in 1957, when the second stage of the cultural revolution was launched, they were again urged to bridge the gap between art and work. At the Bitterfeld writers' conference in 1959 it was agreed that writers should actually join factory brigades and experience the reality of physical labour

[*Doc. 38*]. In time this did produce, according to Erica Carter, 'some genuine cross fertilization between "high and low", bourgeois and working-class cultures' [*25 p. 444*] as the descriptions of factory and rural life by such writers as Crista Wolf and Erwin Strittmatter indicate [25; 35; 37].

THE WORKERS' AND PEASANTS' STATE

The GDR described itself as a workers' and peasants' state and young people were repeatedly exhorted to make the ideology of the working class their own [88]. Claus Offe has argued that the GDR, lacking a national identity, had only therefore an economic identity and represented 'a pure … form of a socialist economic society' [in 116 *p. 39*]. There was both the right to work but also the duty to work. There was, however, no right to strike. The FDGB was just a mouthpiece of the SED, but the brigades or production units, into which the workers were organized, were able at times to act as legitimate channels of protest and complaint, and so go some way, as Joerg Roesler has argued, towards defusing the 'daily potential for economic and social conflict in the factories and, as a result, also in society as a whole' [114 *p. 809*]. The factory was arguably the most important vehicle for socializing the adult population in the GDR. Routine medical care, the looking after of children in crèches, cultural and social activities, and even shopping all took place within the context of the factory or the brigade [116].

It was into this new 'worker and peasant society' that the 3,254 million expellees, a diverse group of men, women, skilled artisans, agricultural labourers and former members of the Prussian land-owning classes were integrated. By the law of 8 September 1950 they were given modest loans to help buy tools and household furniture and were promised priority in housing, but from then on the state relied on the increasing demand for labour and the expansion of heavy industry to integrate them into society. The term 'worker-settler' was dropped, and the expellee problem was officially deemed to be solved [114].

The GDR may have been a workers' state, but it was not a workers' paradise. Wages and the standard of living were much lower than in the FRG. Basic but not particularly appealing foodstuffs were usually available. In the winter, for instance, the selection of vegetables and fruit might consist of red cabbage, potatoes and apples. There were also frequent shortages of products which were needed for everyday life, such as bicycle valves or children's clothing [88], while the shops were full of shoddy mass-produced goods which nobody wanted. Housing, too, remained poor in the 1950s because the GDR's scarce economic resources were directed towards industrial projects. On the other hand, state subsidies kept the prices of food, rent and transport low, while there was no fear of unemployment since job security was guaranteed. There was also a comprehensive state pension system, for the organization of which the FDGB was made responsible in 1956 [88; 111].

Theoretically, women had complete equality in this new workers' and peasants' state. The Civil Code and the divorce laws were revised much more rapidly than in the FRG. As early as 1949 the relevant sections on the family in the Civil Code were revoked and a year later replaced by the law on the protection of the mother and child, which categorically stated that 'Marriage does not lead to any restrictions or narrowing down of a woman's rights' [111 *p. 13*]. All matters 'pertaining to married life' were to be decided jointly by both partners. In 1954 a new law abolished the principle of guilt in divorce [111].

The preponderance of females over males in the GDR was even greater than in the FRG because many young male expellees had fled westwards, while a large number of POWs had also chosen to take their release in the Western zones. Women were therefore the main labour reserve in the GDR and were indispensable to the construction of a new economy. Through the provision of factory crèches and after-school supervision of children, women were actively encouraged to work. The official line propagated by the state was that there was complete equality of opportunity between the sexes. In reality, however, the women, initially lacking qualifications, occupied the lowest-paid and unskilled jobs. They also suffered under 'the bondage of a double burden', to quote Ina Merkel [116 *p. 376*], in that for the most part they still had to play the key role in looking after the home and children. At times they also met with considerable hostility from their male colleagues when they took on jobs which had traditionally been occupied by males [111; 114; 116].

THE OPPOSITION

While there were aspects of the GDR which were positive, such as its full employment policy and assistance for working women, one fact was nevertheless evident throughout its history: 'a lot of people', as Mary Fulbrook has stressed, 'did not like the GDR' [112 *p. 151*]. The dramatic events of 16–17 June 1953 were the most obvious manifestation of opposition to SED rule until September/October 1989, but recent research has shown that there was a considerable amount of low-key resistance to the party line throughout the history of the GDR [85; 114]. To explain it, historians have drawn on Martin Broszat's concept of resistance to another, albeit more popular dictatorship, the Third Reich. Brozat's analysis of behaviour that effectively contained or ignored the demands of the regime also characterizes the way many East Germans reacted to the Party's totalitarian claims in both work and social life. In most cases people simply wanted to be left alone, and therefore it is important, as Andrew Port has stressed, not to equate 'most non conformists' acts with fundamental protest against the regime' and 'misleadingly transform East Germany into a society of resistance fighters' [114 *p. 807*].

Well beyond 1961 there remained 'pockets of immunity' or 'resistance' [112 *p. 161*] within such groups as former SPD members, older people who could not accept the division of Germany, and the professions, particularly medicine. In some universities like Halle, Leipzig and the Humboldt University in Berlin, there was at times more open criticism of the regime. There were, of course, a few pockets of Nazism left in the 1950s, particularly in the rural areas. From time to time swastikas were daubed on walls, but these graffiti, often scrawled by school students, were more the product of the desire to shock the authorities than evidence of a Nazi revival. Among the factory workers there was, too, a constant undercurrent of grumbling about pay levels, working conditions and production quotas [114]. Sometimes this did erupt into brief work stoppages, critical graffiti or even occasionally acts of industrial sabotage. There was also a considerable reluctance to turn up to FDGB or Party meetings. The SED saw this as politically motivated, but it was as much a product of apathy and boredom with the excruciating tedium of Party or factory meetings, which often took place after working hours [112; 114].

The attitudes of youth were a constant challenge. Like the workers, young people reacted against over-organization by the state. At the universities there were occasional political protests, particularly during the Hungarian revolt of 1956. Possibly more worrying for the authorities was the discovery that East German youth, like its counterpart in the West, was not immune to American fashions in clothing, music and films. In the late 1950s rock and roll fan clubs were set up and there were youth riots in East Berlin and most of the other larger cities. Idolization of Elvis Presley was combined with what one *Stasi* report called 'depraved ravings against leading comrades' [112 *p. 164*; 106].

Psychologically the most effective opposition to the totalitarian claims of the SED was the Evangelical Church, which was the dominant Christian organization in East Germany. It represented 'an alien body' [88] in the socialist society and was also a part of the United German Evangelical Church, and so maintained contacts with West German clergy. Like Marxism-Leninism, the Church had both a comprehensive philosophy and the necessary structure and hierarchy to back it up. It was therefore potentially a formidable opponent. Up to 1948, SMAD had attempted to cooperate with the Church, despite removing the teaching of religion from the school curriculum. Tension with the Party, however, began to escalate when it pulled out of the *Volkskongress* movement. By 1952 Ulbricht had embarked on what amounted to an attempt to liquidate the Church. Members of the Christian youth and student organizations were threatened with expulsion from schools or university unless they gave up their membership, while in the period 1952–53, 72 priests and youth leaders were arrested [88; 112].

Under Soviet pressure in June 1953, Ulbricht was forced to pursue a more conciliatory line and tolerate the Church's youth organizations, but essentially this was just a change of tactics rather than principle. In 1954 the SED introduced, in an effort to marginalize the Churches, the *Jugendweihe*, a secular state ceremony, as an alternative to confirmation. Considerable pressure was brought to bear on families to force them to participate. Inevitably this re-ignited the battle between Church and Party. Under the leadership of Bishop Dibelius, the Chairman of the Executive Council of the Evangelical Church in Germany, the Church initially rejected the *Jugendweihe*, but eventually had little option but to come to terms with it. Ulbricht also began to develop a more subtle approach to the Church, by seeking to divide the pro-Western and the strongly anti-GDR supporters of Dibelius from those pastors who were more prepared to compromise with the regime. In 1958 the SED achieved a considerable success when the East German Church decided that it had to distance itself from the decision taken by the Evangelical Church in West Germany to provide military chaplains for the *Bundeswehr*. It also agreed to 'respect the development towards socialism and contribute to the peaceful construction of the life of the community'. In return it managed to extract the concession from the state that 'every citizen enjoys full freedom of belief and conscience' [112 *p. 101*]. This enabled the Church both to continue to provide an alternative ideology to Communism and to offer a wide range of social organizations that were not under the Party's control. Ultimately, in the 1980s these were to play an important part in the downfall of the regime [112].

CHAPTER ELEVEN

GERMANY FROM DEFEAT TO PARTITION: A RETROSPECTIVE VIEW

In the winter of 1945–46 it was not easy to foresee the future shape of Germany. The total collapse of civilized society and the moon-like landscape of the cities seemed to promise little hope, yet 1945 was not in fact *Stunde Null* ('zero hour'). The economic historians have shown how much productive capacity survived in both zones [92; 101; 103]. The psychological impact of defeat turned many Germans into an apathetic and demoralized people but, led by a small minority, some of whom had been *émigrés*, politics began to revive in both zones, together with plans for political and social reform.

The main theme running through German history from 1945 to 1961 was its partition into two states integrated into mutually hostile blocs. It can be argued that 'the FRG in its early years of existence was effectively a part of the American political, economic and military system, more like a state such as California or Illinois than an independent nation' [61 *p. 305*], while the GDR progressively became very much part of the Soviet system. One of the most controversial issues in post-war German history is whether this partition could have been avoided and the part the Germans themselves played in it. In the 1950s the blame for the division was firmly attributed to Russia by Western politicians, but more recent studies have particularly emphasized the initial role of the Western powers [48; 66], the general reluctance of both Adenauer and many other West Germans to hazard the policy of Western integration for the uncertainties of a neutral, unified Germany [20, Vols 1 and 2; 128], and Ulbricht's own 'revolutionary zeal' [49 *p. xi*]. There were certainly times in June 1948 or spring 1952, for instance, when Stalin would have gladly conceded a neutral but united Germany to stop the integration of West Germany into an American-dominated Western Europe. In many ways the GDR was 'Stalin's unwanted child' [49].

The FRG and the GDR shared a common heritage and traced their roots back to the Reich Bismarck had created in 1871, although each individually covered only a fraction of the old Reich and they were geographically and socio-politically very different structures. Both had to come to terms with their Nazi past. They also faced similar social, psychological and physical problems in rebuilding their societies. There was the same need to integrate expellees from the former eastern territories, repair or rebuild the housing stock, restore labour discipline and reform the welfare system. Their response to these challenges, however, was so varied that by 1961 their social, political and economic structures were radically different.

THE FEDERAL REPUBLIC

As Roseman has pointed out, West German history 'offers no prevailing orthodoxy or defining controversies' [78 *p. 365*], but the reasons for the FRG's stability and the degree to which its political and social structures were 'restorations' have inspired a considerable amount of debate [38; 60; 70]. In 1949 the prospects for the FRG seemed bleak and there were uncomfortable parallels with the Weimar Republic. Yet there was no right-wing backlash, despite the presence of millions of refugees from the lost eastern territories, the frequent intervention of the Allied High Commissioners and the impact of the currency reform on the small saver. On the contrary, in the 1950s the FRG enjoyed an exceptional social, political and economic stability. Why was this? Certainly increasing economic prosperity, co-determination and the Equalization of Burdens law helped to integrate the workers and the expellees into the Bonn republic. The Cold War and Western integration also rapidly ensured the acceptance of the FRG within Western Europe and its access to global markets. This allowed the new political system to take root and gave Adenauer an authority which no chancellor in the Weimar Republic enjoyed. In the 1950s he established a 'Chancellor democracy', based firmly on the CDU/CSU, which was effectively able to bridge the Catholic/Protestant divide in West Germany and appeal to the middle ground. Adenauer was a formidable politician who 'exuded a mixture of patriarchal but determinedly civilian authority and a canny ... and unbombastic rhetorical style' [78 *p. 373*].

The degree to which the FRG was modernized politically, economically and socially in the 1950s is also a matter of considerable debate among historians [79, Vol. 2; 100; 107]. Were the 1950s just a period of reconstruction and restoration, or were they a time of radical modernization and social revolution? From its very beginnings the FRG was a paradox. It was a new state, yet at the same time it was the direct heir to the German Reich. Thus there was bound to be a considerable element of restoration and reconstruction in its early years. This was particularly visible in what Klessmann has called the 'new beginnings with old personnel' in the civil service [46 *p. 254*]. Throughout the West German government machine it was an undeniable fact that, as Karl Jaspers put it, 'Nazis who had once been prominent again became effective and authoritative' [72 *p. 183*]. Ideally, denazification should have been more effective, but in practice a certain continuity of personnel was unavoidable. The crucial difference between Bonn and Weimar was that these officials, whatever their past, were ready to accept a democratic state and its rules. Of course the striking economic success of the FRG, the Cold War and Adenauer's crusade against Communism, which had also been the arch enemy of the Hitler Reich, facilitated this acceptance.

Popular attitudes revealed a 'striking and elusive mixture of restoration and new tones and accents' [107 *p. 11*]. In the early 1950s West German society was characterized by an indifference to politics, a deep pessimism about the future and an intense desire to lead a private life – the *ohne mich* attitude. There was still considerable admiration for Hitler and a reluctance to accept German responsibility for the war. On the other hand, there was a 'new openness' [107 *p. 11*]. In 1951 some 68 per cent of the population favoured European integration and some 80 per cent of the films shown in the cinemas had been made abroad, while in the kitchen, Germans were increasingly ready to experiment with foreign recipes [107].

By the late 1950s the rigid conservatism of the early part of the decade had begun to fade and the contours of a new era could be discerned. The determination of the West Germans to throw themselves into work, which, according to the psychoanalysts Alexander and Margarete Mitscherlich, showed a 'manic touch', the consequence of a 'collective denial of the past' [103 *p. 213*], began to be eroded by the consumer society. The reaction to the *Spiegel* Affair by students and intellectuals anticipated the protest movements of some six years later and the end of the 'amnesia' about the Nazi period. In foreign affairs, disillusionment with Kennedy's handling of the Berlin crisis and the building of the Wall also heralded a more critical attitude towards the USA, which came to a head during the Vietnam War. The Berlin Wall, by consolidating the SED regime, also forced Bonn to rethink its approach to the GDR, which ultimately led to Willy Brandt's *Ostpolitik*. By 1961 the Adenauer era was visibly drawing to an end. The SPD had modernized itself and had a young charismatic leader, Willy Brandt, and the FDP was an increasingly reluctant coalition partner of the CDU/CSU Union, but the pendulum had still a considerable way to swing until an FDP–SDP coalition was formed in 1969 [79 Vol. 3].

THE GERMAN DEMOCRATIC REPUBLIC

The end of the Cold War has enabled historians to begin the more difficult task of placing the GDR within the context of German history and of exploring the degree of support, or at least tolerance, it enjoyed from its citizens. Since its collapse in 1990 much of the GDR's history has been written from the standpoint of the victors and former opponents of the regime under the assumption that it was an illegal dictatorship. Efforts have been made by historians sympathetic to the former regime to 'oppose from left-wing standpoints this attempt to claim the power of interpretation over a significant part of German history' [80 p. 392]. It will take several years before an authoritative history of the GDR can be written, but a start has been made with several objective analyses of its political, social and economic structures [87; 112; 114; 116]. The crucial issues that historians are seeking to answer concern the degree of support the regime actually enjoyed from its citizens, whether its eventual collapse had always been inevitable and to what extent the SED dictatorship was comparable to the tyranny of the Third Reich [80].

The GDR had, as Mommsen puts it, a 'janus face' [86 *p. 28*]. It faced two ways: it was both a Russian satellite, controlled by a relatively small number of collaborators, and the product of the German Communist tradition going back to the 1920s, which had created a strong independent proletarian culture. The vacuum created by the defeat of Nazism and the shell-shocked indifference to politics, or the '*ohne mich*' attitude, of much of the population, together with the legacy of authoritarian structures and traditions, which stretched back to Imperial Germany, assisted the SED's take-over of power. Initially the regime enjoyed some real support from East German Communists and a considerable number of middle-class intellectuals, such as the historian Kuczynski and the playwright Brecht, who all believed that only the root-and-branch destruction of capitalism through Marxism would render a future renaissance of Nazism impossible. There were therefore certain reserves of support for the SED in 1949, although the Politbureau in 1950 had no illusions about being able to win a genuinely free election.

Whom did the GDR directly benefit? In the 1950s it offered the children of workers and peasants, the so-called Hitler Youth generation, unique chances to study and form a new socialist elite, it gave women equality of sorts and made the right to work a reality. These were not inconsiderable achievements, but they were accomplished at an immense cost to personal and political freedom and the standard of living. It was no wonder, then, the FRG so consistently exercised a magnet-like draw on the population of the GDR. Adenauer was regarded by many in the GDR as the natural leader of Germany.

How then did the GDR survive up to 1961? Was it through the combination of Russian bayonets and the creation of a totalitarian dictatorship similar to the Third Reich? The SED established a dictatorship that was in essentials very different from the Third Reich. For a start it was much less popular. Ulbricht was no charismatic leader, and indeed for a time after 1953 he paid lip-service to the idea of a collective leadership. While the system of mass organizations was similar to the affiliated organizations of the Third Reich, the apparent multi-party structure, which, of course, was dominated by the SED, had no parallel in the Third Reich, where the Nazi Party was the only official party. The SED's system of democratic centralism with clear vertical lines of command was again different from the chaos of competing agencies that made up the Third Reich [80]. The SED was also dependent on a foreign power, Russia, whereas the *raison d'être* of the Nazis was to free Germany from foreign influences. Finally, although the SED employed the *Stasi*, imprisoned and, in the early 1950s, tortured political dissidents, it did not unleash a world war and genocide. The open frontier in Berlin until August 1961 also ensured that many critics, dissidents and large numbers of ambitious young workers and professionals left the GDR rather than staying to oppose the SED.

Mitter and Wolle [85] argue that the GDR's eventual collapse was inevitable after the 1953 uprising, even though it lingered on for another 36 years. They see its history as 'decline and fall in stages' (to quote the title of their book, *Untergang auf Raten*) from 1953 onwards but, as Mary Fulbrook points out, this interpretation ignores the fact that there was ' a rise ... from the baseline of 1953 to a period of comparative tranquility in the early 1970s' [112 *p. 72*]. This was helped by the construction of the Berlin Wall in 1961 which gave the GDR a 'second chance'.

A COMPARISON BETWEEN THE TWO STATES

Hartmut Kaeble has observed that 'apart from the language and the history up to 1945' [116 *p. 573*] the two Germanies had very little in common by 1990. In the 1950s they were already rapidly growing apart with radically different legal, political and educational systems. Although both societies could be described as 'work societies', the factory-centred society of the GDR was very different from the FRG where work and leisure were two distinct worlds. The GDR was a secular society, whereas in the FRG the Churches, particularly the Catholic Church, still exercised considerable influence on both the government and the people. The position of women, too, was very different. In the GDR there was a real legal equality, and women were desperately needed in the work force, even though they were not always accepted as equals. In the FRG, while a large number of single women had to work, and led independent lives, the government actively encouraged their withdrawal into the family. In both states rural life was revolutionized. In the FRG, farming was mechanized and the numbers working on the land declined rapidly. In the GDR, the population in the countryside remained constant, but collectivization revolutionized the structure of rural life [25; 115]. The middle classes also fared very differently in the two states. In the FRG there was a considerable continuity of personnel in business, law, the teaching professions and local government, while in the GDR, apart from the Church, only in Medicine and to a much smaller

1.   WESTERN GERMANY IN JULY 1945

2.   LIFE IN BERLIN AT THE END OF MAY 1945

3.   STARVATION IN BRESLAU, JULY 1945

4.   CONDITIONS ON ONE OF THE FIRST TRAINS CARRYING GERMAN
     EXPELLEES FROM LOWER SILESIA IN FEBRUARY 1946 AS DESCRIBED BY
     THE ARCHBISHOP OF MEISSEN

5.   THE REFUGEE PROBLEM IN SCHLESWIG-HOLSTEIN

6.   ULBRICHT RECALLS A CONVERSATION WITH THE MAYOR OF THE VILLAGE
     OF SCHLAITZ IN THE SUMMER OF 1945 DURING HIS TRAVELS THROUGH
     THE SOVIET ZONE

7.   EXTRACTS FROM THE POTSDAM AGREEMENT, 2 AUGUST 1945

8.   THE DENAZIFICATION OF THE AMERICAN ZONE

9.   THE DEVELOPMENT OF FOOD SUPPLIES, 1947–48

10. CREATING THE SED

11. GERMAN PROTEST AT THE SOVIET REQUISITION POLICY

12. THE BLACK MARKET

13. THE SED AS A PARTY OF THE NEW TYPE

14. THE BASIC LAW OF THE FEDERAL REPUBLIC OF GERMANY, 23 MAY 1949

15. THE RHÖNDORF CONFERENCE, AUGUST 1949

16. ADENAUER INFORMS THE HIGH COMMISSIONERS OF THE FORMATION OF
     HIS GOVERNMENT, SEPTEMBER 1949

17. SCHUMACHER REJECTS A BIPARTISAN APPROACH

18. ADENAUER'S REPUTATION

19. THE GDR ELECTIONS OF OCTOBER 1950

20. ULBRICHT AT WORK

21. THE FRG ELECTION RESULTS, 1949–51

22. THE WEST GERMAN GOVERNMENT'S REACTION TO THE SOVIET NOTE OF
     10 MARCH 1952

23. THE CENTRAL COMMITTEE OF THE SOVIET COMMUNIST PARTY ISSUES AN
     ULTIMATUM TO THE SED, 2 JUNE 1953

24. 17 JUNE 1953 IN THE GDR

25.   THE GENERAL TREATY ON GERMANY, 23 OCTOBER 1954

26.   THE TREATY BETWEEN THE GDR AND THE USSR, 20 SEPTEMBER 1955

27.   THE HALLSTEIN DOCTRINE

28.   ADENAUER AND GERMAN UNITY

29.   KHRUSHCHEV'S SPEECH ON BERLIN, 10 NOVEMBER 1958

30.   THE DECISION TO BUILD THE WALL

31.   ADENAUER'S MESSAGE TO THE EAST GERMANS AFTER THE CLOSING OF THE FRONTIER IN BERLIN, DELIVERED BEFORE A SPECIAL SESSION OF THE *BUNDESTAG*, 18 AUGUST 1961

32.   THE *SPIEGEL* AFFAIR

33.   ERHARD ON COLLECTIVISM

34.   PRODUCTIVITY IN THE FRG

35.   ECONOMIC EXPANSION AT ROBERT BOSCH, GmbH

36.   THE POSITION OF WOMEN IN POST-WAR GERMANY

37.   SETTING UP HOME IN THE FRG IN THE 1950s

38.   THE ROLE OF WRITERS AND ARTISTS IN THE GDR

DOCUMENT 1   WESTERN GERMANY IN JULY 1945

Strang was surprised not so much by the extent of the destruction in the British Zone as by how untouched the countryside had been by the war and by how healthy the population looked. Later in his diary he expresses astonishment, for instance, that the owner of the house in the small Westphalian town of Lübbecke, which he occupied, still had a cook, 'two young housemaids', a laundry maid and a gardener. Documents 2 and 3 give a more sombre account of life in Germany in the summer of 1945. Yet Strang did foresee 'widespread malnutrition and something near to starvation', unless coal production increased dramatically and large supplies of grain were imported.

First, the general aspect of the country. A smiling countryside, beautifully farmed with bountiful crops growing to the roadside and hedgerows: villages and small towns off the main roads quite intact: towns and villages at important communication points badly smashed. Larger centres like Münster or Osnabrück, half or three-quarters devastated; industrial cities like Dortmund almost totally in ruins, except round the outer fringes. The population more healthy looking, better dressed, and showing less sign of strain than one would have expected, even in the more heavily damaged urban areas. The official ration is low, but in the country it is at present supplemented from stocks and garden produce. The position in the large towns is difficult, and the workers certainly do not receive enough to sustain heavy labour. We were told at Dortmund that signs of malnutrition are beginning to appear, and that administrative staffs are beginning to show signs of over-work, bad temper and tiredness, from shortage of food. But I cannot say that, even in the Ruhr, from a casual inspection, we saw obvious or widespread signs of acute distress. What the winter may bring is another story; and what the position may be in the Soviet zone is also another story. It is strange to see people going serenely and even cheerfully about their business in their ruined towns and cities. I asked the Commander of the military government detachment at Dortmund where the 400,000 inhabitants of Dortmund found place to live. He said that they had moved out to the less devastated periphery, several families to a house. I asked how, if that was so, it came about that the main streets in the centre were thronged with people. He explained that although Dortmund is in ruins, the life of the city goes on in cellars and on ground floors. Some factories are working; some banks are open; some shops are doing business; exchange of goods and services goes on. Roads still lead in and out of Dortmund (though it is like threading a maze to find one's way about them), and where those roads meet the life of the community continues to spring and begins to reorganise itself. I asked whether he thought that Dortmund would ever be re-built. He said certainly, sooner or later. The city authorities were already thinking ahead and actively debating alternative schemes: he himself had been brought into consultation.

Sir William Strang (Political Adviser to the Military Governor of the British Zone), *Diary of a Tour through the British Zone, 1–6 July 1945*, PRO FO 371 46933, p. 9.

DOCUMENT 2   LIFE IN BERLIN AT THE END OF MAY 1945

The following extract, which is part of the life story of two Berlin sisters, is typical of its times. Two sisters, one widowed with a child, manage to find a refuge in their grandmother's flat in Berlin. It shows how 'families became the main refuge for those who had been dislocated and lost their possessions' [102 p. 27].

We then lived in this two-and-a-half room flat, my grandmother, we two and little Jack. My mother was still in the Black Forest with her sister, but we had her officially registered as occupant of the flat. In this way we did not have to take in refugees even though my mother was not yet living with us. She joined us as soon as she was able to get through. And then, the whole struggle for survival began. The main problem was getting food for the baby. The four of us just had to help together, everyone as best as she could. We four adults each held ration cards grade five for housewives, we called them 'ascension cards' at the time. The baby was entitled to grade two rations. But it was virtually impossible to survive on the rations alone. ... The worse thing was that we never had enough to eat. My mother always dreamt that one could buy bread rolls again. And then she would cover the bread roll with smoked bacon which would be big enough to hang down the sides. Such a roll with a bacon-border, this is what she wished for.

Kolinsky, [102], pp. 27–8.

DOCUMENT 3   STARVATION IN BRESLAU, JULY 1945

Father Paul Peikert describes the situation to a colleague.

Already now 300 to 400 people die in Breslau a day, that is 10,000 to 12,000 people a month. Now the same methods of extermination are applied to us as we applied to other peoples, only with the one outward appearance of humanity that the Russians and the Poles do not murder senselessly as did our *Waffen SS* and *Gestapo* in the occupied territory to the horror of the whole world. But if one considers the intention, it amounts to the same thing.

Siebel-Achenbach, [63], p. 127.

CONDITIONS ON ONE OF THE FIRST TRAINS CARRYING GERMAN EXPELLEES FROM LOWER SILESIA IN FEBRUARY 1946 AS DESCRIBED BY THE ARCHBISHOP OF MEISSEN

As early as March 1945 the Provisional Government of the Polish Republic set up the new administrative district of Lower Silesia. Siebel-Achenbach has calculated that in mid-June there were still 1.8 to 2 million Germans in Lower Silesia. In November 1945 the Allied Control Council in Berlin agreed that 6,650,000 ethnic Germans from Poland and the Sudetenland would have to be resettled in Germany. On 22 February the first train load of expellees left Lower Silesia for the British Zone. Although the Polish government was supposed to ensure that the expellees had sufficient food, water and sanitary facilities, in practice this usually did not happen. Owing to a lack of coal for the locomotives, damaged track, destroyed bridges, etc., the journey into Western Germany took 'days if not weeks' [63 p. 140] with the dreadful consequences described below.

The people, men, women, and children all mixed together, were tightly packed in the railway cars, these cattle-wagons themselves being locked from the outside. For days on end, the people were transported like this, and in Görlitz the wagons were opened for the first time. I have seen with my own eyes that out of one wagon alone ten corpses were taken and thrown into coffins which had been kept on hand. I noted further that several people had become deranged in these wagons. The people were covered with excrement, which led me to believe that they were so tightly packed together that there was no longer any possibility for them to relieve themselves at a designated place.

Siebel-Achenbach, [63], pp. 141–2.

THE REFUGEE PROBLEM IN SCHLESWIG-HOLSTEIN

As it was predominantly rural this Land had to accept 40 per cent of the 2.5 million refugees from the East German territories in the British Zone. This caused severe problems, as the letter from the Regional Governor, Land Schleswig-Holstein to the Deputy Military Governor, British Zone, 30 May 1947, indicates.

… About two and a half million refugees have been accepted in the British Zone. 48% of these have come to Schleswig-Holstein, whose population was previously only 7.8% of that of the whole zone.

In this Land [sic] now, there are nearly as many refugees as indigenous population. 47% of the people of the Land are refugees, whose coming has increased the population of the Land by 80% of the 1939 figure. The average figures for the whole British Zone on these two counts are only 17.6% and 20% respectively, for the American Zone 16.7% and 20%, and for the French Zone only 3.3% and 3% respectively. On a basis of former population, therefore, Schleswig-Holstein has been forced to absorb a very much higher population of refugees than any other part of Western Germany.

... In the matter of estimating available living accommodation also, Schleswig-Holstein seems to have suffered far more in comparison with the other Lander [*sic*].

At the time when allocations of refugees to the various Lander [*sic*] was made, information about living space was scanty and unreliable; factors such as sanitation were not given adequate consideration, and the original estimates of living space available have resulted in greater overcrowding in the Land than in any other.

Here the average number of persons per room is 1.5 with a floor space of 5.5 square metres per person. The average for the Zone as a whole is 1.1 persons per room with a floor space of 6.1 square metres per person. The average floor space per person is 7.6 square metres in the American Zone, and 9.5 square metres in the French Zone.

Air Vice Marshall H.V. Champion de Crespigny to the Deputy Military Governor, British Zone, 30 May 1947, PRO FO 1006/93, p. 3A.

DOCUMENT 6   **ULBRICHT RECALLS A CONVERSATION WITH THE MAYOR OF THE VILLAGE OF SCHLAITZ IN THE SUMMER OF 1945 DURING HIS TRAVELS THROUGH THE SOVIET ZONE**

'How do you make a living?' I asked. His answer was, 'I have two hectares.' 'But you can't make a living or even feed a family from two hectares,' was my rejoinder, to which he responded, 'I know, but I also work on the estate.' 'What,' I asked in astonishment, 'you people still have landlords here?'...

Then we went to his house and talked with him and some other peasants. 'Look here,' I said, 'you have a very strange democracy in your village. The mayor has to work for the big landlord who gives the orders. What kind of mayor are you? What kind of village council do you have? The landlord has the economic power – the land – while he lets you hold occasional council meetings as window dressing.' Comrade Heilemann agreed: 'You're right, but how can we change it?' 'That's simple,' we advised him. 'Take the landlord's property.'

Stern, [21], pp. 107–8.

DOCUMENT 7   EXTRACTS FROM THE POTSDAM AGREEMENT, 2 AUGUST 1945

By the time the Allies met at Potsdam in July 1945, the Grand Alliance was under great strain, as it was only the war against Hitler that had kept it united. The policies on which there was a genuine Allied consensus were the measures to eliminate Nazism and German militarism and secure disarmament. The political principles, as can be seen in this extract, were 'sufficiently ambivalent' [26 p. 11] to enable the powers to paper over their disagreements and reach a temporary agreement.

It is not the intention of the Allies to destroy or enslave the German people. It is the intention of the Allies that the German people be given the opportunity to prepare for the eventual reconstruction of their life on a democratic and peaceful basis. If their own efforts are steadily directed to this end, it will be possible for them in due course to take their place among the free and peaceful peoples of the world....

A. POLITICAL PRINCIPLES

1. In accordance with the Agreement on Control Machinery in Germany, supreme authority in Germany is exercised, on instructions from their respective governments, by the Commander-in-Chief of the armed forces of the United States of America, the United Kingdom, the Union of Soviet Socialist Republics, and the French Republic, each in his own zone of occupation, and also jointly, in matters affecting Germany as a whole, in their capacity as members of the Control Council...
2. So far as is practicable, there shall be uniformity of treatment of the German population throughout Germany.
3. The purposes of the occupation of Germany by which the Control Council shall be guided are:
  I. The complete disarmament and demilitarisation of Germany and the elimination or control of all German industry that could be used for military production...
  II. To convince the German people that they have suffered a total military defeat and that they cannot escape responsibility for what they have brought upon themselves, since their own ruthless warfare and the fanatical Nazi resistance have destroyed the German economy and made chaos and suffering inevitable.
  III. To destroy the National Socialist Party and its affiliated and supervised organisation, to dissolve all Nazi institutions, to ensure that they are not revived in any form, and to prevent all Nazi and militarist activity or propaganda.

IV. To prepare for the eventual reconstruction of German political life on a democratic basis and for eventual peaceful co-operation in international life by Germany...

9. The administration of affairs in Germany should be directed towards the decentralisation of political structure and the development of local responsibility. To this end...

IV. For the time being no central German government shall be established. Notwithstanding this, however, certain essential central German administrative departments headed by State Secretaries, shall be established, particularly in the fields of finance, transport, communications, foreign trade, and industry. Such departments will act under the direction of the Control Council...

B. ECONOMIC PRINCIPLES

14. During the period of occupation Germany shall be treated as a single economic unit. To this end common policies shall be established in regard to:

(a) mining and industrial production and allocation;
(b) agriculture, forestry, and fishing;
(c) wages, prices, and rationing;
(d) import and export programs for Germany as a whole;
(e) currency and banking, central taxation and customs;
(f) reparations and removal of industrial war potential;
(g) transportation and communications.

In applying these policies account shall be taken, where appropriate, of varying local conditions.

Jarausch and Gransow (eds), [3], pp. 4–5.

DOCUMENT 8   THE DENAZIFICATION OF THE AMERICAN ZONE

In a telegram to the American War Department, Clay outlines the problems involved in large-scale denazification.

15 December 1946   C7373   SECRET
From CLAY Personal for ECHOLS

On my return to Germany I find that as a result of my talk with the Laenderrat [*sic*] [Council of States] there has been a vigorous upswing in execution of the denazification program. However, it has become apparent that due to the large number of people chargeable under the law (estimated at approximately three million) the administrative difficulties will require at least two years and perhaps longer for full completion of the program. Obviously, political stability in Germany cannot be obtained fully until the program is completed. Therefore, it appears most desirable to reduce the numbers chargeable under the law, emphasising that this reduction is to permit German administration to concentrate on the punishment of active Nazis who were or are in places of prominence in German life.

Extract from Smith (ed.), [7], Vol. 1, p. 285.

DOCUMENT 9   **THE DEVELOPMENT OF FOOD SUPPLIES, 1947–48**

Throughout 1947–48 food supplies in the Bizone failed to improve largely because of the inefficiency of the Bizonal administration, the increase in the population due to the arrival of the expellees, the world food shortage and the inability of West German industry to export its manufactures and so pay for food imports. Inevitably, the low level of rations, an example of which can be seen below, weakened worker productivity and delayed economic recovery.

Rations distributed in calories per day in Hamburg

6 Jan.–2 Feb *1947*	1,149
3 Mar.–30 Mar.	1,566
26 May–22 June	1,130
21 July–17 Aug.	1,135
15 Sept.–12 Oct.	1,417
10 Nov.–7 Dec.	1,371
5 Jan.–1 Feb *1948*	1,441
March	1,444
May	1,553
July	1,986
September	1,846
November	1,837
December	1,189

Kramer, [103], pp. 76–7.

DOCUMENT 10   **CREATING THE SED**

As early as June 1945 Stalin was anxious to secure the unity of the SPD and KPD. Increasing opposition from SPD members led to growing Soviet pressure. Grotewohl indeed complained to Christopher Steel, the head of the Political Division in the British Military Government, that they were being 'tickled by Soviet bayonets' [49 p. 31]. On 11 February 1946 the Central Executive of the SPD agreed to unity by a vote of eight to three and the actual unification congress was held in Berlin on 21–22 April. Below is an extract from the resolution that was carried.

It is the historical task of the unified workers' movement to organise the struggle of the working class and all constructive elements of the population in a conscious and uniform manner. The Socialist Unity Party of Germany must direct the present endeavours of the working class towards the struggle for socialism and must lead the working class and all constructive elements of the population in the achievement of this, its historical mission.

The Socialist Unity Party of Germany can pursue its struggle successfully only if it unites the best and most progressive forces of the working population and by representing their interests becomes *the party of the constructive elements of the population.*

This campaign organisation is founded on the democratic right of its members to make resolutions, the democratic election of all party officers, and the obligation of all members, deputies, representatives, and officers to be bound by democratically agreed resolutions.

The interests of working people are the same in all countries where the capitalist mode of production is found. The Socialist Unity Party of Germany therefore declares itself at one with the class-conscious workers of all countries. It feels solidarity with the peace-loving and democratic peoples all over the world.

The Socialist Unity Party of Germany, as an independent party, campaigns in *its own* country for the true national interests of *its own* people. As a German socialist party it is the best and most progressive national force; it stands with all its strength and all its energy against all particularist tendencies and for *the economic, cultural, and political unity of Germany.*

The Socialist Unity Party of Germany will draw up a programme based on these principles and demands, which is to be presented to the membership by the committee and to be adopted at the next full party congress.

The Socialist Unity Party of Germany is the best guarantee for the unity of Germany! It will ensure victory for socialism! Socialism is the banner of the future!

Under this flag we shall be victorious!

Thomanek and Mellis, [8], pp. 19–20.

DOCUMENT 11   **GERMAN PROTEST AT THE SOVIET REQUISITION POLICY**

This popular ditty was frequently sung in the Halle area according to reports from the Soviet Military Administration in 1947.

Welcome, liberators!
You take from us eggs, meat, and butter, cattle and feed.
And also watches, rings, and other things.
You liberate us from everything, from cars and machines.
You take along with you train cars and rail installations.

From all of this rubbish – you've liberated us!
We cry for joy.
How good you are to us.
How terrible it was before – and how nice now.
You marvellous people!

Naimark, [53], p. 181.

DOCUMENT 12   THE BLACK MARKET

Viktor Agartz, Director of the Economic Administration of the British Zone in Minden, informed the British Military Government in the summer of 1946 of the following.

The system of organised barter between industrial enterprises and farmers and the illegal allocation of rationed consumer goods to industrial workers so that they may exchange them for food has reached such vast dimensions that prosecutions in individual cases no longer have any deterrent effect. These unregulated barter deals are at present the norm. Industrial commodities can hardly be obtained any more through normal purchasing or allocation. This whole system of barter and compensation deals is carried on quite openly, and so it is seen by most people as being absolutely correct and above board. My staff have discovered, for example, that workers exchange coal for potatoes. There is a fixed exchange rate of one hundredweight (50 kilos) of potatoes for 15 hundredweight of coal.

Kramer, [103], p. 87.

DOCUMENT 13   THE SED AS A PARTY OF THE NEW TYPE

To discuss the programme for the First SED Party Conference, Pieck, Grotewohl and Oelssner went to Moscow in December 1948. Although Stalin did not at this stage want the SED to turn East Germany into a 'people's democracy', or in other words a Communist state, as he still wished to keep open the option of a unified neutral Germany, he nevertheless agreed that the SED should become a party 'of the new type'. The following extract from a resolution at the Party Conference on 28 January 1949 shows what this meant.

The characteristics of a party of the new type are:

The Marxist-Leninist party is the conscious vanguard of the working class. That is, it must be a workers' party which primarily has in its ranks the best elements of the working class, who are constantly heightening their class consciousness. The party can only fulfil its role as the vanguard of the proletariat if it has mastered Marxist-Leninist theory, which gives it insight into the laws of development of society. Therefore the first task in the development of the SED into a party of the new type is the political and ideological education of the membership and particularly of the office-bearers in the spirit of Marxism-Leninism.

The role of the party as vanguard of the working class is realised in the day-to-day strategic guidance of party activity. This makes it possible to direct all aspects of party activity in the areas of government, economy, and cultural life. To achieve this it is necessary to form a collective strategic party leadership by electing a Political Bureau (Politburo)....

The Marxist-Leninist party is founded on the principle of democratic centralism. This means strictest adherence to the principle that leading bodies and officers are subject to election and that those elected are accountable to the membership. This internal party democracy is the basis for the tight party discipline which arises from members' socialist consciousness. Party resolutions are binding on all party members, particularly for those party members active in parliaments, governments, administrative bodies, and in the leadership of the mass organisations.

Democratic centralism means the development of criticism and self-criticism within the party and supervision to ensure that resolutions are rigorously carried out by the leadership and by members.

Toleration of factions and groupings within the party is not consistent with its Marxist-Leninist character.

The Marxist-Leninist party is strengthened by the struggle against opportunism. The working class is not a closed group. The spirit of opportunism is constantly being imported into it by bourgeois elements and calls forth uncertainty and vacillation in its ranks. Therefore the remorseless struggle against all opportunistic influences is an indispensable precondition for strengthening the party's campaigning power.

The highest class vigilance is the absolute duty of every party member. It is also necessary to prevent the infiltration of spies and agents of the secret services and of Schumacher's Eastern Bureau into the party and the democratic bodies.

The Marxist-Leninist party is permeated with the spirit of internationalism. This internationalism determines its place in the worldwide conflict between the war propagandists and the forces of peace, between reaction and progress, between capitalism and socialism. In this struggle the Marxist-Leninist party is firmly allied with the forces of peace and democracy, side by side with the People's Democracies and the revolutionary workers' parties all over the world. It recognises the leading role of the CPSU ... in the struggle against imperialism and declares it to be the duty of all working people to support the socialist Soviet Union with all their might.

Thomanek and Mellis, [8], pp. 48–9.

DOCUMENT 14   THE BASIC LAW OF THE FEDERAL REPUBLIC OF
GERMANY, 23 MAY 1949

On 1 July 1948 the Military Governors handed over the London Recommendations which charged the eleven Minister-Presidents of the three West German zones to call a constitutional convention to create a federal republic. Initially, a draft constitution was hammered out by a committee of political and constitutional experts who met on an island in the Herrenchiemsee. They carefully avoided the use of the word 'constitution' for two reasons: (a) the 1919 constitution of the Weimar Republic had never been legally abrogated; (b) to stress that the new West German government was merely a provisional one until unification occurred. On 1 September, the 65 members (elected by the Land *parliaments) of the Parliamentary Council met. Seven committees were set up to work on different aspects of the constitution, while an eighth prepared the final text of the constitution. This was approved by the Military Governors on 12 May 1949 and was officially published in the* Federal Gazette, *extracts of which are quoted below, on 23 May.*

Preamble:
The German people in the *Länder* of Baden, Bavaria, Bremen, Hamburg, Hesse, Lower Saxony, North Rhine-Westfalia [*sic*], Rhineland-Palatinate, Schleswig-Holstein, Württemberg-Baden, and Württemberg-Hohenzollern, conscious of its responsibility before God and man, animated by the resolve to preserve its national and political unity, and to serve the peace of the world as an equal partner in a united Europe, desiring to give a new order to political life for a transitional period, has enacted, by virtue of its constituent power, this Basic Law of the FRG. It has also acted on behalf of those Germans to whom participation was denied.

The entire German people is called on to achieve by free self-determination the unity and freedom of Germany ...

Article 20: (1) The FRG is a democratic and social federal state.

(2) All state authority emanates from the people. It is exercised by the people by means of elections and voting and by separate legislative, executive, and judicial organs.

(3) Legislation shall be subject to the constitutional order; the executive and the judiciary shall be bound by the law ...

Article 21: (1) The parties participate in the shaping of the political will of the people. Their foundation is free, their inner structure must correspond to democratic principles, they have to account for the source of their funds in public.

(2) Parties which are inclined to harm or to overthrow the free democratic order or to endanger the existence of the FRG according to their

goals or to the behaviour of their supporters are unconstitutional. The Federal Constitutional Court decides on the question of constitutionality. ...

Article 23: For the time being, this basic law applies in the territory of the *Länder* of Baden, Bavaria, Bremen, Hamburg, Hesse, Lower Saxony, North Rhine-Westfalia, Rhineland-Palatinate, Schleswig-Holstein, Württemberg-Baden, and Württemberg-Hohenzollern. In other parts of Germany, it shall be put into force on their accession...

Article 116: (1) This Basic Law understands as German, except for other legal stipulations, whoever has German citizenship or whoever lived as a refugee or expellee of German ethnic origin or as his spouse or descendant on the territory of the German Empire on 31 December 1937.

Jarausch and Grasnow (eds), [3], pp. 6–7.

DOCUMENT 15   **THE RHÖNDORF CONFERENCE, AUGUST 1949**

Adenauer sums up his arguments against a Grand Coalition with the SPD.

There is a great difference between ourselves and the Social Democrats regarding the principles of Christian conviction. Moreover, there is an unbridgeable gap between ourselves and the Social Democrats in the matter of economic structure. There can only be either a planned economy or a social market economy. The two shall not mix. In view of these differences it would not even be possible to have a Christian Democrat as Minister of Economics and a Social Democrat as Under-Secretary of State. We could never get things moving. We have got to steer a steady course. Only then can there be a good parliamentary opposition.

Adenauer, [9], pp. 180–1.

DOCUMENT 16   **ADENAUER INFORMS THE HIGH COMMISSIONERS OF THE FORMATION OF HIS GOVERNMENT, SEPTEMBER 1949**

General Sir Brian Robertson, the British High Commissioner, was an admirer of Konrad Adenauer. Until Robertson was moved to the Middle East in June 1950, his advice was greatly valued by Adenauer. In this weekly report to the Foreign Secretary, Robertson describes the brief ceremony on 21 September when Adenauer introduced his Cabinet to the High Commissioners and the entry into force of the Occupation Statute was announced. What Robertson does not report is that Adenauer was uncomfortable with the ceremony, as the Occupation Statute was, after all, an unpleasant reminder of Germany's status as a 'conquered nation' [9 p. 183]. When Adenauer and his ministers met the High Commissioners at the Petersberg (the headquarters of the High Commission in the hotel where Chamberlain had met Hitler in September 1938), they had taken up position on an ornate carpet, while Adenauer was expected to stand before them. However when François-Ponçet, the French High Commissioner, stepped forward to greet the Chancellor, Adenauer adroitly stepped on the carpet. None of the High Commissioners objected.

The Occupation Statute came into force, and the High Commission into existence at 11 am on the 21st of September when the Chancellor, Dr Adenauer, called on the High Commissioners at Petersberg accompanied by a selection of his Ministers and reported the formation of his Government. He was received with a guard of honour of gendarmes and British and American military police, and the black, red and gold flag of the Federal Republic was hoisted for his visit. Adenauer made an excellent speech stressing the desire of the new state to earn and obtain the confidence of its European neighbours and expressing Germany's gratitude for the aid provided by the Occupying Powers, to which François Ponçet [*sic*] returned a suitable though somewhat tutorial reply. In commenting on events in Bonn and in particular upon Adenauer's declaration of policy to the *Bundestag* the Soviet licensed press has not ceased to gnash its teeth in ill-concealed fury.

Personal weekly report from the British High Commissioner to the Foreign Secretary, 28.9.49,
PRO FO 371 76652 (C7509, p. 1).

DOCUMENT 17   SCHUMACHER REJECTS A BIPARTISAN APPROACH

Blankenhorn, one of Adenauer's most trusted advisers on foreign affairs, reports on a discussion with Carlo Schmid, the SPD Chairman of the Foreign Relations Committee in the Bundestag, on 12 November 1949, on the dismantling issue and other foreign policy issues.

Two-hour discussions with Carlo Schmid, who gives an impression of utter exhaustion. With a swollen, pale, tired face, he sits opposite me and has the posture of a despairing, depressed and disappointed man. Most disappointed at his own party people and at Schumacher, whom he calls introverted, and whose touchiness is the reason for the powerful attacks on Adenauer's policy. I explain emphatically to Schmid that I regard the efforts to reach a joint approach with the Opposition in the area of foreign policy as being in serious danger. Schumacher's interview has let the dogs loose in the streets and it will take great deal of effort and patience to get joint discussions going again. I looked forward with serious concern to the debate on Tuesday. Carlo Schmid largely shared this view. He accused the Chancellor of being insufficiently informed about the essential problems of the Ruhr and of the European Union. ...

Schwarz, [20], Vol. 1, p. 482.

DOCUMENT 18   ADENAUER'S REPUTATION

Heinrich Brüning, Reich Chancellor, 1930–32, wrote the following in November 1949 to the CDU Bundestag member, Hermann Pünder.

I regard Adenauer as best suited for the post he has, because of his temperament, his gift for handling people and tactical skill – also because he can rule and he can put up with a great deal of hype for himself by his apparatus. (The journalists here report that people in Germany see him as equal to Bismarck and as the man who is completing the work that defeated Stresemann.) Today, especially in their effect here, such strong words are necessary to awaken interest in a man if he can withstand it. But that does not last. What is important then is that he does not lose the measure of things. ...

Schwarz, [20], Vol. 1, p. 452.

DOCUMENT 19   THE GDR ELECTIONS OF OCTOBER 1950

The rescheduling of the general election in the GDR to October 1950 and the agreement of the CDUD and the LDPD to present the voters with one united list of candidates supporting common policies ensured that the SED would not face any real challenge. The following extract is from the Proclamation of 15 May 1950 on the elections by the National Council of the National Front of Democratic Germany.

The successful policies of the government of the German Democratic Republic form the basis which made it possible for the October elections to take place in the context of the programme of the National Front of democratic Germany. This will carry our struggle for the consolidation of peace, the strengthening of the democratic order, and the unity and independence of the whole of Germany a significant step forward. Accordingly the National Council of the National Front of democratic Germany welcomes the Democratic Bloc's decisions to put forward a common election programme and a common list of candidates from the National Front of democratic Germany for the elections on 15 October. The National Council calls on the many thousand active members of the committees of the National Front of democratic Germany to prepare for the coming elections by convincing every single citizen of the correctness of our path, the struggle for a single, free, democratic Germany, for the conclusion of a peace treaty and the re-achievement of Germany's independence.

Thomanek and Mellis, [8], p. 39.

DOCUMENT 20   ULBRICHT AT WORK

Heinz Lippmann, a senior official in the FDJ, describes how Ulbricht tried to diminish the authority of the Politbureau by summoning officials to his office to tell them of decisions of which it was not informed.

9–11 A.M.: conference with Minister and Department Heads of the Agricultural Ministry; 11 A. M.–12 noon: conference with Gustav Robelen, SED Central Committee Department Head for Army and State Security, and the head of Political Administration for the People's Army, on problems of political work in the army; noon–3 P.M.: conference with the heads of the Democratic League of Women, during which lunch is served; 4–6 P.M.: report by Secretary of Free German Youth on current campaigns; 6–7 P.M.: reports by Glückauf and Verner on some problems of work in West Germany; conversation with Joos on political aspects of personnel problems. (Ulbricht was always very thorough on this problem since it involved his own method of picking and training personnel.) Around 9 P.M., as a rule, he would talk with the Soviet Zone authorities, although he usually called them several times a day. ... In the evening, he generally met with Central Committee Department heads and dictated specific instructions connected with that day's conferences.

Ulbricht usually had six to eight conferences a day at which basic problems of policy, the economy, culture, etc., were taken up. ... During these meetings, decisions were made that frequently never reached the Politburo. At these conferences, Ulbricht always had notes prepared on questions he considered important. First, the invited functionaries would report, then Ulbricht would explain how he viewed future developments, and finally, he would give concrete directions on what he wanted done.

Stern, [21], pp. 123–4.

DOCUMENT 21   THE FRG ELECTION RESULTS, 1949–51 (PERCENTAGE OF VOTES CAST)

The first federal election of 1949 was fought by sixteen parties, many of which were small regional groups like the Deutsche Partei *from Lower Saxony (others not included in the table below were the* Notgemeinschaft *[Emergency Association] in Württemberg-Baden and the* Südschleswigsche Wählerverband *[South Schleswig Voters' League]. Twelve gained seats in the* Bundestag. *On the extreme left, the KPD inevitably suffered from association with the Soviet Zone and the SED. It was declared illegal by the Constitutional Court in 1956. On the extreme right, the DRP (the German Reich Party) attempted to rally the core Nazi vote made up of fanatical*

Nazis, ex-professional soldiers and the victims of denazification. The two big parties, the CDU/CSU and the SPD, each received roughly 30 per cent of the vote. It was not until 1972 that the SPD was again to come so close to challenging its main rival. By 1953 the CDU/CSU had forged ahead, largely at the expense of the smaller parties, six of which failed to gain 5 per cent of the total of second votes cast or three directly elected members and so won no seats in the Bundestag. *One new party, the BHE, however, did just manage to gain 5 per cent of the vote and 15 seats. In the 1957 election for the first time in German electoral history one party, the CDU/CSU, gained a clear majority. By 1961 voters were beginning to tire of Adenauer, but the main beneficiary of this was the FDP rather than the SPD. The other small parties failed to clear the 5 per cent hurdle.*

Year	Turn-out	CDU-CSU	SPD	FDP	BHE	KPD	DP	DRP
1949	78.5	31.0	29.2	11.9		5.7	4.0	1.8
1953	85.8	45.2	28.8	9.5	5.9	2.2	3.3	1.1
1957	87.8	50.2	31.8	7.7			3.4	1.0
1961	87.7	45.3	36.2	12.8				0.8

Pulzer, [27], p. 187.

DOCUMENT 22   **THE WEST GERMAN GOVERNMENT'S REACTION TO THE SOVIET NOTE OF 10 MARCH 1952**

Otto Lenz, Secretary of State in the Bonn Chancellery, made the following entry in his diary about the reaction of the Cabinet on 11 March to Stalin's note.

Jakob Kaiser thinks that the note is certainly aimed at the Western governments, but we must adopt a positive attitude at all costs. Federal Chancellor thinks it is directed primarily at France, in order to bring it back to its old, traditional policy with Russia. Under no circumstances must we arouse suspicion that we are wavering in our policy. He also thinks it necessary to have an agreed terminology for dealing with the press. Rather vehement debate between Jakob Kaiser and the Federal Chancellor. Jakob Kaiser takes the view that a national German army would be more valuable than a European one. Federal Chancellor points out that the European states alone would not be in a position to defend themselves.

Schwarz, [20], Vol. 1, p. 652.

THE CENTRAL COMMITTEE OF THE SOVIET COMMUNIST PARTY ISSUES AN ULTIMATUM TO THE SED, 2 JUNE 1953

After Stalin's death in March 1953, Ulbricht was worried that the new Soviet leaders – Malenkov, Beria and Molotov – might try to compromise on the German question and force him to abandon his economic and social programmes. His public statements in March and April indicated that he had no desire to support the Soviet peace programme. The GDR, however, was dependent on Moscow and could hardly pursue an independent policy. Thus when Ulbricht, Oelssner and Grotewohl were summoned to Moscow on 2 June they had to accept from the Soviet leadership a document which was in reality an ultimatum ordering them to make reforms. The document started with the following hard-hitting observation.

The pursuit of a wrong political line in the German Democratic Republic has produced a most unsatisfactory political and economic situation. There are signs of bitter dissatisfaction – among broad masses of the population, including the workers, the farmers, and the intellectuals – with the political and economic policies of the GDR. The most conspicuous feature of this dissatisfaction is the mass flight of East German residents to West Germany. From January 1951 through April 1953, 447,000 people have fled to West Germany; over 120,000 during the first four months alone. Working people make up a substantial number of the defectors. An analysis of the social composition of defectors reveals the following: 18,000 workers; 9,000 medium and small farmers, skilled workers, and retirees; 17,000 white-collar workers and intellectuals; and 24,000 housewives. It is striking that 2,718 members and candidates of the SED and 2,619 members of the FDJ were among the defectors to West Germany in the first four months of 1953.

It should be recognised that the main cause of this situation is the false course adopted during the Second Party Conference of the SED – and approved by the Central Committee of the Communist Party of the Soviet Union – accelerating the pace of the construction of socialism in East Germany, without the necessary domestic and foreign policy preconditions.

Ingimundarson, [123], p. 473.

17 JUNE 1953 IN THE GDR

In the immediate aftermath of the disturbances of 17–18 June it seemed that Ulbricht was doomed, but he was saved by the arrest of Beria on 26 June. He was then able to accuse his critics of being 'factionalists' and supporters of the disgraced Beria. By the time the Central Committee met on 24–26 July Ulbricht was secure. The Committee's hard-line resolution, which is quoted below, must be viewed in the context of these events.

As tools of American imperialism, West German monopoly capitalist and Junker circles played an important role in preparing the fascist putsch attempt on June 17. Ever since the power of the workers was established in the GDR, ever since the capitalist monopolies and Junkers were expropriated and banned, these circles, which hold power in West Germany, have been waging a bitter battle for restoration of the old capitalist order in the GDR. They shrink from no crime in order to subvert popular control and the peaceful construction of the GDR, and to take back the factories from the workers and the land from the peasants. Their political representatives, Adenauer and Kaiser, openly announced the fascist Day 'X' in advance. The particular focus of the hatred of these reactionary circles is the SED, the leading force in creating the foundations of the popular democratic order.

The intentions of West German monopoly capitalists and Junkers were reflected on June 17 in the hostile demands of fascist provocateurs for the overthrow of the government of the GDR and restoration of the power of big capitalists and Junkers.

Jarausch and Gransow (eds), [3], pp. 8–9.

DOCUMENT 25   THE GENERAL TREATY ON GERMANY, 23 OCTOBER 1954

In 1952 West Germany signed the General Treaty and agreed to enter the EDC. When the French National Assembly rejected the EDC treaty on 30 August 1954, the Western Allies in the London and Paris Conferences speedily negotiated a new settlement. The text of the General Treaty was substantially incorporated into a new treaty, and further protocols were signed admitting the FRG into NATO. These agreements 'recast the relationships of the Western European nations more decisively than any other event since the war' [29, Vol. 1 p. 330].

Article 1. (1) When this treaty goes into effect, the United States of America, the United Kingdom of Great Britain and Northern Ireland, and the French Republic (in this treaty and supplementary treaties thereafter also referred to as the 'Three Powers') will end the occupation regime in the Federal Republic, repeal the occupation statute and dissolve the Allied High Commission and the offices of the State Commissioners in the Federal Republic.

(2) The Federal Republic will thereby have the full powers of a sovereign state over its internal and external affairs.

Article 2. In view of the international situation, which until now prevented German reunification and the conclusion of a peace treaty, the Three Powers retain the rights and duties exercised or held by them with regard to Berlin and Germany as a whole, including German reunification and a peace settlement. The rights and duties retained by the Three Powers in regard to stationing armed forces in Germany and protecting the security of these forces are determined by Articles 4 and 5 of this Treaty ...

Article 7. (1) The signatory states agree that a significant goal of their joint policies is a settlement for all of Germany through a peace treaty freely agreed to by Germany and its former opponents, which will form the basis for a lasting peace. They further agree that a final determination of Germany's borders must be postponed until such a settlement is reached.

(2) Until conclusion of a peace treaty settlement, the signatory states will co-operate by peaceful means to implement their common goal: a reunited Germany possessing a free, democratic constitution similar to the Federal Republic and integrated into the European Community ...

(4) The Three Powers will consult the Federal Republic in all matters affecting the exercise of their rights with regard to Germany as a whole ...

Jarausch and Gransow, (eds), [3], pp. 10–11.

DOCUMENT 26   THE TREATY BETWEEN THE GDR AND THE USSR, 20 SEPTEMBER 1955

This treaty marked the end of the period when the GDR appeared to be a temporary structure which could possibly be sacrificed by the Soviet leadership to create a united but neutral Germany. It opened the way to increasing economic and military integration into the Eastern bloc.

The President of the GDR and the Presidium of the Supreme Soviet of the Soviet Union ... in view of the new situation which has arisen owing to the coming into force of the Paris Agreement of 1954; convinced that the concerted efforts of the GDR and the Soviet Union to co-operate in the preservation and consolidation of peace and of security in Europe, to restore the unity of Germany as a peace-loving and democratic state, and to bring about a peace settlement with Germany in the form of a treaty are in accordance with the interest of the German people and the Soviet people and alike with the interests of the other European peoples; taking into consideration the obligations of the GDR and the Soviet Union under the international agreements that concern Germany as a whole, have decided to conclude this treaty ...

The contracting parties solemnly confirm that the relations between them are based on complete equality of rights, mutual respect of sovereignty, and non-interference in domestic affairs.

In accordance with this, the GDR is free to decide on questions of its internal and foreign politics, including those pertaining to its relations with the FRG, as well as those pertaining to the development of relations with other states ...

The Soviet troops at present stationed on the territory of the GDR in accordance with the existing international agreements, remain temporarily in the GDR with the approval of the government of the GDR on conditions to be settled by an additional agreement between the government of the GDR and of the Soviet Union.

The Soviet troops temporarily stationed on the territory of the GDR will not interfere with internal affairs of the GDR and with the social and political life of the country.

There is accord between the contracting parties that it is their main aim to bring about a peaceful settlement for the whole of Germany by means of appropriate negotiations. In accordance with this, they will make the necessary efforts toward a settlement by a peace treaty and toward the restoration of the unity of Germany on a peaceful and democratic basis.

Jarausch and Gransow (eds), [3], pp. 11–12.

DOCUMENT 27   THE HALLSTEIN DOCTRINE

Following the establishment of diplomatic relations with the USSR after his trip to Moscow in early September, Adenauer was determined that his government's claim that the FRG was the only legitimate German state should not be placed in jeopardy. He was concerned that the exchange of ambassadors with the USSR, which had just signed a treaty of friendship with the GDR on 20 September, might lead to other states recognizing the GDR. Thus on 22 September Hallstein and another official in the Foreign Office, Wilhelm Grewe, drew up what became known as the Hallstein Doctrine, the essence of which is explained below by Adenauer.

On the occasion of establishing diplomatic relations between the government of the FRG and the government of the USSR, I declare:

1. The establishment of diplomatic relations between the government of the FRG and the government of the USSR does not represent any recognition of present territorial possessions on both sides. Final determination of the German boundaries remains reserved for a peace treaty.

2. The establishment of diplomatic relations with the government of the Soviet Union does not signify any change in the legal standing of the FRG

regarding its authority to represent the German people in international affairs and the political relationship in those German areas which presently lie outside its effective jurisdiction ...

These reservations eliminate the possibility that third nations misinterpret our decision to establish diplomatic relations with the Soviet Union. All states having diplomatic relations with us can clearly see that the standpoint of the FRG toward the so-called 'GDR' and to boundary issues has not changed in the least ...

A settlement of Germany's territorial situation that is binding under international law does not yet exist. Such a settlement can be made only within the scope of a peace treaty to be concluded with a freely elected all-German government. The position of the government of the Federal Republic toward the government of the Soviet zone – as follows from the first reservation – will not be affected by the establishment of diplomatic relations between the Soviet Union and the FRG. The government of the so-called 'GDR' was not formed on the basis of truly free elections and therefore has not received any real authorisation by the people. In fact, it is rejected by the overwhelming majority of the population; there is neither legal protection nor freedom in the Soviet occupied zone, and the constitution exists only on paper.

The FRG therefore remains the only free and legal German government, with sole authorisation to speak for all of Germany. ... We have notified the Soviet government of our viewpoint in order to remove any doubts whatsoever as to the firmness of our position. If the Soviet government nevertheless established diplomatic relations with us, it is doing so, though without granting approval, with full knowledge of our stand toward the so-called 'GDR' and our claim to speak for all of Germany. Where third nations are concerned, we also maintain our standpoint regarding the so-called 'GDR'. I must clearly and in no uncertain terms declare that the government of the FRG will interpret as an unfriendly act the establishment of diplomatic relations with the 'GDR' by third nations with which it has official relations, as this act would serve to deepen the division of Germany.

Jarausch and Gransow (eds), [3], pp. 12–13.

DOCUMENT 28   ADENAUER AND GERMAN UNITY

Sir Ivone Kirkpatrick, the Permanent Under-Secretary of State at the Foreign Office, reports on a conversation with the West German Ambassador, Herbert Blankenhorn, in December 1955.

The German ambassador told me yesterday that he wished to make a particularly confidential communication to me on this subject. I would recollect that I had told him on my return from Geneva that I had come to the conclusion that we might eventually have to be more elastic than the Americans were prepared to be and that we might have to move to a position in which we declared that, provided Germany was unified by means of free elections and provided that unified German Government had freedom in domestic and foreign affairs, we should sign any reasonable security treaty with the Russians.

The Ambassador told me that he had discussed this possibility very confidentially with the Chancellor. Dr Adenauer wished me to know that he would deprecate reaching this position. The bald reason was that Dr Adenauer had no confidence in the German people. He was terrified that when he disappeared from the scene a future German Government might do a deal with Russia at the German expense. Consequently he felt that the integration of Western Germany with the West was more important than the unification of Germany. He wished us to know that he would bend all his energies towards achieving this in the time which was left to him, and he hoped that we would do all in our power to sustain him in this task.

Steininger, [128], pp. 118–19.

DOCUMENT 29   KHRUSHCHEV'S SPEECH ON BERLIN, 10 NOVEMBER 1958

By 1958 Ulbricht was convinced that the time had come to adopt a much tougher line towards the FRG. Krushchev was initially cautious. At first he advised Ulbricht once again to propose four-power negotiations on Berlin. When there was no response from the Western powers, Khrushchev decided against the advice of his own Foreign Office experts to follow a more uncompromising line. Hence, on 10 November, in a tough speech, an extract of which is quoted below, he called for a German peace treaty, and then on 27 November he issued his ultimatum. The ensuing crisis lasted until the construction of the Berlin Wall on 13 August 1961.

Is it not time for us to draw appropriate conclusions from the fact that the key items of the Potsdam Agreement concerning the maintenance of peace in Europe and, consequently, throughout the world, have been violated, and that certain forces continue to nurture German militarism, prompting it in the direction in which it was pushed before the Second World War, that is, against the East? Is it not time for us to reconsider our attitude to this part of the Potsdam Agreement, and to denounce it? The time has obviously arrived for the signatories of the Potsdam Agreement to renounce the remnants of the occupation regime in Berlin, and thereby make it possible to create a normal situation in the capital of the German Democratic Republic. The Soviet Union, for its part, would hand over to the sovereign

German Democratic Republic the functions in Berlin that are still exercised by Soviet agencies. This, I think, would be the correct thing to do.

Morgan, [4], pp. 77–8.

DOCUMENT 30   **THE DECISION TO BUILD THE WALL**

An extract from the Resolution of the GDR Council of Ministers, 12 August 1961.

To stop hostile activities by revanchist and militaristic forces in West Germany and West Berlin, a border control will be introduced at the borders to the GDR, including the border with western sectors of Greater Berlin, as is common on the borders of sovereign states. Borders to West Berlin will be sufficiently guarded and effectively controlled in order to prevent subversive activities from the West. Citizens of the GDR will require a special permit to cross these borders. Until West Berlin is transformed into a demilitarised, neutral free city, residents of the capital of the GDR will require a special certificate to cross the border into West Berlin. Peaceful citizens of West Berlin are permitted to visit the capital of the GDR (democratic Berlin) upon presentation of a West Berlin identity card. Revanchist politicians and agents of West German militarism are not permitted to enter the capital of the GDR (democratic Berlin). For citizens of the West German Federal Republic wishing to visit democratic Berlin, previous control regulations remain in effect. Entry by citizens of other states to the capital of the GDR will not be affected by these regulations.

Jarausch and Gransow (eds), [3], p. 15.

DOCUMENT 31   **ADENAUER'S MESSAGE TO THE EAST GERMANS AFTER THE CLOSING OF THE FRONTIER IN BERLIN, DELIVERED BEFORE A SPECIAL SESSION OF THE *BUNDESTAG*, 18 AUGUST 1961**

In the immediate aftermath of the crisis of 13 August, Adenauer 'wrapt himself in silence' [32 p. 164]. He did not go to West Berlin until 22 August. His dignified but resigned statement on 18 August to the Bundestag *essentially depicts his view that little could be done in the short term to help the East Germans.*

Let me finally say a few words to the inhabitants of the Eastern sector of Berlin and the Soviet zone of Germany. Your sorrow and suffering are our sorrow and suffering. In your particularly difficult situation you were able at least to derive some comfort from the thought that, if your lot should become quite unbearable, you could mend it by fleeing. Now it looks as if you had [*sic*] been deprived of this comfort, too. I request you with all my heart: do not abandon all hope of a better future for yourselves and your children. We are convinced that the Free World, and particularly we here, shall some day be successful in our efforts to obtain freedom for you. The right to self-determination will continue in its victorious march throughout the world and will not halt at the boundary of the Soviet zone. Believe me, the day will come when you will be united with us in freedom. We do not stand alone in the world; justice is on our side, and so are all the nations who love freedom.

Heidelmeyer and Hindrichs (eds), [2], p. 288.

DOCUMENT 32   THE *SPIEGEL* AFFAIR

Sebastian Hafner, moderate Conservative journalist, commented as follows on the affair in the Süddeutsche Zeitung, *early November 1962.*

What is usually referred to as 'the accompanying circumstances of the *Spiegel* affair' is in reality the affair itself. The fateful question for Germany which is being raised at this time is not whether the *Spiegel* has – in some articles that may be weeks or months old – crossed the uncertain and flexible limit that distinguishes legitimate public information on defence matters from treason. Let the lawyers calmly decide that point for themselves. The question is whether the Federal Republic of Germany is still a free and constitutional democracy, or whether it has become possible to transform it overnight by some sort of *coup d'état* based on fear and arbitrary power.

Bark and Gress, [29], Vol. 1, p. 505.

DOCUMENT 33   ERHARD ON COLLECTIVISM

This extract from Erhard's bestseller, Wohlstand für Alle (Prosperity through Competition) *sums up his belief in the importance of the individual and his scepticism towards socialism, collectivism and excessive bureaucracy.*

The position of the individual within the State, or better still the attitude of the citizen to the State, should be a constant consideration of the politically responsible. On this point I want to make my position clear as a comment on the eagerness to organise (not to say craze for organisation) which permeates the 20th century. Now the inherent passion of the German for associations, formerly much ridiculed, has taken on a new and dangerous guise. It has encouraged the conviction that, if only big and strong organisations can be built up, which would be in a position to demonstrate their aims in a politically powerful manner, then the State when faced by these interests would capitulate. Obviously many large pressure groups act in accordance with this principle. If the conviction grows, the State will necessarily become the plaything of pressure groups.

Hand in hand with this development goes another, which might almost be called tragic: the experience which I have gained over the many years in which I have been responsible for economic policy has taught me again and again that, in these collective expressions of opinion, 'mistakes in translation' of the worst kind take place. What the individual, of whatever rank or occupation, professes, has hardly anything in common with what the organisation representing him makes of its mandate, i.e. what it puts forward as demands.

Erhard, [99], p. 141.

DOCUMENT 34   **PRODUCTIVITY IN THE FRG (1950 = 100)**

Year	All industry	Mining industry	Basic production and goods industry	Investment goods industry	Consumer goods industry	Food and stimulants industry
1951	109.6	107.2	108.0	113.8	107.2	109.7
1952	114.2	112.4	110.8	121.4	109.6	114.9
1953	122.1	114.8	118.9	124.6	119.7	129.5
1954	129.2	118.6	128.0	134.2	125.3	132.9
1955	138.3	126.9	138.0	145.0	132.2	140.5
1956	144.5	132.1	144.7	150.5	139.3	145.4
1957	155.1	138.9	157.4	158.9	150.3	166.1
1958	163.1	145.4	166.9	167.3	155.7	166.1
1959	179.8	158.1	186.1	180.5	167.9	174.5

Productivity as defined by output per man-hour. Figures exclude electricity power generation and the construction industry.

Kramer, [103], p. 206.

This company report for 1955 shows the pace of economic growth and the challenges created by it as experienced by one of the FRG's most dynamic companies.

As a consequence of the general growth of the economy there was a rise in demand for parts for motor vehicles and engines as well as for other Bosch products. Altogether our turnover increased by nearly 25 per cent, while supplies to the motor manufacturing industry for engine and chassis parts showed an above-average increase. ...

Turnover in bicycle lights improved in the autumn months and was in general satisfactory.

Foreign and inland trade in household equipment made gratifying progress. The turnover of refrigerators and kitchen equipment has increased steadily and we have begun to market these products abroad. Sales of refrigerators and freezers for commercial use have also proved to be a sound development.

Since we broadened our range of electric tools we have registered a substantial increase in sales. ...

Exports of Bosch products of all kinds were 15 per cent up on the previous year and went through the DM 100 million barrier for the first time. This figure does not include indirect exports of products built into motor vehicles or engines, which would probably even exceed direct exports. Unfortunately we still do not yet have free world trade, the rationing and licensing regulations still in existence in many countries hamper the mutual exchange of goods. In various countries we have opened new agencies with well-equipped customer service workshops. All over the world experienced Bosch experts now ensure once again the meticulous maintenance of our products. ...

Although raw material prices continued to rise and there were especially steep increases in the price of copper, the expansion of output and the successes in the rationalisation have made it possible to cut prices in a number of products.

In financial terms the year once again brought strains. The urgent necessity of raising money for rationalisation purposes coincided with the need to acquire more factory floor space, machine tools, and other manufacturing equipment to meet the rising level of demand. As a result the need for outside capital was inescapable. Unfortunately the worsening situation on the capital markets since August has prevented the planned consolidation of the short and middle-term credits. ...

There is no doubt that productivity at a time of full employment cannot be increased unless we rationalise. This means, apart from organisational measures, the use of labour-saving machines and equipment and therefore investment. ...

During the year we increased employment by 5,034, and by the end of the year 31,505 persons were employed by Robert Bosch GmbH, not counting apprentices and student trainees. There were 26,116 wage-earners and 5,289 salaried staff. ... Our subsidiary companies employed 6,492 (not including apprentices and trainees).

In view of the general shortage of skilled workers we paid special attention, as always, to the training of good junior staff. Altogether 160 industrial and clerical apprentices and trainees and 75 student trainees completed their education in the past year. In addition, we trained another 108 employees as detail constructors, setters, assistant mechanics, machine tool operators, and draughtsmen assistants; 105 employees trained for work abroad. On 31 December 1955 altogether 774 persons were in education and training ...

Year	Bosch average hourly wages including overtime and shift allowances (1949 = 100)	Cost of living index (1949 = 100)	National average hourly wage (1949 = 100)
1949	100.0	100.0	100.0
1950	110.0	106.7	111.3
1951	126.5	104.0	121.7
1952	135.2	106.5	127.0
1953	139.8	105.1	133.0
1954	143.7	104.5	137.6
1955	149.4	105.7	141.3

The salaries of white-collar staff showed a similar improvement.

As a result of progressive rationalisation through the use of modern machines and other equipment there has been a continuous reduction of the wage quota (salaries and wages including additional costs), while in the economy as a whole the wage quota has remained constant.

Year	Wage quota (1949 = 100)
1949	100.0
1950	93.9
1951	84.6
1952	83.8
1953	81.2
1954	78.4

The sinking wage quota does not, however, mean declining wages. On the contrary the development of earnings in our companies shows that increasing mechanisation and automation of production is accompanied by rising wages. The idea that unemployment will rise as a result of rationalisation is contradicted by the facts. Today we have full employment and a lack of labour.

Robert Bosch, GmbH, Company Report, 1955. In Kramer, [103], pp. 285–7.

DOCUMENT 36   THE POSITION OF WOMEN IN POST-WAR GERMANY

(a) Walther von Hollander, writing in the women's magazine, Constanza, *in 1948, describes the tensions between men and women in immediate post-war Germany.*

I know a great many women who try everything in their power to make sure that their husband does not notice the helpless and humiliating position in which he finds himself. In addition to the worries where the daily bread will come from and to the efforts of providing something resembling civilised living, women find the strength to encourage their husbands and to put up with his passivity and weakness. But the situation really becomes intolerable when the helpless man then acts like a domestic tyrant. A powerless tyrant – a disgusting type. And however many excuses one may find for his behaviour in the adverse circumstances of our times, his demands simply are too much for the woman who is already stretched beyond her physical and emotional strength.

Kolinsky, [102], pp. 29–30.

(b) Helga Prolins, in another article in Constanza *in 1949, describes the desperate search for a man.*

The hunt for a man has assumed unprecedented proportions: 'a kingdom for a man' – regardless of how he is! Every other woman becomes a dangerous rival in the fight for the man. Therefore, grab him with all means of seduction even if it should cost one's comfortable home or even one's personality. … And the man? Well, as the sought-after object he sits on his throne and has the best offers presented to him. It goes without saying that his character will not improve with all the uncritical and exaggerated pampering he receives. He used to woo, and is now being wooed. Who knows how it will affect him in the long run to be spoilt only to be conquered? One thing is clear: the situation is bad for both sides, the women who panic to land themselves a man, and the men who turn into real Good-For-Nothings [Paschas].

Kolinsky, [102], p. 30.

DOCUMENT 37   SETTING UP HOME IN THE FRG IN THE 1950s

This extract comes from the reminiscences in the early 1980s of a tool-maker who set up home with his wife in 1950.

Today, the young people start a marriage with owning a car, and we had nothing at all when we started. We could not help it, it was impossible to get anything. And we did not earn the big money, we had to save every penny. ... We had lots of problems to begin with. The flat was very small, a converted attic. We had to saw the beds shorter to get them into the tiny room where we slept. Every time I turned, I hit my knee on the roof and woke up. We lived for six years in that place. ... In 1957, we moved into this apartment, and bought everything at once: furniture for the bedroom, the kitchen, the living room. We had saved all our money for seven years. ... Only after 1957 could we purchase larger items, and we bought our first car in 1962 ... and since then we have replaced a lot of things, bought a new three piece suite, a wardrobe, a stereo, a fitted bedroom and kitchen ...

Kolinsky, [102], pp. 78–9.

DOCUMENT 38   THE ROLE OF WRITERS AND ARTISTS IN THE GDR

An extract from Ulbricht's speech at the Authors' Conference held in the Palace of Culture of the Bitterfeld Electrochemical Combine, 24 April 1959.

On the basis of the decisions of the 5th Party Conference we must state that the discussions represent an important contribution towards the development of a further blossoming of socialist culture in the German Democratic Republic. The new feature is that instead of a small circle of writers and authors trying to discuss and solve these tasks by themselves, everything is being done to develop all the talents and potential present in the population in order to *give socialist culture a very broad base.*

Young writers are to be developed from the working class, the ranks of the workers, correspondents, etc. They are to be given every opportunity to develop their talents. We must at the same time implement practical measures *to enable the workers to storm the heights of culture.*

The task is to create the new socialist national culture on the foundation of the construction of socialism and to use it in the struggle to overcome the remnants of capitalist ideology, of capitalist and bourgeois habits. The task is at the same time to carry on the struggle with artistic means against imperialist and fascist ideology and bourgeois decadence which exert their influence from the West.

Our literature, our art, the fine arts in general must be given a new socialist content and must be made accessible to the whole people. In the context of the great social transformation which has taken place on our territory in the last 14 years, the creative activity of the working people here in the heart of Europe proved what great capacities and what strength are present in the people to develop the new socialist order of society, the socialist economy, and the new socialist culture.

What is the task our writers have been assigned by history?

Their task is to give artistic form to what is new in life, in people's social relationships, in their struggle for the construction of socialism and the socialist reorganisation of all aspects of life, so that they inspire people by their artistic achievements and so help to speed up and advance the tempo of development. Working people expect writers to make their great contribution to socialist reorganisation in the German Democratic Republic. The major forms of popular education – books, television, film, radio, the press – offer the writer the most varied opportunities to develop his talents.

Thomanek and Mellis, [8], pp. 306–7.

CHRONOLOGY

1945

7–8 May	The unconditional surrender of the German armed forces.
17 July–2 August	The Potsdam Conference.

1946

21–22 April	The forced amalgamation of the KPD and the SPD in the Soviet Zone to create the SED.

1947

1 January	The creation of Anglo-American Bizone.
10 March–24 April	The Moscow Conference fails to resolve the German question.
4 June	SMAD sets up German Economic Commission (DWK).
5 June	Marshall announces the European Recovery Programme (Marshall Plan).
15 December	The London Foreign Ministers' Conference breaks up.

1948

22 February	The Communist coup in Czechoslovakia.
7 June	The London six-power Conference recommends calling of a West German constituent assembly.
20 June	Currency reform in the Western zones.
24 June	The Berlin blockade begins.
5 September	The Parliamentary Council meets in Bonn.

1949

4 April	NATO is set up.
12 May	The USSR lifts the Berlin blockade.
23 May	The Basic Law is announced in the FRG.
30 May	The Third *Volkskongress* approves the GDR Constitution.
15 September	Adenauer is voted Chancellor by one vote in the *Bundestag*.
22 September	Occupation Statute comes into force in the FRG.
12 October	GDR provisional government under Grotewohl is confirmed in power by the *Volkskammer*.
22 November	Petersberg Treaty.

1950

8 February	Ministry for State Security (*Stasi*) is created in the GDR.
25 June	The outbreak of the Korean War.
9 August	The FRG Constitution is extended to West Berlin.
8 September	The GDR joins Comecon.
15 October	The Election to the *Volkskammer*.
26 October	Blank is appointed Commissioner for Security Matters in the FRG.

1951

15 March	The West German Foreign Office is set up under Adenauer.
18 April	The European Coal and Steel Community replaces the Ruhr Authority.
1 December	The first Five Year Plan is launched in the GDR.

1952

10 March	Stalin's note, proposing a neutral united Germany.
26 May	The General Treaty is signed in Bonn.
27 May	The EDC Treaty is signed in Paris.
9–12 July	The second SED Congress.
23 July	The *Länder* are dissolved in the GDR.

1953

5 March	Stalin dies.
28 May	'Norms' in the GDR are increased by 10 per cent.
16–18 June	Strikes and riots in the GDR.
6 September	The FRG election: Adenauer retains power.

1954

1 January	The USSR ends reparation payments from the GDR.
31 August	The EDC is rejected by the French Assembly.
19–23 October	The nine-power Conference in London agrees to the FRG's sovereignty and membership of NATO.

1955

5 May	The FRG becomes a sovereign state.
9 May	The FRG joins NATO.
14 May	The Warsaw Pact is formed.
9–13 September	Adenauer visits Moscow.
20 September	The USSR recognises GDR sovereignty.
22 September	The Hallstein Doctrine is announced.

1956

18 January	The National People's Army is created in the GDR.
14–25 February	The Twentieth Party Congress is held in Moscow; Khrushchev condemns Stalinism.
21 July	Military service is introduced into the FRG.
23 October– 4 November	The Hungarian uprising is suppressed.

1957

25 March	The Treaty of Rome is signed.
15 September	The CDU/CSU wins a majority in the general election.

1958

9 January	The second Five Year Plan.
28 May	Rationing ends for meat and sugar in the GDR.
27 November	Khrushchev's Berlin ultimatum.

1959

1 October	The Seven Year Plan replaces the Five Year Plan.
13–15 November	The SPD Party Congress adopts the Godesberg Programme.

1960

January–April	Collectivization of the remaining independent farms in the GDR is completed.

1961

13 August	The border between East and West Berlin is sealed off.
17 September	Adenauer retains power in the FRG election.

1962

26 October	The *Spiegel* Affair; Strauss resigns on 9 November.

1963

22 January	The Elysée Treaty is signed.
25 June	The 'New Economic System' starts in the GDR.
15 October	Adenauer is succeeded by Erhard.

GLOSSARY

Bank deutscher Länder The Federal Central Bank (renamed *Bundesbank* in 1957). It is legally required to manage the money supply and regulate the banking system independently of the government.

Bloc parties In July 1945 SMAD created the anti-Fascist bloc of parties in the Soviet Zone. After 1946 it was dominated by the SED. By 1948 it was composed of the CDUD, LDPD, DBD, NDPD and SED, the first four of which accepted the leading role of the SED.

Bundesrat The Federal Council or Upper House in which the *Länder* of the FRG are represented by their ministers or their delegates.

Bundesrepublik The Federal Republic of Germany.

Bundestag The Federal Diet or Lower House of the FRG. It is elected by a combination of proportional and majority representation. Every voter has two votes: one for the local constituency and one for a party list of candidates, elected according to proportional representation.

Bundeswehr The Federal Army of the FRG.

Central Committee The Central Committee of the SED acted on behalf of the Party Congress when it was not sitting. All important officials and Party members belonged to it.

Collectivization The replacement of private farms by LPGs (agricultural production cooperatives), which took place between 1952 and 1960. Individual land holdings, although at first legally still owned by the original farmers, were amalgamated and farmed collectively as one unit. By the early 1960s over 90 per cent of German farms were collectivized and the independent agricultural sector virtually disappeared.

Comecon The Committee for Mutual Economic Assistance, set up in Moscow in April 1949 for economic cooperation between the states of the Soviet bloc.

Cominform Communist Information Bureau, set up by Stalin in September 1947 in response to the Truman Doctrine and the Marshall Plan.

Decartelization The breaking up of cartels or trusts into smaller units.

IG Farben (Interessen Gemeinschaft der deutschen Farbenindustrie) A large dye and chemical cartel which produced synthetic materials for the Nazi Four Year Plan and developed Zyklon B gas. After the Second World War it was broken up into some 50 smaller companies.

Land A federal state such as Bavaria.

Landtag A state assembly.

Marxism-Leninism The Communist doctrine, based on the teachings of Marx and Lenin, which was the guiding philosophy of the SED.

National Front of Democratic Germany Formed 1949 in GDR; all parties and mass organizations belonged to it. Its role was both to campaign for a united socialist Germany and to enable the SED to control the bloc parties and present a united programme in elections.

[Ober]bürgermeister [Lord] Mayor.

Ohne mich Literally 'Without me'. The wish not to be politically involved, which was much in evidence in both Germanies in the 1950s.

Ostpolitik The 'Eastern policy' conducted by the FRG towards the GDR and the Eastern bloc after 1969.

Politbureau The Political Bureau of the SED based on the Russian model; it was the key decision-making body in the GDR.

Reichswehr The German Army, 1920–35.

Stasi The GDR Ministry for State Security (Ministerium für Staatssicherheit – MfS) was set up in February 1950. It was usually referred to as the *Stasi,* which was a combination of the first two syllables of the German words for state and security.

Union (of CDU/CSU) The CSU exists only in Bavaria where the CDU has no branches at all. On the other hand, the CDU operates in the other German *Länder.* Consequently, the two parties do not compete against each other, and in the *Bundestag* form a single group of *Fraktion.*

Volkskammer The Lower House of the GDR parliament. Theoretically it was the most important constitutional body in the GDR, but in reality it met only on symbolic occasions and real power rested in the Politbureau and Central Committee of the SED.

Volkskongress The People's Congress, of which three were called: December 1947, February 1948 and May 1949.

Wehrmacht German armed forces, 1935–45.

Werwolf The name given to what was planned to be a Nazi resistance movement in 1945.

Westpolitik The German policy towards the West.

WHO'S WHO

Ackermann, Anton (born Eugen Hanisch) *(1905–73)* Member of Central Committee and State Secretary in the GDR Foreign Ministry, 1949–53; forced to resign from the Central Committee in 1954 for supporting the Zaisser–Herrnstadt group.

Adenauer, Konrad (1876–1967) Oberbürgermeister of Cologne, 1917–33, March–April 1945; Chairman of the CDU in the British Zone, 1946–49; President of the Parliamentary Council, 1949; Chancellor of the FRG, 1949–63; Chairman of the CDU, 1950–66.

Arnold, Karl (1901–58) Oberbürgermeister of Düsseldorf, 1946; CDU prime minister of North Rhineland-Westphalia, 1947–55; president of the *Bundesrat*, 1949–53.

Augstein, Rudolf (1924–) Founder and editor of the *Spiegel* magazine, January 1947–.

Bahr, Egon (1923–) Salesman, journalist and adviser to Willy Brandt on foreign policy; the main originator of *Ostpolitik*.

Baudissin, Lieutanant-General Wolf Graf von (1907–93) Founding member of the *Bundeswehr*, 1950–58; serving officer in the *Bundeswehr* and NATO, 1958–67.

Beria, Lavrentii (1899–1953) Chief of the NKVD; Deputy Prime Minister of the USSR, 1952–53.

Bevin, Ernest (1881–1951) British Foreign Secretary, 1945–51.

Blank, Theodor (1905–72) Trade union general secretary, Dortmund, 1931–33; dismissed by Nazis; security adviser to Adenauer, 1950–55; Defence Minister, 1955–56; Justice Minister, 1957–65.

Blankenhorn, Herbert (1904–91) Diplomat, 1929–45; minister and director of the Office for Foreign Affairs in the Chancellery, 1950–51; director of the political division of the West German Foreign Office, 1951–55; the FRG's representative to NATO, 1955–59; ambassador to Paris, Rome and London, 1959–70.

Böckler, Hans (1875–1951) Joined the SPD in 1894; leading official of the General Metal Workers Association, 1920–33; SPD member of the *Reichstag*, 1928–33; arrested by the Nazis, 1933–34; Chairman of the DGB, 1949–51.

Böll, Heinrich (1917–85) Novelist and member of *Grüppe 47*.

Brandt, Willy (1913–92) Joined the Socialist Workers' Party in 1931; a resistance fighter in Norway, 1940–45; *Bürgermeister* of West Berlin, 1957–66; candidate for the Chancellorship in the 1961 and 1965 elections; Foreign Minister, 1966–69; Chancellor, 1969–74; leader of the SPD, 1964–88.

Brecht, Bertolt (1898–1956) Playwright and poet; in exile, 1933–47; resident in East Berlin, 1947–56.

Brentano, Heinrich (1904–64) Lawyer; CDU/CSU party whip, 1949–55; Foreign Minister, 1955–61.

Byrnes, James (1879–1972) US Secretary of State, 1946–47.

Churchill, Winston (1874–1965) British Prime Minister, 1940–45, 1951–55.

Clay, General Lucius (1897–1978) Military Governor of the American Zone, 1945–49.

Dahlem, Franz (1892–1981) KPD member of the *Reichstag*, 1928–33; interned in a concentration camp, 1941–45; member of the SED Politbureau and Central Committee, 1949–53; forced to resign in 1953; rehabilitated in 1956.

De Gaulle, General Charles (1890–1970) French Prime Minister, 1944–46; President, 1958–69.

Dehler, Thomas (1897–1967) FDP leader, 1954–57; FRG Minister of Justice, 1949–53; quitted the coalition in 1956.

Dertinger, Georg (1902–68) General–Secretary of the CDUD, 1946–49; GDR Foreign Minister, 1949–53; imprisoned, 1953–64.

Dibelius, Otto (1888–1967) Bishop of Berlin-Brandenburg, 1945–66; Chairman of Executive Council of the Evangelical Church in Germany, 1949–61.

Dönitz, Grand Admiral Karl (1891–1980) Hitler's successor, 30 April–23 May 1945; sentenced to 10 years' imprisonment at Nuremberg, 1946.

Dulles, John Foster (1888–1959) American Secretary of State, 1953–59.

Eden, Sir Anthony (1897–1977) British Foreign Secretary, 1935–38, 1940–45, 1951–55; Prime Minister, 1955–56.

Eisenhower, General Dwight (1890–1969) Supreme Commander of the American forces in Europe, 1942–45; Supreme Commander of NATO, 1950–52; President of the USA, 1953–61.

Erhard, Professor Ludwig (1897–1977) Economics lecturer, 1928–45; minister for trade and commerce in Bavaria, 1945–47; Director of Economics, Bizone, 1948–49; Minister of Economics, 1949–63; Chancellor, 1963–66.

Etzel, Franz (1902–70) CDU member of the *Bundestag*, 1949–61; Vice-president of the ECSC, 1951–57; federal minister of finance, 1957–61.

Faulhaber, Cardinal Michael von (1896–1952) Archbishop of Munich, 1917–52; Cardinal, 1921–52.

Fechner, Max (1892–1973) Member of SPD, 1922–33; imprisoned by the Nazis; GDR Minister of Justice, 1949–53; dismissed and imprisoned, 1953–56.

François-Ponçet, André (1887–1978) French ambassador in Berlin, 1931–38; High Commissioner in the FRG, 1949–55; ambassador in Bonn, May–September 1955.

Globke, Hans (1898–1973) Civil servant, 1929–45; drafted the Nuremberg Laws of 1935; adviser to Adenauer, 1949–53; State Secretary in Chancellery, 1953–63.

Grass, Günter (1927–) Writer and artist.

Grotewohl, Otto (1894–1964) SPD member of the *Reichstag*, 1925–33; imprisoned, 1938–39; co-founder of the SED, 1946; Prime Minister of the GDR, 1949–60.

Hallstein, Professor Walter (1901–82) Academic lawyer; State Secretary in the Office of the Chancellor, 1950–51; State Secretary in the Foreign Ministry, 1951–57; president of the EEC, 1958–67.

Hamann, Karl (1903–73) Co-founder of the LDPD; chairman of the LDPD and the GDR Agricultural Minister, 1949–52; imprisoned, 1952–57; moved to the FRG in 1957.

Harich, Wolfgang (1923–) Lecturer at Humboldt University; dissident and critic of Ulbricht, 1956–57; imprisoned, 1957–67.

Heinemann, Gustav (1899–1976) Lawyer; *Oberbürgermeister* of Essen, 1946–49; Minister of the Interior, 1949–52; resigned from the CDU in 1952; chaired the all-German synod, 1949–55; founded the United German People's Party, 1953; joined the SPD in 1957; Minister of Justice, 1966–69; President of the FRG, 1969–74.

Heisenberg, Professor Werner Karl (1901–76) Physicist and founder of quantum mechanics. He was professor in Leipzig, then Göttingen; Nobel Prize winner in 1932; he opposed a nuclear-equipped *Bundeswehr*.

Herrnstadt, Rudolph (1903–68) Editor of *Neues Deutschland*, 1949–53; publisher and member of the Politbureau; expelled from the Central Committee in July 1953 and from the SED in 1954.

Herzfeld, Hans (1892–1982) History professor at Free University, West Berlin, 1950–60.

Heuss, Theodor (1884–1963) Writer; Democratic Party MP, 1924–33; minister for education, Baden, 1945–46; Chairman of the FDP, 1948–49; FRG President, 1949–59.

Honecker, Erich (1912–94) Member of the German Communist Youth organization, 1926–35; imprisoned by the Nazis, 1935–45; set up and led the FDJ, 1945–55; in charge of security, 1957; first secretary of the SED, 1971–89.

Janka, Walther (1914–94) Dissident and head of the *Aufbau Verlag* in the GDR, 1952–57; arrested and imprisoned, 1957.

Jaspers, Karl (1883–1969) Philosopher and Rector of Heidelberg University, 1945–48; moved to a chair in Basel; highly critical of the FRG; he argued in *Wohin treibt die Bundesrepublik?* [72] in 1966 that the West Germans still did not understand democracy.

Jendretzky, Hans (1897–1992) Joined the KPD, 1920; imprisoned by the Nazis, 1933–38; Chairman of the FDGB, 1946–48; dismissed from the Politbureau, 1953; rehabilitated in 1958; Chairman of the FDGB group in the *Volkskammer*, 1965–90.

Kaiser, Jakob (1888–1961) Christian trade union official, 1920–33; member of the German resistance to Hitler; co-founder of the CDU in 1945; chairman of CDUD in the Soviet Zone, 1945–47; Minister for All German Affairs in the FRG, 1949–57.

Kastner, Hermann (1886–1957) Chairman of the LDPD, 1949; deputy prime minister (GDR), 1949–50; fled to the FRG, 1956.

Khrushchev, Nikita (1894–1971) Elected to the USSR Politbureau, 1939; First Secretary of Russian Communist Party, 1953–64: Premier, 1958–64.

Kopf, Hinrich (1893–1961) SPD prime minister of Lower Saxony, 1946–55, 1959–61.

Kraft, Waldemar (1898–1977) Leader of the BHE.

Kuczynski, Jürgen (1904–97) Joined the SED in 1946; Director of the German Economic Institute, 1949–52; Professor of Political Economy and Economic History at Humboldt University, 1946–70.

Külz, Wilhelm (1875–1948) DDP member of the *Reichstag*, 1920–32; *Oberbürgermeiste*r, Dresden, 1931; Chairman of the LPDP, 1946–48.

Lemmer, Ernst (1898–1970) DDP member of the *Reichstag*, 1924–33; co-founder of the CDU in the Soviet Zone and deputy chairman, 1946–49; fled to West Berlin, 1950; elected to the *Bundestag*, 1952–70; Minister for all German questions, 1957–62; and for expellees, 1964–65.

Lübke, Heinrich (1894–1972) Centre Party member of the Prussian *Landtag*, 1931–33; minister of food for North Rhine-Westphalia, 1947–52; federal agriculture minister, 1953–59; President of the FRG, 1959–69.

Macmillan, Harold (1894–1986) British Foreign Minister, 1955; Prime Minister, 1957–63.

Malenkov, Georgi (1902–88) Deputy Prime Minister of the USSR, 1953–55.

Mann, Thomas (1875–1955) Journalist and novelist.

Marshall, General George (1880–1959) American Secretary of State, 1947–49; Defence Minister, 1950–51.

Matern, Hermann (1893–1971) Joined the KPD in 1920; co-founder of the National Committee of Free Germany, 1943; member of the Central Committee and the Politbureau, 1950.

Mende, Erich (1916–) FDP member of the *Bundestag*, 1949–70; FDP party leader, 1960–68; minister of all German affairs, 1963–66; joined the CDU in 1970.

Merkatz, Hans-Joachim von (1905–1982) DP member of the *Bundestag*, 1949–60; CDU member, 1960–69; minister for *Bundesrat* affairs, 1955–62; also Minister of Justice, 1956–57 and Minister for Expellees, 1960–61.

Merker, Paul (1894–1969) Joined the KPD in 1920; Secretary of Free German Movement in Mexico, 1942–45; member of the Politbureau and State Secretary in the GDR Ministry for Agriculture and Forestry, 1949–50; deprived of all offices in 1950.

Molotov, Vyacheslav (1890–1986) Soviet Foreign Minister, 1939–46, 1953–56.

Monnet, Jean (1888–1979) Drew up the French modernization plan in 1946 and the Schuman Plan in 1950; president of the ECSC, 1952–55.

Morgenthau, Henry (1891–1967) Secretary of US Treasury, 1933–45; general chairman of the United Jewish Appeal, 1947–67.

Neumayer, Fritz (1884–1973) FDP *Bundestag* member, 1949–56; joined the *Freie Volkspartei*, 1956; Minister of Housing, 1953; Minister of Justice, 1953–56.

Niemöller, Martin (1892–1984) U-boat captain, 1914–18; pastor in Dahlem, 1931; had a key role in organizing the confessing church in 1933; interned in a concentration camp, 1937–45; in charge of the Evangelical Church's foreign relations department, 1946–56; President of the World Council of Churches, 1961–68.

Nuschke, Otto (1883–1957) Leader of the CDUD, 1948–57.

Oelssner, Fred (1903–77) Joined the KPD in 1920; director of the German section of Moscow Radio, 1941–45; member of the Central Committee and Politbureau; expelled from the SED, 1958; partially rehabilitated in 1965.

Ollenhauer, Erich (1901–63) Leader of the SPD youth movement, 1928–33; emigrated, 1933–45; Vice-chairman of the SPD, 1946–53; chairman and parliamentary leader 1952–63.

Pfleiderer, Karl (1899–1957) Diplomat, 1926–45; FDP *Bundestag* member, 1949–55; ambassador to Yugoslavia, 1955–57.

Pieck, Wilhelm (1876–1960) Joined the KPD in 1918; KPD member of the Prussian *Landtag*, then the *Reichstag*, 1920–33; co-founder in Moscow of the Free German Committee, 1943; President of the GDR, 1949–60.

Pleven, René (1901–93) French Prime Minister, July 1950, 1951–52.

Robertson, Sir Brian (1896–1974) Deputy Military Governor, then Governor of the British Zone, 1945–49; High Commissioner, 1949–50.

Roosevelt, Franklin (1882–1945) American President, 1932–45.

Röpke, Professor Wilhelm (1899–1966) Liberal economist; professor at Graz University, 1928–29; Marburg University, 1929–33; taught at the University of Istanbul, 1933–37; and at Geneva University, 1937–66.

Schäffer, Fritz (1888–1967) Head of the provisional Bavarian government, 1945; co-founder of the CSU; federal Finance Minister, 1949–57; Justice Minister, 1957–61.

Schiller, Professor Karl (1911–95) SPD economics Senator in Hamburg, 1948–53; Senator of Economic Affairs in West Berlin, 1961–65; Federal Economics Minister, 1966–71; Federal Economics and Finance Minister, 1971–72.

Schirdewan, Karl (1907–) Imprisoned by the Nazis, 1934–45; member of the SED Politbureau, 1953–58; dismissed in 1958.

Schmid, Carlo (1896–1979) Son of a French mother and German father; studied international law; in the Second World War served with the German occupation force in France; later appointed (by the French) head of the German administration in Württemberg-Hohenzollern; joined the SPD and chaired the principal committee within the parliamentary Council; member of the *Reichstag*, 1949–72; deputy leader of the SPD and candidate for the presidency of the FRG, 1959.

Schnabel, Professor Franz (1887–1966) German historian; professor at Munich University, 1951–59.

Schröder, Gerhard (1910–89) Lawyer and CDU member of the *Bundestag*, 1949–80; Minister of the Interior, 1953–61; Foreign Minister, 1961–66; Defence Minister, 1966–69.

Schumacher, Kurt (1895–1952) SPD member of the *Reichstag*, 1930–33; interned in Dachau concentration camp, 1933–43; leader of the SPD, 1946–52.

Schuman, Robert (1886–1963) French Prime Minister, 1947–48; Foreign Minister, 1948–52; Minister of Justice, 1955.

Seebohm, Hans-Christoph (1903–67) Member of the DP, 1949–60 (thereafter the CDU) and FRG Transport Minister, 1949–66.

Selbmann, Fritz (1899–1975) Joined the KPD in 1922; KPD member of the *Reichstag*, 1932–33; imprisoned by the Nazis, 1933–45; economics minister, Saxony, 1946–48; Minister for Mines and Metallurgy, 1949–55; member of the Central Committee, 1954–58; writer.

Stalin, Marshal Joseph (1879–1953) General Secretary, 1922–53; President of the Council of Ministers of the USSR, 1946–53.

Stammberger, Wolfgang (1920–82) FDP member of the *Bundestag*; FRG Minister of Justice, 1961–62; joined the SPD in 1964.

Strauss, Franz Josef (1915–88) Co-founder of the CSU in 1946; elected to the Bizone Economic Council, 1948; CSU *Bundestag* member, 1949–88; Defence Minister, 1957–62; Finance Minister, 1966–69; Chancellor candidate, 1980.

Strittmatter, Erich (1912–) GDR writer and novelist.

Ulbricht, Walther (1893–1973) Joined the KPD in 1919; KPD member of the *Reichstag*, 1928–33; in Moscow, 1933–45; co-founder of the National Committee for Free Germany; General-Secretary/First Secretary of the SED, 1946–71; Chairman of the State Council, 1960–73.

Wolf, Christa (1929–) Novelist; member of the West Berlin Academy of Arts, 1981; national (GDR) prize for art and literature, 1987.

Wollweber, Ernst (1893–1958) Joined the KPD in 1919; KPD *Reichstag* member, 1932–33; in exile in Denmark, Sweden, and the USSR, 1933–45; director of inland shipping, in the Soviet Zone, 1947–49; state secretary in the transport ministry, 1949–55; Minister for State Security, 1955–58.

Zaisser, Wilhelm (1893–1958) Joined the KPD in 1919 and the Russian Communist Party in 1932; lecturer in the anti-Fascist school, 1943–45; Minister of Interior, 1949; Minister of State Security, 1950–53; expelled from the SED in 1954.

Ziller, Gerhart (1912–1957) Joined the KPD in 1919; imprisoned by the Nazis; engineering minister, 1950; member of the Central Committee, 1953; committed suicide in 1957.

BIBLIOGRAPHY

DOCUMENTS

1   *Documents on Germany, 1944–61. Committee on Foreign Relations, US Senate, 1961*, US Printing Office, Washington, DC, 1961.
2   Heidelmeyer, W. and Hindrichs, G. (eds), *Documents on Berlin, 1943–63*, Oldenbourg Verlag, Munich, 1963.
3   Jarausch, K.H. and von Gransow, V. (eds), *Uniting Germany. Documents and Debates 1944–93*, Berg, Oxford/Providence, 1994.
4   Morgan, R., *The Unsettled Peace*, BBC Books, London, 1974.
5   Ruhm, von O. (ed.), *Documents on Germany under Occupation, 1944–55*, Oxford University Press, Oxford, 1955.
6   Schweitzer, C.C. et al. (eds), *Politics and Government in the Federal Republic of Germany: Basic Documents*, Berg, Leamington Spa, 1984.
7   Smith, J.E. (ed.), *The Papers of General Lucius Clay: Germany 1945–49* (2 vols), Indiana University Press, Bloomington, IN, 1974.
8   Thomanek, J.K.A. and Mellis, J. (eds), *Politics, Society and Government in the GDR: Basic Documents*, Berg, Oxford/New York, 1988.

DIARIES AND MEMOIRS

9   Adenauer, C., *Memoirs*, Weidenfeld and Nicolson, London, 1966.
10 Andreas-Friedrich, R., *Schauplatz Berlin: Tagebuchaufzeichnung, 1945 bis 1948*, Suhrkamp, Frankfurt/M, 1984.
11 Brandt, W., *My Life in Politics*, Hamish Hamilton, London, 1992.
12 Clay, J.D., *Division in Germany*, Heinemann, London, 1950.
13 Leonhard, W., *The Child of the Revolution*, Collins, London, 1957.
14 Montgomery, B.L., *Memoirs*, Collins, London, 1958.
15 Tjulpanow, S., *Deutschland nach dem Krieg (1945–9)*, Dietz, Verlag, East Berlin, 1986.

BIOGRAPHIES OF GERMAN POLITICIANS

16 Edinger, L.J., *Kurt Schumacher*, Stanford University Press, Stanford, CA, 1965.
17 Marshall, B., *Willy Brandt: A Political Biography*, Macmillan, London/Basingstoke, 1997.
18 Prittie, T., *Konrad Adenauer, 1876–1967*, Tom Stacey, London, 1972.
19 Prittie, T., *Willy Brandt*, Weidenfeld and Nicolson, London, 1974.
20 Schwarz, H.-P., *Konrad Adenauer. A German Politician and Statesman in a Period of War, Revolution and Reconstruction*, Vol. 1: *From the German Empire to the Federal Republic.* Vol. 2: *The Statesman*, Berghahn, Oxford/Providence, 1995–97.

21   Stern, C., *Ulbricht: A Political Biography*, Pall Mall, London, 1965.

GENERAL HISTORIES

Of Germany (dealing with both the FRG and GDR)

22   Berghahn, V., *Modern Germany* (2nd edn), Cambridge University Press, Cambridge, 1987.
23   Fulbrook, M., *Germany, 1918–1990: The Divided Nation*, Fontana, London, 1991.
24   Fulbrook, M., *The Two Germanies, 1945–1990: Problems of Interpretation*, Macmillan, London/Basingstoke, 1992.
25   Fulbrook, M. (ed.), *German History since 1800*, Arnold, London, 1997.
26   Kettenacker, L., *Germany since 1945*, Oxford University Press, Oxford, 1997.
27   Pulzer, P., *German Politics, 1945–1955*, Oxford University Press, Oxford, 1995.
28   Turner, H.A., *Germany from Partition to Reunification*, Yale University Press, New Haven, CT, 1992

Of the FRG

29   Bark, D.L. and Gress, D.R., *A History of West Germany*, Vol. 1: *From Shadow to Substance 1945–63*. Vol. 2: *Democracy and its Discontents, 1963–1991* (2nd edition), Blackwell, Oxford 1991.
30   Benz, W. (ed.), *Die Bundesrepublik Deutschland* (3 vols), Fischer, Frankfurt/M, 1983.
31   Glees, A.G., *Reinventing Germany. German Political Development since 1945*, Berg, Oxford/Washington, DC, 1996.
32   Nicholls, A.J., *The Bonn Republic*, Longman, London, 1997.

Of the GDR

33   Dennis, M., *German Democratic Republic*, Pinter, London, 1988.
34   Krisch, H., *The German Democratic Republic*, Westview Press, Boulder, CO, 1985.
35   McCauley, M., *The GDR since 1945*, Macmillan, London/Basingstoke, 1983.
36   Staritz, D., *Geschichte der DDR, 1949–85*, Suhrkamp, Frankfurt/M, 1985.
37   Weber, H., *Die DDR 1945–1986*, Oldenbourg Verlag, Munich, 1988.

THE OCCUPATION AND DIVISION OF GERMANY, 1945–49

38   Autorenkollektiv (Huster, E.U. and Kraiker, G., et al., *Determinanten der Westdeutschen Neuordnung, 1945–52*, Suhrkamp, Frankfurt/M, 1977.
39   Broszat, M., Henke, K.-D. and Wolle, H. (eds), *Von Stalingrad zur Währungsreform: Zur Sozialgeschichte des Umbruchs in Deutschland*, Oldenbourg Verlag, Munich, 1988.

40   Donnison, F., *Civil Affairs and Military Government. North West Europe, 1944–46*, HMSO, London, 1961.

41   Eschenburg, T., *Jahre der Besatzung (1945–9)*, Vol. 1: *Geschichte der Bundesrepublik Deutschland*, Deutsche Verlags-Anstalt/Brockhaus, Stuttgart/Wiesbaden, 1983.

42   Farquharson, J., 'Land Reform in the British Zone, 1945–47', *German History*, vol. 6, no. 1, 1988, pp. 35–6.

43   Gimbel, J., *The American Occupation of Germany, 1945–9*, Stanford University Press, Stanford, CA, 1968.

44   Hearndon, A. (ed.), *The British in Germany: Educational Reconstruction after 1945*, Hamish Hamilton, London, 1978.

45   James, H., 'The Prehistory of the Federal Republic', *Journal of Modern History*, vol. 63, March 1991, pp. 99–115.

46   Klessmann, C., *Die doppelte Staatsgründung*, Vandenhoeck and Ruprecht, Göttingen, 1988.

47   Knapp, M. (ed.), *Von der Bizonengründung zur ökonomisch-politischen Westintegration*, Haag und Herchen Verlag, Frankfurt/M, 1984.

48   Kuklick, B., *American Policy and the Division of Germany*, Cornell University Press, Ithaca, NY, 1977.

49   Loth, W., *Stalin's Unwanted Child. The Soviet Union, the German Question and the Founding of the GDR*, Macmillan, London/Basingstoke, 1998.

50   Mai, G., 'Deutschlandpolitische Entscheidungen im Allierten Kontrolrat, 1945–48', in W. Loth (ed.), *Die Deutsche Frage in der Nachkriegszeit*, Akademie Verlag, Berlin, 1994, pp. 29–66.

51   Marshall, B., *The Origins of Post-War German Politics*, Croom Helm, London, 1988.

52   Merkl, P., *The Origins of the West German Republic*, Oxford University Press, Oxford, 1963.

53   Naimark, N.M., *The Russians in Germany: A History of the Soviet Zone of Occupation 1945–9*, Harvard University Press, Cambridge, MA, 1995.

54   Nettl, J.P., *The Eastern Zone and Soviet Policy in Germany, 1945–50*, Oxford University Press, Oxford, 1951.

55   Niethammer, L., *Die Mitläuferfabrik: Die Entnazifierung am Beispiel Bayerns*, Dietz Verlag, East Berlin, 1982.

56   Otto, W., 'Deutscher Handlungsspielraum und sowjetischer Einfluss', in E., Scherstjanoi (ed.), *Protocoll des Kolloquiums. Die Gründung der DDR*, Akademie Verlag, Berlin, 1993, pp. 138–44.

57   Petersen, E.N., *Retreat to Victory. American Occupation of Germany*, Wayne State University Press, Detroit, MI, 1977.

58   Pike, D., *The Politics of Culture in Soviet Occupied Germany, 1945–9*, Stanford University Press, Stanford, CA, 1993.

59   Rodenbach, von, H.-J., 'Die Berliner Blockade und die staatliche Teilung Deutschlands', in *Studien zur Deutschlandfrage*, Vol. 12: *Die Deutschlandfrage von Jalta und Potsdam bis zur staatlichen Teilung Deutschlands, 1949*, Duncker and Humblot, Berlin, 1993, pp. 91–115.

60   Schmidt, E., *Die verhinderte Neuordnung, 1945–52*, Europäische Verlagsanstalt, Hamburg, 1970.

61 Schwartz, T.A., *America's Germany. John J. McCloy and the Federal Republic of Germany*, Harvard University Press, Cambridge, MA, 1991.
62 Sharp, T., *The Wartime Alliance and the Zonal Division of Germany*, Oxford University Press, Oxford, 1975.
63 Siebel-Achenbach, S., *Lower Silesia from Nazi Germany to Communist Poland, 1942–49*, Macmillan, London/Basingstoke, 1994.
64 Suckut, S., ' "Wenn die Nation erhalten bleibt, werden alle administrativen Spaltungmassnahmen eines Tages zergehen und zerfallen" – Zur Vorgeschichte der DDR-Gründung', in *Studien zur Deutschlandfrage*, Vol. 12: *Die Deutschlandfrage von Jalta und Potsdam bis zur staatlichen Teilung Deutschlands, 1949*, Duncker and Humblot, Berlin, 1993, pp. 117–46.
65 Turner, I.D., 'British Occupation Policy and its Effects on the Town of Wolfsburg and the Volkswagenwerk, 1945–9', unpublished PhD thesis, University of Manchester, 1984.
66 Turner, I.D. (ed.), *Reconstruction in Post-War Germany*, Berg, Oxford/New York, 1989.
67 Williamson, D.G., *A Most Diplomatic General. The Life of General Lord Robertson of Oakridge*, Brassey's, London, 1996.
68 Willis, F., *The French in Germany, 1945–49*, Stanford University Press, Stanford, CA, 1962.
69 Zink, H., *The United States in Germany, 1944–55*, Greenwood Press, Westport, CT, 1974.

POLITICAL AND GENERAL HISTORY OF THE FRG AND GDR, 1949–89

The FRG

70 Allemann, F., *Bonn ist nicht Weimar*, Kiepenheuer und Witsch, Cologne, 1956.
71 Abenheim, D., *Reforging the Iron Cross*, Princeton University Press, Princeton, NJ, 1989.
72 Jaspers, K., *Wohin treibt die Bundesrepublik?*, Piper, Munich, 1966.
73 Klessmann, C., *Zwei Nationen, eine Nation. Deutsche Geschichte, 1955–70*, Vandenhoeck and Ruprecht, Göttingen, 1988 (this includes chapters on the GDR).
74 Larres, K. and Panayi, P. (eds), *The Federal Republic since 1949*, Longman, London, 1996.
75 Miller, S. and Potthoff, H., *A History of German Social Democracy*, Berg, Leamington Spa, 1986.
76 Paterson, W.E. and Southern, D., *Governing Germany*, Blackwell, Oxford, 1991.
77 Pridham, G., *Christian Democracy in Western Germany*, Croom Helm, London, 1977.
78 Roseman, M., 'Division and Stability: The Federal Republic of Germany, 1949–1989', in M. Fulbrook (ed.), *German History since 1800*, Arnold, London, 1997, pp. 365–90.

79   Schwarz, H.-P., *Die Ara Adenauer*, Vol. 2 *1949–57*, Vol. 3, *1957–63* of *Geschichte der Bundesrepublik Deutschland*, Deutsche Verlags-Anstalt/ Brockhaus, Stuttgart/Wiesbaden, 1981, 1983.

The DDR

80   Allinson, M., 'The Failed Experiment: East German Communism', in M. Fulbrook (ed.), *German History since 1800*, Arnold, London, 1997, pp. 391–410.

81   Baring, A., *Uprising in East Germany*, Cornell University Press, Ithaca, NY, 1972.

82   Grieder, P., 'Tension, Conflict and Opposition in the Leadership of the Socialist Unity Party (SED), 1946–73', unpublished PhD thesis, University of Cambridge (no. D196726), Cambridge, 1995.

83   Henkel, R., *Im Dienste der Staatspartei. Über Parteien und Organisationen der DDR*, Nomos Verlagsgesllschaft, Baden Baden, 1994.

84   Lammers, K.C., 'The German Democratic Republic as History', *Contemporary European History*, vol. 6, no. 3, 1997, pp. 419–25.

85   Mitter, A. and Wolle, S., *Untergang auf Raten*, Bertelsmann Verlag, Munich, 1993.

86   Mommsen, W., 'Der Ort der DDR in der Geschichte', in J. Kocka and M. Sabrow (eds), *Die DDR als Geschichte: Fragen-Hypothesen – Perspektive*. Akademie Verlag, Berlin, 1994, pp. 26–39.

87   Pritchard, G., *The Making of the GDR*, Manchester University Press, Manchester, 2000.

88   Schroeder, K. (Unter Mitarbeit von S. Alisch), *Der SED Staat*, Hauser, Munich, 1998.

89   Sontheimer, K. and Bleek, W., *The Government and Politics of East Germany*, Hutchinson, London, 1975.

90   Spittmann, I. (ed.), *Die SED in Geschichte und Gegenwart*, Verlag Wissenschaft und Politik, Cologne, 1987.

ECONOMIC AND SOCIAL HISTORY

91   Schaffer, H., *Women in the Two Germanies*, Pergamon, Oxford, 1981.

The FRG

92   Abelshauser, W., *Wirtschaftsgeschichte der Bundesrepublik*, Suhrkamp, Frankfurt/M, 1983.

93   Berghahn, V.R., *The Americanization of West German Industry*, Berg, Leamington Spa, 1986.

94   Berghahn, V.R., 'Resisting the Pax Americana? West German Industry and the United States, 1945–55' in M. Ermath (ed.), *America and the Shaping of German Society*, Berg, Oxford/New York, 1993, pp. 85–100.

95   Braun, H., 'Das Streben nach Sicherheit in den 50 Jahren', *Archiv fur Sozialgeschichte*, vol. xviii, 1978, pp. 279–306.

96 Conze, W. and Lepsius, R., *Sozialgeschichte der Bundesrepublik Deutschland: Beiträge zum Kontinuitätsproblem.* Industrielle Welt. Schriftenreihe des Arbeitskreises fur moderne Sozialgeschichte, no. 34, Klett-Cotta, Stuttgart, 1983.

97 Dahrendorf, R., *Society and Democracy in Germany*, Weidenfeld and Nicolson, London, 1968.

98 Diefendorf, J.M., *In the Wake of War. Reconstruction of German Cities after World War II*, Oxford University Press, Oxford, 1993.

99 Erhard, L., *Prosperity Through Competition*, Thames and Hudson, London, 1958.

100 Ermath, M. (ed.), *America and the Shaping of German Society 1945–55*, Berg, Oxford/New York, 1993.

101 Giesch, H., Paque, K.H. and Schmieding, H., *The Fading Miracle*, Cambridge University Press, Cambridge, 1992.

102 Kolinsky, E., *Women in Contemporary Germany. Life, Work and Politics*, (2nd edition), Berg, Oxford/New York, 1993.

103 Kramer, A., *The West German Economy*, Berg, Oxford/New York, 1991.

104 Nicholls, A.J., *Freedom with Responsibility: The Social Market Economy in Germany*, Oxford University Press, Oxford, 1994.

105 Overy, R., 'The Economy of the Federal Republic since 1949', in K. Larres and P. Panayi (eds), *The Federal Republic since 1949*, Longman, London, 1996, pp. 3–34.

106 Pommerin, R. (ed.), *The American Impact on Postwar Germany*, Berghahn, Oxford/Providence, 1995.

107 Rosen, M., 'Reconstruction and Modernization: The Federal Republic and the Fifties', *Bulletin*, vol. XIX, no. 1, May 1997, pp. 5–16, German Historical Institute, London.

108 Sywottek, A., 'The Americanization of daily life', in M. Ermath (ed.), *America and the Shaping of German Society, 1945–55*, Berg, Oxford/New York, 1993.

109 Willett, R., *The Americanization of Germany*, Routledge, London, 1989.

The GDR

110 Childs, D., *The GDR: Moscow's German Ally* (2nd edition), Allen and Unwin, London, 1988.

111 Edwards, G.E., *GDR Society and Social Institutions*, Macmillan, London/Basingstoke, 1985.

112 Fulbrook, M., *Anatomy of a Dictatorship. Inside the GDR, 1949–89*, Oxford University Press, Oxford, 1995 (paperback, 1997).

113 Goeckel, R., *The Lutheran Church and the East German State*, Cornell University Press, Ithaca, NY, 1990.

114 Hübner, P. and Tenfelde, K. (eds), *Arbeiter in der SBZ–DDR*, Klartext Verlag, Essen, 1999.

115 Humm, Antonia Maria, *Auf dem Weg zum sozialistischen Dorf?* Vandenhoeck and Ruprecht, Göttingen, 1999.

116 Kaeble, H., Kocka, J. and Zwar, H. (eds), *Sozialgeschichte der DDR*, Klett-Cotta, Stuttgart, 1994.

117   Kopstein, J., *Economic Decline in East Germany, 1945–1989*, University of North Carolina Press, Chapel Hill, NC and London, 1997.
118   Roesler, J., 'The Rise and Fall of the Planned Economy in the German Democratic Republic, 1945–89', *German History*, vol. 9, no.1, 1991, pp. 46–61.
119   Stokes, R.G., 'Autarky, Ideology and Technological Lag: The Case of the East German Chemical Industry, 1945–64', *Central European History*, vol. 208, no. 1, pp. 29–45.

FOREIGN POLICY, *OSTPOLITIK* AND THE UNITY QUESTION, 1949–88

120   Gaddis, J.L., *We Now Know, Rethinking Cold War History*, Oxford University Press, Oxford, 1997.
121   Gillingham, J., *Coal, Steel and the Rebirth of Europe, 1918–1955*, Cambridge University Press, Cambridge, 1991.
122   Graml, H., 'Die Aussenpolitik', in W. Benz (ed.), *Die Bundesrepublik Deutschland* (vol. I), Fischer, Frankfurt/M, 1983.
123   Ingimundarson, V., 'Cold War Misperceptions: The Communist and Western Responses to the East German Refugee Crisis in 1953', *Journal of Contemporary History*, vol. 29, 1994, pp. 463–81.
124   Jacobsen, H.A. et al., *Drei Jahrzehnte Aussenpolitik der DDR*, Oldenbourg Verlag, Munich, 1979.
125   Larres, K., 'Germany and the West: The "Rapallo Factor" in German Foreign Policy from the 1950s to the 1990s', in K. Larres and P. Panayi (eds), *The Federal Republic of Germany since 1949*, Longman, London, 1996, pp. 278–326.
126   Milward, A.S., *The Reconstruction of Western Europe, 1945–51*, Methuen, London, 1984.
127   Moreton, E. (ed.), *Germany between East and West*, Cambridge University Press/Royal Institute of International Affairs, Cambridge/London, 1987.
128   Steininger, R., *The German Question, the Stalin Note of 1952 and the Problem of Reunification*, Columbia University Press, New York, 1990.
129   Wendler, J., *Die Deutschlandpolitik der SED, 1952–58*, Bohlau Verlag, Köln, 1991.
130   Wettig, G., 'Stalin and German Reunification', *Historical Journal*, vol. 37, no. 2, 1994, pp. 411–19.
131   Willis, R., *France, Germany and the New Europe, 1945–67*, Oxford University Press, Oxford, 1968.

INDEX

Ackermann, A., 90, 91, 154
Adenauer, Konrad
  administrations
    (1949–53), 54–7
    (1953–57), 58–63
    (1957–61), 63–5
    (1961–63), 65–6
  attacks *Halbstarken*, 80
  and the Berlin crisis (1958–61), 48–50
  and the *Bundeswehr*, 62
  CDU leader in the British Zone, 22
  and choice of Bonn as capital, 33
  crusade against Communism, 113
  domestic policy aims, 59–60
  establishes 'Chancellor democracy', 112
  and European Integration, 40, 45–6, 50
    (*see also* ECSC, EDC and EEC)
  friction with Erhard, 63–4, 66
  and German unity, 42–3, 45–7, 49,
    139–40, 141–2 (*see also* Globke, plans)
  and the Hallstein Doctrine, 46–7, 138–9
  and the market economy, 53
  and NATO, 40, 42, 45
  Oberbürgermeister of Cologne, 22
  paradoxical nature of Adenauer era, 77–8
  payment of reparations to Israel, 41
  the Petersberg Agreement, 39, 55–6
  President of the Parliamentary Council,
    31
  relations with the FDP, 60–1, 65–6
  relations with the SPD, 55–7, 58, 64–6
    (*see also* Schumacher)
  relations with the USSR, 43–50
  relations with the Western Allies
    France, 39–41, 46, 50 (*see also* de
      Gaulle; Saar)
    Great Britain, 47–9, 50
    USA, 39, 41, 45–50 (*see also* Kennedy)
  retirement, 66
  and Rhöndorf Conference, 53, 130
  and the *Spiegel* Affair, 65–6
  success in elections, 133–4
    (1949), 33, 53
    (1953), 59
    (1957), 63
    (1961), 65
  views on West German rearmament, 40–1
  see also co-determination; Equalization of
    Burdens Act

Agartz, V., 73, 87
agriculture, 71, 74, 77 (*see also*
  collectivization of agriculture)
Ahlen Programme, 22
Allies, wartime, 3–4, 5–8, 11–24ff.
  aims in Germany, 3–4, 7–8, 123–4 (*see
    also* Conferences, Potsdam *and* Yalta)
  break-up of alliance over German
    question, 25–31
  Western, 25–31ff., 39–50ff., 136–7
  see also Germany, Allied occupation of;
    Control Council, Allied;
    High Commission, Allied
Armies
  American, 6, 46
  British, 6, 47
  German, *see Bundeswehr*; *Nationale
    Volksarmee*
  Russian, 6, 19, 88
Arnold, K., 53, 154
Augstein, R., 65–6, 154 (*see also Spiegel*
  Affair)

Baden-Württemberg, 16
Basic Law, 30–3, 78
Baudissin, Lieutenant-General W. von, 61,
  154
Bavaria
  and the Basic Law, 33
  1946 constitution of, 16
  denazification in, 13
  elections in, 56
  expellees in, 71–2
  particularism in, 16
  political conflict in, 60
  under US occupation, 3
  see also Christian Social Union (CSU)
Bavarian Party, 54, 60
Beria, L., 44, 89, 154
Berlin, 3, 5, 6
  blockade, 28–30
  crisis (1958–61), 48–50, 63, 65
  disturbances in (1953), 87–8
  East, 29, 87–8, 125, 141
  life in (1945), 120
  ultimatum (1958), 48, 140
  Wall, 93–4, 98, 115, 116, 141
  West, 33, 48, 64–5, 141
Bevin, E., 27, 154

Bitterfeld, 88, 103, 147
Bizone, the (Bizonia)
    administrative and political developments
        in, 25–6, 28, 68
    econonic developments in, 20, 69
    formation of, 19
    see also Erhard, L.
blackmarket, 18, 69, 127
Blank, T., 61, 62, 154
Blankenhorn, H., 47, 154
Böckler, H., 23, 57, 71, 154 (*see also*
    Deutsche Gewerkschaftsbund)
Böhm, F., 67
Böll, H., 79, 154
Brandenburg, 16
Brandt, W., 64–5, 113, 154
Brecht, B., 79, 154
Bremen, 14
Brentano, H. von, 78, 155
Bund der Heimatvertriebenen und
    Entrechteten (BHE), 60, 68
Bundesrat, 32, 53, 61
Bundestag, 33
    (1949–53), 53–9
    (1953–57), 59–64
    (1957–61), 63–5
    (1961–65), 65–6
Bundeswehr, 59–62, 66

cartels, 20, 74 (*see also* decartelization)
Central Bank, 69, 70, 72–3
Central Committee (of the SED), 83, 86, 89,
    90, 92, 135
    constitution of, 83
Christian Democratic Union
    and the Catholic Church, 23, 60
    and Christian Socialism, 22, 70
    coalition with the FDP, 53–4, 59, 60–1,
        68
    divisions over the Elysée Treaty, 50
    electoral successes (1949–61), 33, 41,
        58–9, 63, 65
    and end of Adenauer era, 66
    foundation of, 21–2
    growing impatience with Adenauer, 62,
        64
    joins the Frankfurt Coalition, 25–6, 68
    organization of, 55, 153
    Protestant wing of, 54, 60
    relations with the SPD, 55–8, 65–6
    role in the Parliamentary Council, 31
Christian Democratic Union of Germany
    (CDUD)
    and democratic bloc, 83, 85
    joins anti-Fascist bloc (June 1945), 21
    leaders join Grotewohl's cabinet, 84
    member of the *Volkskongress*, 28, 34
Christian Social Union (CSU)
    in Bavaria, 60, 153

Erhard as chairman, 33
    foundation of, 22
    in the Parliamentary Council, 32
    see also Christian Democratic Union
Churches
    Catholic (in the FRG), 22, 77, 79, 60
    Evangelical (in the FRG), 56, 57; (in the
        GDR), 87, 106–7
Churchill, W., 40, 45, 155
Civil Code (in the FRG), 78; (in the GDR),
    105
civil law, 78
civil service, 7, 17, 59, 77–8
Clay, General Lucius, 14, 18–19, 32
coal, 13, 17, 74, 95
co-determination, 57
collectivization of agriculture, 86, 87, 93,
    98–100, 115
Cologne, 5
COMECON, 48, 97, 115
COMINFORM, 34
Conferences
    Berlin, (1954), 45
    Foreign Ministers'
        London (1947), 27
        Moscow (1947), 25
        Paris (1946), 19; (1949), 35
    Foreign Minister's deputies (1951), 43
    Potsdam, 7–8
    Six Powers (London, 1948), 28, 29
    Summit
        Geneva (1955), 45; (1959), 48
        Paris (1960), 49
    Yalta, 3, 6, 19
consumer age, 77
Control Council, Allied
    agreement on expellees, 121
    and education, 14
    first meeting, 6
    laws on denazification, 13
    plans for, 3, 123
    reparations, 18
    Russian representatives withdraw from,
        28
    and works councils, 24
    see also Germany, Allied Occupation of
counter-part funds, 70
Cuba, 47
Cuba Crisis, 65
currency reform, 29, 112
    in East Germany, 95
    in West Germany, 68–9

Dahlem, F., 83–4, 91, 155
de Gaulle, 46, 50, 155
decartelization, 7, 20, 73–4
Dehler, T., 60–1, 155
Democratic Republic of Germany (GDR), *see*
    Germany, the Democratic Republic of

denazification, 7, 11–13, 59
Dertinger, G., 84, 87, 155
Deutsche Gewerkschaftsbund (DGB), 23, 57, 71
Deutsche Wirtschaftskommission, 20, 26, 28, 96
Dibelius, O., Bishop, 107, 155
divorce, 78, 105
Dönitz, K., Grand Admiral, 6, 155
Dulles, A., 41, 45, 155
Düsseldorf, 60

education, 14–15, 60, 77, 102–3
Eisenhower, President, D., 45, 49, 155
Eisler, G., 35
elections
    to the *Bundestag*, (1949), 33, 53; (1953), 59; (1957), 63; (1961), 65, 133–4
    demands for free elections, 89
    in the GDR, (1950), 84–6; (1954), 90
    in the *Länder* (FRG), 56, 58, 60, 66
    in occupied Germany, 16
Elysée Treaty, 50
Equalization of Burdens Act, 58–9
Erhard, L., 155
    Economic Director of the Bizone, 33, 68–70
    Economics Minister, 54, 71–5ff.
    friction with Adenauer, 63
    and heir to Adenauer, 65–6
    reservations about the EEC, 50, 62, 74–5
    and the social market economy, 5, 62–3, 67–8, 70, 71, 74
Etzel, F., 63, 155
Eucken, W., 67
European Coal and Steel Community (ECSC), 40–1
European Defence Community (EDC), 40–1
European Economic Community (EEC), 45, 46, 50, 62, 63, 74–5
European Recovery Programme, *see* Marshall Plan
expellees, 5–6, 55, 58–9, 71, 76, 104–5, 112, 120–2 (*see also Bund der Heimatvertriebenen und Entrechteten*; Germany, Democratic Republic of, flight from the GDR to the FRG)

Faulhaber, M. von, Cardinal, 77, 155
Fechner, M., 89, 155
Federal Constitutional Court, 58, 60, 64
Federal Republic of Germany (FRG), *see* Germany, Federal Republic of
Fibag Construction Company, 65
films, 113
food shortages, 5, 17, 19, 87, 100, 104, 120, 124–5, 127, 131

France
    aims in Germany, 4
    and the Berlin crisis (1958–61), 49
    and the ECSC, 40
    and the EDC, 40–1
    favours a federal West Germany, 32
    Franco-Germany Treaty of (1963), 50
    friction with the Anglo-Saxon powers, 45
    and Marshall Aid, 32
    and the Saar, 4, 19, 28, 39–40, 42
    Western integration and entente with FRG, 46
    see also Germany, Allied Occupation of
François-Ponçet, A., 55, 155
Free Democratic Party (FDP)
    break with, 60–1
    coalition with the CDU/CSU, 53–60, 65–6
    coalition with the SPD in North Rhine-Westphalia, 61
    formation of, 23
    and Frankfurt coalition, 26
    and the Parliamentary Council, 26
Free German Youth (FDJ) 83, 101–2

Gastarbeiter, 74
General Treaty, 41, 58
German Democratic Party (DDP), 23
Germany
    the collapse of the Third Reich, 4–7
    and comparisons with the GDR, 90, 114
    and economy of, 3, 5
    legacy of, 5, 79, 111
    the legacy of the Bismarckian Reich, 39, 75, 79, 111
    legacy of the Weimar Republic, 31
Germany, Allied Occupation of, 1945–49
    Allied policies in
        denazification, 12–13
        education, 14–15
    economy in, 17–21
    emergence of political parties, 21–3
    legacy of Occupation, 24
    new *Länder* created in, reform of local government, 16–17
    Zones of Occupation
        American, 3, 12, 13, 14, 16, 17, 20
        British, 6, 13, 15, 16, 20
        French, 3, 6, 13, 14, 27
        Russian, 3–4, 12, 14, 16–17
    see also Bizone, the; *Deutsche Wirtschaftskommission*
Germany, the Democratic republic of (GDR)
    and the Berlin Wall, 93–4
    collectivization of agriculture in, 98–100
    consolidated by the Wall, 48–50, 93–4
    de-Stalinization crisis, 91–2

Germany, the Democratic republic of
    (GDR) (*continued*)
  economic problems and attempts to
    overcome them by the planned
    economy, 89, 96–8
  flight from the GDR to the FRG, 73, 87,
    93, 96, 98, 99, 103, 114, 115, 135,
    141–2
  formation of, 35
  gains sovereignty, 45
  indifference and opposition to the regime,
    105–7
  initial provisional nature of, 43–4
  the 'Janus face' of , 114
  the 'New Course', 89–90, 99
  role of education and art in creating a
    socialist state, 101–4
  SED dictatorship established, 34–5, 83–6,
    92–3
  shaken by events of 17 June 1953, 86–90
  workers and peasants in, 104–5;
  see also Socialist Unity Party of Germany;
    Ulbricht, W.
Germany, division into two states, 4, 25–35,
    43–5, 50, 113
Germany, the Federal Republic of (FRG)
  achieves sovereignty, 41–2
  constitution of, 31–3
  economic 'miracle' of, 67, 72–5
  foreign policy of, 39–42, 45–50
  formation of, 33, 130–1
  impotence of during the Berlin crisis
    (1958–61), 48–50
  politics in, 53–66
  relations with GDR, 46–7
  the 'restoration' debate, 17, 113
  the spirit of the 1950s in, 76–80
  and Western integration, 39–41, 45–6,
    115, 140
  see also Adenauer, Konrad; Christian
    Democratic Union; Social Democratic
    Party of Germany
Globke, H., 54, 155
  plans, 47, 49
Glückauf, E., 44
Görlitz, 88, 121
  Treaty of, 48
Grass, G., 79, 155
Great Britain
  Adenauer's distrust of, 46, 48
  and the Berlin blockade, 29–30
  and the Berlin crisis (1958–61), 48–9
  and the Bizone, 19
  and the creation of the FRG, 28–9
  decline of its power in the Mediterranean,
    45
  economic weakness, 5, 19, 25
  and the EEC, 50, 74–5
  its German policy, 4, 25, 27

  and Marshall Aid, 70
  and Suez crisis, 46
  and tactical nuclear weapons in the FRG,
    47
Grotewohl, O., 43, 44, 87, 155
Gründig, M., 18
Grüppe 47, 79

Halbstarken, 80
Hallstein, W., 41, 47, 50, 98, 156
  Doctrine, 47, 138–9
Hamann, K., 87, 156
Hamburg, 17, 22, 125
Hanover, 5
Harich, W., 92, 156
Heinemann, G., 54, 56, 156
Heisenberg, Professor W., 77, 156
Hemingway, E., 79
Hennecke, A., 96–7
Herrnstadt, R., 89, 80, 156
Hesse, 1, 16, 56
Heuss, T., 23, 53, 64, 156
High Commission, Allied, 41, 54, 56, 84,
    130–1
Hitler, A., 6, 71, 84
Hitler period, 90
Hitler Youth, 5, 114
Honecker, E., 44, 93, 156
housing, 58, 72, 76, 104, 122, 147
Hungarian uprising, 91

inflation, 17–18, 72

Janka, W., 92, 156
Jaspers, K., Professor, 12, 112, 156
jazz, 79

Kaiser, J., 22, 43, 54, 134, 156
Kastner, H., 84, 156
Kennedy, J., 49, 113
Khrushchev, N., 45, 48–50ff., 91, 93, 98,
    140, 157
Klöckner, 77
Kommunistische Partei Deutschlands
    (KPD)
  banned in the FRG, 55, 133
  in the Ruhr, 27
  union with SPD, 21–2
Kopf, H., 54, 157
Korean War, 56, 72, 85
Kraft, W., 63, 157
Kuczynski, J., 114, 157
Külz, W., 84, 157

land reform, 20–1 (*see also* collectivization
    of agriculture)
Lemmer, E., 28, 157
Level of industry plans, 18, 47
Liberal parties, 22–3

Liberaldemokratische Partei Deutschlands (LDPD), 34, 83, 84 (*see also* German Democratic Party; Free Democratic Party)
Lower Saxony, 15, 54
Lübke, H., 59, 64, 157

Macmillan, H., 49, 157
Mann, T., 79, 157
Mannesmann, 77
Marshall, G., 16, 157
Marshall Plan, 26–7, 68, 70–1, 73
Marxism-Leninism, 22, 91, 86, 91, 103, 106, 127–8
Matern, H., 89, 157
Mecklenburg, 16
Mende, E., 65, 66, 157
Merkatz, H.-J. von, 78, 157
Military government, see Germany, Allied Occupation of, 1945–49
Military Governors, 29, 31, 33, 70
   American, 14, 18–19, 32, 124
   British, 27, 30
Monnet, J., 40, 157
Morgenthau, H., 4, 157
Morgenthau Plan, 4
Munich, 13, 16, 22

National Front, 85
Nationale Volksarmee (NVA), 91
NATO, 40, 42, 45, 48, 90
Nazis
   ex-Nazis in the FRG, 13, 133
   ex-Nazis in the GDR, 89, 106
   and the Nuremberg trials, 12
   and the police, 7
   suspension of Nazi teachers, 14
   see also Germany, collapse of the Third Reich; Germany, Allied Occupation of, 1945–49
Neumayer, F., 63, 157
New Course, 87–90, 99
Niemöller, M., Pastor, 56, 57, 158
Nölting, E., 68
North Rhine-Westphalia, 15, 61
Nuremberg trials, 12
Nuschke, O., 28, 84, 88, 158

Occupation Statute, 29, 39, 130–1
Occupation, Allied, see Germany, Allied Occupation of 1945–49
Oder River, 3
Oder–Neisse line, 7
Oelssner, F., 89, 92, 158
Ollenhauer, E., 59, 158
Order 234, 20, 96
Organization for European Economic Cooperation (OEEC), 26

Parliamentary Council, 31
pensions, 63, 74, 105
Petersberg Agreement, 39, 55
Pfleiderer, K., 47, 158
Phoenix tyre factory, 18
Pieck, W., 28–9, 158
Pleven Plan, 40, 57
Poland
   annexations of German territory, 3
   expulsion of Germans, 5, 120–1
   and Görlitz Treaty, 48
Polish October, 48, 91
Politbureau, 83, 84, 85, 92 (*see also* Socialist Unity Party of Germany)
Potsdam Conference, 7–8
Potsdam Agreement, 11, 14, 15, 17, 18, 23, 140
Prussia, 15, 17
   former ruling class of, 4–5, 77

Radford Plan, 46
rationing, 17, 68, 69, 87
reparations, 7–8, 18
   Allied disagreement on, 18–19, 25
   concessions to the FRG on, 55
   final settlement for the FRG, 41
   the GDR and payment to, 96
   Marshall Aid as substitute for, 70–1
   SAGs returned to GDR ownership, 90
   Soviet interest in, 4, 19, 27
Rhöndorf Conference, 53, 130
Robertson, Sir Brian, General, 27, 121, 130, 158
Rock and Roll, 80
Roosevelt, F., 3
Ruhr, 3, 4, 5, 13, 17, 25, 27
   industrialists, 74, 77
   see also ECSC
Ruhr Authority, 28, 39
Ruhr Statute, 39–41
Russia, see the USSR

Saar, 16, 28, 40, 42
Saxony, 14, 16, 20
Schäffer, F., 59, 63, 158
Schiller, Professor K., 64, 158
Schirdewan, 92, 158
Schleswig–Holstein, 6, 15, 58, 71–2, 121–2
Schmid, C., 31, 64, 131, 158
Schröder, 65, 50, 59, 158
Schumacher, K., 21, 22, 42–3, 55–7, 159
Schuman, R., 40, 59, 159
Schuman Plan, 40 (*see also* ECSC)
Seebohm, H.–C., 159
Selbmann, F., 92, 159
Sethe, P., 43–4
Social Democratic Party of Germany (SPD)
   amalgamation in Soviet Zone with SED, 21–2

Social Democratic Party of Germany (SPD)
   (*continued*)
   'black–red' coalition talks, 65, 66
   cooperation with CDU/CSU, 55, 57
   economic programme of, 56, 70
   and European integration, 42, 57, 63
   Godesberg Programme, 64
   in *Länder* politics, 56, 60
   and Parliamentary Council, 31–2
   re-emergence, 21
   represented on Economic Council, 25
   showing in the *Bundestag* elections, 134;
      (1949), 33; (1953), 59; (1957), 63;
      (1961), 65
   tactics in opposition, 55
   talk of coalition with the FDP, 61
social market economy, 53, 59, 67–8, 71,
   74, 130 (*see also* Erhard, L.)
Socialist Unity Party of Germany (SED)
   and the Berlin Wall, 93
   comparisons with Nazi Germany, 114
   creation of, 21–2
   dependence on Stalin, 30–1
   and dictatorship of, 83–6, 92, 101
   and division of Germany, 27–9, 34–5
   economic policy of, 95–100
   educational policy of, 102–3
   and the FDJ, 101–3
   internal divisions on unification question,
      43–4, 87–90, 92
   organization of, 83–4, 127–8
   party conferences
      1st (1949), 127–8
      2nd (1952), 86, 97, 99
      3rd (1956), 91
   party congresses
      4th (1954), 90
      5th (1958), 92, 97
   recruitment of the party elite, 101
   and 17 June 1953, 88–90
Soviet Military Administration (SMAD), 16,
   20, 26, 27, 28, 35, 84, 96, 106
Sowjetische Aktiengesellschaft (SAG), 13,
   19, 90
Spiegel Affair, 65–6
Stalin, J., 4, 30, 34, 43, 57, 73, 159
   Stalin's note, 43–4, 99
Stalingrad, 3
Stammberger, W., 66, 159
Stasi (*Ministerium für Staatssicherheit*), 85,
   86, 90, 93, 111
Strauss, F. J., 50, 59, 62, 63, 65–6, 159 (*see*
   also Spiegel Affair)
strikes
   in the FRG, 57, 70, 73
   in the GDR, 88–9, 91
Suez crisis, 91

Thuringia, 16

Trade Unions
   in the FRG, 23–4, 57, 70, 73
   in the GDR, 23, 83, 106

Ulbricht, W., 159
   attitude towards the Churches, 106–7
   defeats rivals, 92
   and de-Stalinization crisis, 91–2
   and division of Germany, 34, 35, 43, 84
   policies on socialism and collectivization,
      86–7, 90, 98–100
   position in the GDR, 83–4, 89–90, 133
   returns to Germany, 4, 122
   and 2nd Party Conference, 86
   survives 17 June 1953, 86–90, 136
   views on role of writers, 147–8
   see also Germany, Democratic Republic
      of; Socialist Unity Party of Germany
unemployment, 71, 76, 104–5
USA
   aims in Germany, 3, 4, 8
   'Americanization' of the FRG, 74,
      79–80
   backs setting-up of the FRG, 27–9
   and Berlin crisis (1958–61), 48–50, 113
   and the Bizone, 8, 25–6
   desire for *détente* with USSR
   and Marshall Aid, 26–7, 70–1
   Occupation policies, 11–24ff.
   policy during the Berlin blockade, 29–30
   policy on tactical nuclear weapons, 47
   relations with the FRG, 41, 45, 59
   supports European integration, 111
   supports West German rearmament, 40
   see also Germany, Allied Occupation of,
      1945–49, American Zone of Occupation
USSR
   advance into Germany, 5
   aims in Germany, 4, 7
   attitude of the USSR to the GDR, 34–5,
      45–6, 137–8
   attitude of the USSR to German unity, 35,
      43–5, 111
   its Communist Party provides the model
      for the SED, 83–5
   consequences of de-Stalinization on the
      GDR, 91
   helps SED delay the 1950 election (1949),
      84
   isolated at the London Conference, 27
   military intervention in the GDR, 17 June
      1953, 88
   and the Moscow Conference, 25
   and the occupation of Germany, 11–24ff.
   pressure put on SED to change course,
      87, 135
   relations between Ulbricht and the Soviet
      leadership, 83–94ff., 98, 107
   and reparations, 7–8, 19, 126–7

USSR (*continued*)
  responds to Western currency reform with
    Belin blockade, 29–30
  response to the Marshall Plan, 26–7
  sets up DWK, 20, 28
  triggers Berlin crisis (1958–61), 48–50,
    140–1

Volkseigener Betrieb (VEBs), 95
Volkskammer, 24, 35
Volkskongress movement, 27–8, 34, 35

Wandel, P., 14, 102
Wolff, Otto, 77
Wollweber, E., 92, 159

women, 5, 78, 105, 114, 120, 146
workers
  during the Allied Occupation, 18, 20–1
  in the FRG, 57, 71, 76–7, 145–7
  in the GDR, 88, 91, 96–7, 104–6

Yalta Conference, 3, 16, 19
youth
  in the FRG, 80
  in the GDR, 101–2, 106–7
  see also Hitler Youth
Yugoslavia, 47

Zaisser, 89, 90, 159
Ziller, G., 92, 159

SEMINAR STUDIES IN HISTORY

General Editors: Clive Emsley & Gordon Martel

The series was founded by Patrick Richardson in 1966. Between 1980 and 1996 Roger Lockyer edited the series before handing over to Clive Emsley (Professor of History at the Open University) and Gordon Martel (Professor of International History at the University of Northern British Columbia, Canada and Senior Research Fellow at De Montfort University).

MEDIEVAL ENGLAND

The Pre-Reformation Church in England 1400–1530 (Second edition)
Christopher Harper-Bill   0 582 28989 0

Lancastrians and Yorkists: The Wars of the Roses
David R Cook   0 582 35384 X

TUDOR ENGLAND

Henry VII (Third edition)
Roger Lockyer & Andrew Thrush   0 582 20912 9

Henry VIII (Second edition)
M D Palmer   0 582 35437 4

Tudor Rebellions (Fourth edition)
Anthony Fletcher & Diarmaid MacCulloch   0 582 28990 4

The Reign of Mary I (Second edition)
Robert Tittler   0 582 06107 5

Early Tudor Parliaments 1485–1558
Michael A R Graves   0 582 03497 3

The English Reformation 1530–1570
W J Sheils   0 582 35398 X

Elizabethan Parliaments 1559–1601 (Second edition)
Michael A R Graves   0 582 29196 8

England and Europe 1485–1603 (Second edition)
Susan Doran   0 582 28991 2

The Church of England 1570–1640
Andrew Foster   0 582 35574 5

STUART BRITAIN

Social Change and Continuity: England 1550–1750 (Second edition)
Barry Coward   0 582 29442 8

James I (Second edition)
S J Houston   0 582 20911 0

The English Civil War 1640–1649
Martyn Bennett   0 582 35392 0

Charles I, 1625–1640
Brian Quintrell   0 582 00354 7

The English Republic 1649–1660 (Second edition)
Toby Barnard   0 582 08003 7

Radical Puritans in England 1550–1660
R J Acheson   0 582 35515 X

The Restoration and the England of Charles II (Second edition)
John Miller   0 582 29223 9

The Glorious Revolution (Second edition)
John Miller   0 582 29222 0

EARLY MODERN EUROPE

The Renaissance (Second edition)
Alison Brown   0 582 30781 3

The Emperor Charles V
Martyn Rady   0 582 35475 7

French Renaissance Monarchy: Francis I and Henry II (Second edition)
Robert Knecht   0 582 28707 3

The Protestant Reformation in Europe
Andrew Johnston   0 582 07020 1

The French Wars of Religion 1559–1598 (Second edition)
Robert Knecht   0 582 28533 X

Phillip II
Geoffrey Woodward   0 582 07232 8

The Thirty Years' War
Peter Limm   0 582 35373 4

Louis XIV
Peter Campbell   0 582 01770 X

Spain in the Seventeenth Century
Graham Darby   0 582 07234 4

Peter the Great
William Marshall   0 582 00355 5

EUROPE 1789–1918

Britain and the French Revolution
Clive Emsley   0 582 36961 4

Revolution and Terror in France 1789–1795 (Second edition)
D G Wright   0 582 00379 2

Napoleon and Europe
D G Wright   0 582 35457 9

Nineteenth-Century Russia: Opposition to Autocracy
Derek Offord   0 582 35767 5

The Constitutional Monarchy in France 1814–48
Pamela Pilbeam   0 582 31210 8

The 1848 Revolutions (Second edition)
Peter Jones   0 582 06106 7

The Italian Risorgimento
M Clark   0 582 00353 9

Bismark & Germany 1862–1890 (Second edition)
D G Williamson   0 582 29321 9

Imperial Germany 1890–1918
Ian Porter, Ian Armour and Roger Lockyer   0 582 03496 5

The Dissolution of the Austro-Hungarian Empire 1867–1918 (Second edition)
John W Mason   0 582 29466 5

Second Empire and Commune: France 1848–1871 (Second edition)
William H C Smith   0 582 28705 7

France 1870–1914 (Second edition)
Robert Gildea   0 582 29221 2

The Scramble for Africa (Second edition)
M E Chamberlain   0 582 36881 2

Late Imperial Russia 1890–1917
John F Hutchinson   0 582 32721 0

The First World War
Stuart Robson   0 582 31556 5

EUROPE SINCE 1918

The Russian Revolution (Second edition)
Anthony Wood   0 582 35559 1

Lenin's Revolution: Russia, 1917–1921
David Marples   0 582 31917 X

Stalin and Stalinism (Second edition)
Martin McCauley   0 582 27658 6

The Weimar Republic (Second edition)
John Hiden   0 582 28706 5

The Inter-War Crisis 1919–1939
Richard Overy   0 582 35379 3

Fascism and the Right in Europe, 1919–1945
Martin Blinkhorn   0 582 07021 X

Spain's Civil War (Second edition)
Harry Browne   0 582 28988 2

The Third Reich (Second edition)
D G Williamson   0 582 20914 5

The Origins of the Second World War (Second edition)
R J Overy   0 582 29085 6

The Second World War in Europe
Paul MacKenzie   0 582 32692 3

Anti-Semitism before the Holocaust
Albert S Lindemann   0 582 36964 9

The Holocaust: The Third Reich and the Jews
David Engel   0 582 32720 2

Germany from Defeat to Partition, 1945–1963
D G Williamson   0 582 29218 2

Britain and Europe since 1945
Alex May   0 582 30778 3

Eastern Europe 1945–1969: From Stalinism to Stagnation
Ben Fowkes   0 582 32693 1

The Khrushchev Era, 1953–1964
Martin McCauley   0 582 27776 0

NINETEENTH-CENTURY BRITAIN

Britain before the Reform Acts: Politics and Society 1815–1832
Eric J Evans   0 582 00265 6

Parliamentary Reform in Britain c. 1770–1918
Eric J Evans   0 582 29467 3

Democracy and Reform 1815–1885
D G Wright   0 582 31400 3

Poverty and Poor Law Reform in Nineteenth-Century Britain, 1834–1914:
From Chadwick to Booth
David Englander   0 582 31554 9

The Birth of Industrial Britain: Economic Change, 1750–1850
Kenneth Morgan   0 582 29833 4

Chartism (Third edition)
Edward Royle   0 582 29080 5

Peel and the Conservative Party 1830–1850
Paul Adelman   0 582 35557 5

Gladstone, Disraeli and later Victorian Politics (Third edition)
Paul Adelman   0 582 29322 7

Britain and Ireland: From Home Rule to Independence
Jeremy Smith   0 582 30193 9

TWENTIETH-CENTURY BRITAIN

The Rise of the Labour Party 1880–1945 (Third edition)
Paul Adelman   0 582 29210 7

The Conservative Party and British Politics 1902–1951
Stuart Ball   0 582 08002 9

The Decline of the Liberal Party 1910–1931 (Second edition)
Paul Adelman   0 582 27733 7

The British Women's Suffrage Campaign 1866–1928
Harold L Smith   0 582 29811 3

War & Society in Britain 1899–1948
Rex Pope   0 582 03531 7

The British Economy since 1914: A Study in Decline?
Rex Pope   0 582 30194 7

Unemployment in Britain between the Wars
Stephen Constantine   0 582 35232 0

The Attlee Governments 1945–1951
Kevin Jefferys   0 582 06105 9

The Conservative Governments 1951–1964
Andrew Boxer   0 582 20913 7

Britain under Thatcher
Anthony Seldon and Daniel Collings   0 582 31714 2

INTERNATIONAL HISTORY

The Eastern Question 1774–1923 (Second edition)
A L Macfie   0 582 29195 X

The Origins of the First World War (Second edition)
Gordon Martel   0 582 28697 2

The United States and the First World War
Jennifer D Keene   0 582 35620 2

Anti-Semitism before the Holocaust
Albert S Lindemann   0 582 36964 9

The Origins of the Cold War, 1941–1949 (Second edition)
Martin McCauley   0 582 27659 4

Russia, America and the Cold War, 1949–1991
Martin McCauley   0 582 27936 4

The Arab–Israeli Conflict
Kirsten E Schulze   0 582 31646 4

The United Nations since 1945: Peacekeeping and the Cold War
Norrie MacQueen   0 582 35673 3

Decolonisation: The British Experience since 1945
Nicholas J White   0 582 29087 2

The Vietnam War
Mitchell Hall   0 582 32859 4

WORLD HISTORY

China in Transformation 1900–1949
Colin Mackerras   0 582 31209 4

US HISTORY

America in the Progressive Era, 1890–1914
Lewis L Gould   0 582 35671 7

The United States and the First World War
Jennifer D Keene   0 582 35620 2

The Truman Years, 1945–1953
Mark S Byrnes   0 582 32904 3

The Vietnam War
Mitchell Hall   0 582 32859 4

American Abolitionists
Stanley Harrold   0 582 35738 1

The American Civil War, 1861–1865
Reid Mitchell   0 582 31973 0